ASH
OF
STARS

ASH
OF
STARS

On the Writing of Samuel R. Delany

EDITED BY JAMES SALLIS

UNIVERSITY PRESS OF MISSISSIPPI *Jackson*

Acknowledgments

"The Languages of Science Fiction: Samuel R. Delany's *Babel-17*" copyright © 1993 Carl Malmgren, originally appeared in *Extrapolation*, Vol. 34, No. 1, published by The Kent State University Press. Reprinted by permission of the author.

"To See What Condition Our Condition Is In: Trial by Language in *Stars in My Pocket Like Grains of Sand*" copyright © 1996 Mary Kay Bray. Appears for the first time here.

"Debased and Lascivious? Samuel R. Delany's *Stars in My Pocket Like Grains of Sand*" copyright © 1986, 1996 Russell Blackford, originally appeared in *Australian Science Fiction Review*, Second Series, Vol. 1, No. 4, September 1986. Reprinted (with minor revisions) by permission of the author.

"The Politics of Desire in Delany's *Triton* and *Tides of Lust*" copyright © 1984 Robert Elliot Fox, originally appeared in *Black American Literature Forum*, Vol. 18, No. 2, Summer 1984. Reprinted by permission of the author and *Black American Literature Forum* (now *African American Review*).

"On *Dhalgren*" copyright © 1977 Jean Mark Gawron, originally appeared as introduction to Gregg Press library edition of *Dhalgren* (Boston: 1977). Reprinted by permission of the author.

" 'This You-Shaped Hole of Insight and Fire': Meditations on Delany's *Dhalgren*" copyright © 1996 Robert Elliot Fox. Appears for the first time here.

"Necessary Constraints: Samuel R. Delany on Science Fiction" copyright © 1994 by The Science Fiction Foundation, originally appeared in *Foundation: The Review of Science Fiction*, No. 60, Spring 1994 (UK). Reprinted here, in abridged form, by permission of the author.

"Nevèrÿon Deconstructed: Samuel R. Delany's *Tales of Nevèrÿon* and the 'Modular Calculus,' " copyright © 1985, 1996 Kathleen L. Spencer, appeared in an earlier form (as "Deconstructing *Tales of Nevèrÿon:* Delany, Derrida, and the Modular Calculus Parts I-IV") in *Essays in Arts and Sciences*, vol. XIV, May 1985. Reprinted, revised and expanded for this book, by permission of the author.

"Delany's Dirt" copyright © 1995 Ray Davis, originally appeared in *The New York Review of Science Fiction*. Reprinted by permission of the author.

"Subverted Equations: G. Spencer Brown's *Laws of Form* and Samuel R. Delany's Analytics of Attention" copyright © 1996 Ken James. Appears for the first time here.

99 98 97 96   4 3 2 1

The paper in this book meets the guidelines for permanence and durability of the Committee on Production Guidelines for Book Longevity of the Council on Library Resources.

Library of Congress Cataloging-in-Publication Data

Ash of stars : on the writing of Samuel R. Delany / edited by James Sallis.
    p. cm.
    Includes bibliographical references (p.   ) and index.
    ISBN 0-87805-852-4 (cloth : alk. paper). — ISBN 0-87805-895-8 (pbk. : alk. paper)
    1. Delany, Samuel R.—Criticism and interpretation.   2. Science fiction, American—History and criticism.   I. Sallis, James, 1944–   .
PS3554.E437Z55   1996
813'.54—dc20   95-39443
                                                                                         CIP

British Library Cataloging-in-Publication data available

To Chip

*It has indeed
been a long
and a fine
friendship*

CONTENTS

INTRODUCTION

Over the past thirty-odd years, as our Alice Walkers, John Updikes and Norman Mailers pursued celebrated careers, out of the light and at the edge of many campfires one writer, with almost no public career at all, has quietly worked to produce what is certainly among the most important bodies of work in American letters. Umberto Eco speaks of him as a fascinating writer who has invented a new style. Fredric Jameson called his Nevèrÿon series "a major and unclassifiable achievement in contemporary American literature."

So a hush falls on the convocation as Samuel R. Delany strokes his full white beard (for, yes, he looks quite the literary lion these days) and as, slowly, the force, the pressure, builds. New Delany books and reissues of old ones—novels, stories, interviews, criticism—appear at a startling rate: at least a dozen in the two years *this* book's been underway. Profiles and reviews abound in such publications as the *Village Voice*, *Callaloo* and *Science Fiction Studies*.

What (historians and arbiters of literature begin to ponder, stroking their own beards) are we ultimately to make of these books, of this body of work floating up out of the waters of American literature, of this most individual of America's individualist writers? Delany (they begin to admit) is not going to go away. We are going to have to deal with him.

What we are going to have to do is embrace him. We are going to have to accept these books, that body of work, as a major landmark in our literature. To admit how important this work is, both for itself and for the influence it has already had and will continue to have. To recognize that such books as *Dhalgren*, the Nevèrÿon quartet and *Hogg* find their natural company in those of Julio Cortazar and Gabriel Garcia Marquez, Thomas Pynchon, Gunter Grass, William Gaddis, Richard Powers.

The scope, ambition and achievement of Delany's work, the discomfort it causes us personally, the challenges with which it confronts us collectively, must be accepted. "Once what Delany is doing, or attempting to do, is understood," Russell Blackford writes herein, "it is difficult to be satisfied with the ambitions of any other sf writer, much less the overwhelming bulk of mainstream fiction."

Following seven years as a professor of comparative literature at the University of Massachusetts, during which time teaching and academic affairs claimed all his attention, Samuel R. Delany has rededicated himself to writing and publishing. Recent and forthcoming books include (from Wesleyan University Press) reissues of older works alongside new collections of stories, essays, criticism and interviews, and (from small presses) a handful of new fiction.

Atlantis: Model 1924 is a remarkable novella erected at the intersection of Delany's father's (actual) arrival as a young man in New York City and (wholly imagined) meeting with Hart Crane on the Brooklyn Bridge, a work as packed, as densely layered with allusion and substance, as anything Joyce wrote. *Hogg* dates from the '70s and is contemporaneous with what many consider Delany's masterpiece, *Dhalgren*. It is also, itself, a masterpiece. *The Mad Man*, finished just days before publication in 1994, re-creates the Upper West Side, where Harlem-born Delany now lives, as a kind of scatological idyll. Equal parts murder mystery and morality play, a meditation on the nature and duplicity of identity, an abutment of pornographic fantasy with real-warts-on-imaginary-frogs realism, it's like nothing any of us has ever read before, a truly new, truly original novel cut, like so much of Delany's work, to its own unique pattern.

The literary world, particularly in America, it seems, has difficulty with writers and work not easily categorized. Even as a science fiction writer, and unquestionably he is one of the field's preeminent stylists, a major influence on two generations of writers, Delany rarely stood in the spot assigned him. He was interested in space opera and stories set on other worlds when the field's most exciting new writers had turned away from such preoccupations. Fabulously popular, he began producing work so divergent and difficult that in science fiction circles to this day mere mention of a title such as *Triton* or *Dhalgren* can call up whole realms of posturing and polemics. Then his efforts carried still further afield, away from fiction entirely, into autobiography, complex modes of criticism, literary theory.

In addition, beginning early in his career with articles for science fiction fan magazines, moving on to his book on a single Tom Disch short story (*The American Shore*) and ever more complex pieces for the *New York Review of Science Fiction* and academic journals—burrowing ever closer to the heart of what he and his chosen field were all about—Delany has become a major critic and theorist for science fiction.

The shelf containing those dozen-plus science fiction novels, then, holds as well several collections of essays, a remarkable autobiography, a series of *sui generis* postmodern fantasies, short-story collections, finely-wrought memoirs of growing up black and gay, addresses and polemics on gay affairs, literary and pornographic novels, and hundreds upon hundreds of pages of criticism ranging from the abstract and theoretical (how do we go about, word by word, reconstructing a world in our language, in our thought?) to the most specific (as in his close readings of fellow science fiction writers, or of Stephen Crane).

From the first, Delany's reach has been encyclopedic. This shows in the scope and Balzacian inclusiveness of the initial three-volume epic, *The Fall of the Towers*; in his creation of a self-discrete universe-city in *Dhalgren*; in the social investigations of the Nevèrÿon tales (a major theme of which is the change from barter to a money-based economy); in the epistemological underpinning of much of his later critical writing.

"The fragments of the world we seek always float down to us in bits and pieces—never all at once," Delany wrote, more or less in passing, in a recent sixty-two-page letter. In that letter the sentence is preceded by *but*. That *but*, that exception, that plane between the inclusive and momentary, between perception and apprehension, is where Delany—professor Delany, science fiction writer Delany, autobiographer and memoirist Delany, critic Delany, gay black Delany—resides.

Always, the revolutionary's goal is to create a society in which he will be superfluous. This he holds in one fist of his mind. Another, open hand accepts that he'll never see such a society, that walls *will* come down, but not in his time. He begins by defining himself in opposition, and in discovering what that means, in defining the limits and borders of his opposition, ends by defining himself truly.

Dichterisch wohnet/Der Mensch auf dieser Erde, Holderlin wrote. Poetically, man dwells on the earth. What we understand of the world (as opposed to what we know of it) we understand by metaphor and intuition, approximations, proliferating half-truths. (Perception, apprehension: fragments of the world floating down as we look up.) Yet any true change or transformation must begin in accurate description.

Revolution is created by language, controlled by language, *is* in a sense language. Revolution itself—opposition, redefinition, its voice, its acts and outcome—only fulfills the language of revolution. As George Steiner suggests, language is the chief instrument of man's refusal to accept the world as it is. And so the dialectic is never conclusive, only temporizing: shelters, halfway houses, moments of quiet while the world and our own efforts at comprehension reload.

Endings to be useful must be inconclusive, Delany writes at one point. In his work there seldom *are* endings: one novel, *Nova*, trails off midsentence; *Dhalgren* loops back endlessly, Escherlike, upon itself; the body of work hopfrogs itself, novels and nonfiction feeding into and commenting upon one another, many of them undergoing a kind of continuous revision that puts one in mind of Henry James setting himself in stone with the New York Edition—or, more appropriately, of Whitman's lifelong re-creation of America and self in successive, endless editions of *Leaves of Grass*.

Like that of Georges Bataille, a writer he resembles in many ways, Delany's work has become a kind of exemplar of Barthes's Text, defined as deriving from conscious violation of that hierarchy of discourses on which genre theory, and poetics in general, depend:

> What constitutes the Text is . . . its subversive force in respect of the old classifications. How do you classify a writer like Georges Bataille? The answer is so difficult that the literary manuals generally prefer to forget about Bataille who, in fact, wrote texts, perhaps continuously one single text.

Just so, in the diversity of Delany's work there is a particular, peculiar unity. Not only does he provide us, in the fiction, with the basic materials, the very stuff of that encounter we call reading, he also provides us, both in the criticism and in self-reflective aspects of later fiction, extensive instruction as to how we should read it—then in letters, memoirs, critical pieces and "silent" interviews, circles back yet a third time to question our reading. Sometimes, as in the marvelous self-interrogations of his autobiography *The Motion of Light in Water*, he questions his own readings as well.

I know of no other creative writer—for Delany, but one distinction among many—whose efforts have been so constantly and centrally involved with creating a body of criticism, with trying to ferret out what literature in the late twentieth century is all about, to understand how it is read, published, received, recycled: how it is *done*. Many writers, of course, turn out reviews, critical pieces, even occasional essays on creativity, but with Delany, from the first, criticism has been its own enterprise, one increasingly inextricable from that of the purely creative, so that the body of his critical work—especially if we include the autobiography and memoirs, open letters that can run to sixty or more pages, interviews, lectures and addresses—well may be one of the largest extant and, although episodic, finally one of the most cohesive.

Most likely it's the creative work that will endure, *Dhalgren* and the Nevèrÿon series in particular, but just as these fantastic works, catching the light of our own eyes, reflect back accurate descriptions of the world in which they were created, so does the fiction reflect back the critical writing—and the critical writing, in turn, the fiction.

"The clearest, most memorable feature of art is how it arises, and the world's best works, in telling of the most diverse things, are in fact narrations of their own birth," Boris Pasternak pointed out. For Delany, autobiography is "only another kind of fiction." *Everything* is only another kind of fiction,

"Wherever we go, whatever we do, self is the sole object we study and learn," Emerson tells us—little difference if we travel to Concord or across galaxies. At first, in articles such as many of those collected in *The Jewel-Hinged Jaw*, Delany's self-examination took place apart from his fiction, on a kind of sidetrack. He had always put much of himself, reimagined events from his own life, into his fiction. Then, in *The Einstein Intersection*, the fiction itself became textually self-conscious. Excerpts from journals Delany kept while composing the novel and while travelling in Greece frame the novel's sections, reflecting, questioning.

> I wonder what effect Greece will have on TEI. The central subject of the book is myth.

> When the rain stopped, I walked through the waterfront fish market where the silver fish had their gills pulled out and looped over their jaws so that each head was crowned with a bloody flower. . . . Perhaps on rewriting I shall change Kid Death's hair from black to red.

> In the second story of the old teahouse across the park I sat in a corner away from the stove and tried to wrestle my characters towards their endings. Soon I shall start again. Endings to be useful must be inconclusive.

Delany's central characters are themselves likely to be storytellers— the poet of *Babel-17*, the singers of "Time Considered as a Helix of Semi-Precious Stones," Lobey with his musical machete in *The Einstein Intersection*, *Dhalgren*'s Kid—even if inchoate ones. They are also likely to be outlaws, and in Delany outlaw and artist are often indistinguishable. He creates entire societies in order to depict those at the society's margin. Outlaw, artist, the sexually unconstrained—these embody that revolutionary impulse at the heart of much of Delany's work.

All too often in science fiction, revolution leads simply to inculcation or restoration of contemporary Western values to some land far removed in time or space. By contrast, Delany's revolutions—galactic, societal, personal, sexual, accomplished or anticipated—are real. These are the figures our lives make against the sky, he says again and again. Now consider, think, see, how painfully those figures must change as the sky above them, the worlds around them, change.

David Samuelson remarks in one of the essays herein that Delany's "ultimate goal as a writer seems to be to bring about a recognition of the power of language to decenter the role of conventions in life as well as in fiction," another marker of that central revolutionary urge. In both its use of language (that is, in the sensual surface of the writing itself) and its sexual preoccupations Delany's work is sensual in a way little speculative fiction is; at the same time it is, again, unusually given to intellection. The fragments of the world float down to us in bits and pieces (this is sensation) and of them (by way of intellect, narrative, self-examination) we cobble together meaning. Borders, of course, are both boundary and frontier, and it seems to me that this commingling of sensation and intellect embodies much of what Delany is about.

In the Nevèrÿon books he set out to bring to the surface, "radically to explore," sadomasochistic and homoerotic elements at the heart of the largely infantile genre of sword and sorcery. The genre *is* puerile, Delany says; one well may wonder why a writer would choose to invest such expense of spirit in an enterprise doomed by that fundamental infantilism, able to create at best (Delany again) "a highly specialized verbal inflation— four volumes and seventeen hundred pages worth, so far—of the most limited interest."

In fact, the Nevèrÿon books are a major achievement, one for which there is no real precedent or antecedent, a hearty, surprising stew of magic, aesthetics, savagery, theories of civilization, flying dragons, politics, useful myth, fantasy, autobiography, sexuality. The man who would intellectualize sword and sorcery, we're forced to remember, earlier (in *Tides of Lust*) had cast the Faust legend as pornography.

I'm hardly alone in thinking *Dhalgren* to be among the handful of great contemporary novels, on a level with *The Recognitions*, *Hopscotch*, *Gravity's Rainbow*, *The Tin Drum* or *One Hundred Years of Solitude*. Despite the novel's frank difficulty, despite its essentially noncommercial nature and early attacks from sf reviewers, *Dhalgren* found—and has retained—its audience. Writing in 1977, three years after the book's publication, Mark Gawron observed:

For a novel so obviously ambitious and difficult, one carrying about it the "taint of the experimental," for a science fiction paperback published with little fanfare, which opened to a storm of critical displeasure, *Dhalgren* has done astoundingly well on the marketplace, selling upwards of half a million copies in its first two years of existence, still far short of the hallowed land of the bestseller, but enough to fall comfortably within the ranks of the top ten bestselling science fiction novels of all time. Why?

Obviously, Gawron goes on, because people liked it.

As to why they liked it, those reasons were doubtless as multifaceted and various as the novel is rich. Most of *Dhalgren*'s bad press has come from within the science fiction world (and again, there *were* highly favorable reactions), both fan and professional; and much of its audience, to judge by its unusual numbers, has been drawn from outside that world. It may simply be a question of certain fixed expectations not being met.

Travelling incognito as critical alter ego K. Leslie Steiner, Delany agrees. The novel did indeed find its way to "that most important of audiences, the vertical audience of concerned and alert readers interested in the progress of American fiction." Only this audience, Steiner suggests, could find such a novel truly absorbing. Elsewhere, in his own voice, in a passage marvelously paralleling the novel's own structure and language, Delany notes:

Anyone who finds it helpful may approach *Dhalgren*, without fear of misreading the text because of the approach (though there is, alas, no way to insure a "proper" reading: it may have none) as (and in) an attempt to explore and respond to a small sector of the grammar of the language of human signs.

The novel tries to focus on the grammar of that language, Delany continues, by a science-fictional reorganization of the ways in which these signs are produced and reproduced. *Dhalgren* is an extraordinary novel, one that functions simultaneously on many levels, a virtual *summa* of contemporary modes of fiction.

At the time of its writing Delany had relocated from New York to San Francisco, a city whose spirit richly invests the novel. Beginning work, Delany told himself: I'll write J.G. Ballard's *The Burning World* as it should have been done, the ultimate end-of-the-world novel. *Dhalgren*'s decaying urban landscape, its emphasis on setting, atmosphere and imagery and its apparent eschewal of meaning, reflect much of what was going on both in science fiction's so-called New Wave and in the period's now-classic postmodern fiction, work like Barth's, Coover's and Barthelme's. *Dhalgren*'s baroque effects and proliferation of ideas look back to Alfred

Bester, an admitted influence, and forward to the cyberpunks who without Delany could not have existed. Certainly there's a profound spillover from the art and poetry scene of S.F. at that time, as well as from the rootlessness and social estrangement many of us felt then. I've also long suspected a nod on Delany's part to William Gass's "The Pedersen Kid," who appears from nowhere (he is found frozen in snow), who may or may not be real, flickers into existence in a present that seems at once non- and pan-historical, refuses simple mimeticism and finally sinks back into the obscurity from which he came.

As one looks back on almost forty years of work, it becomes clear that all along Delany has searched for some ideal form, some mode of writing at once true and imagined, real and fictive, that might encompass it all, that might be able to contain the world's multifarious leanings, vectors, veerings and prevarications. Once he thought that science fiction with its ready-made universals and symbolic potential might accomplish that. Further into his career he believed that ontological or epistemological criticism or the discipline of semiotics might. And if not those, then perhaps his Proustian incursions towards (always *towards,* for everything is approximation, everything is measured apprehension) autobiography. And still he longs to tell the true story of change, to say what would happen were *real* freedom ever rendered: to sketch out, from observing, from reading and imagining, from living through its tatters, the lines of what true society might be.

Science fiction, Delany points out again and again, is a recursive genre, and its discourse, which by definition must be continuous, can be carried on extra- as well as inter-textually. Dave Samuelson's essay in this book occasioned a letter of some forty pages from Delany to its author, yet another volley in a correspondence that has come to fill two file drawers and begun to spill over into a third—preemptive, yes, but at the same time striving to bring Samuelson's observations into line with a unity of vision towards which Delany seems always to be struggling.

Not surprisingly, Delany is an inveterate rewriter. Serial versions of new works crowd his friends' mailboxes. New editions of old works arrive with words or whole sentences whited-out, marginal corrections and emendations, interpolated strips of revised text attached. There's a sense, of course, in which *all* Delany's work is a revised, attached text.

I believe, yes, that Delany is among our finest and most important writers. It's been my intention in compiling the book you now hold—the first major study of his work—to assert this. To insist that Delany's writing be afforded the recognition and attention it deserves. To enter my claim that Delany's legacy can only become ever more apparent as years proceed.

Today, of course, there's a much broader critical acceptance of genre writing than at any time in the past. Even our most devoutly literary reviewers and critics pay service to the energy and regenerative influence of such work. Still, here is one final Delany caveat.

> Now there are many SF and fantasy writers who honestly feel that my work for the last fifteen or more years has been wholly misguided, if not deranged. Paradoxically, I feel that such a judgement is finally more informed—without being in any way more correct—than the extra-generic view that sees my enterprise as revolutionary in *terms of the genre*. The only view less informed is the one that sees my enterprise as, somehow, fundamentally literary and having *nothing* to do with the genre.

Finally, too, my own final caveat.

The body of Delany scholarship is just beginning to congeal. With this anthology I provide a way station from which others can go forward, pitch their own expeditions, discover new continents and map the old. Here you'll find a cross-section of current Delany scholarship, from fairly straightforward readings and appreciations (Carl Malmgren, Mary Kay Bray) to extended, densely argued pieces such as those of Ken James and Kate Spencer.

Some of these pieces, like Mark Gawron's on *Dhalgren*, originated close to publication, while others have the benefit of later work and whatever perspective time affords. Some are reprinted from small-circulation journals, *Black American Literature Forum*, *The New York Review of Science Fiction, Extrapolation*; my wish to collect and make these easily accessible became a major impetus to the creation of this book. Several pieces were extensively revised and expanded for publication here. Ken James's brilliant essay on structure and form in Delany's work, Bob Fox's on *Dhalgren* and Mary Kay Bray's on *Stars in My Pocket Like Grains of Sand* all appear here for the first time.

Any book, of course, is the record of a failure—there's never world enough and time. There are so many other pieces, real and imagined, that I should have liked to include, so many other topics I wish I had been able to touch upon. Delany's early work is terribly slighted, for instance. The short stories are mentioned hardly at all. And though it floats along alligatorlike throughout, head just above water, a constant presence, Delany's landmark autobiography *The Motion of Light in Water* doesn't have the separate essay it so distinctly deserves. Perhaps (one hopes) these lacunae will be redeemed in subsequent volumes.

Recent publication of *The Mad Man* and *Hogg* more than anything else has caused me anew to think about just what Delany's been up to all along. I note that reviewers' comments, their befuddlement and obvious confusion, echo those greeting Delany's work at least since the first great apostasy, *Dhalgren*. Generally these proceed: What is this thing we are holding? It's not at all what it's *supposed* to be. How did it get here? And what in the world are we going to do with it? All good questions. Essential questions.

I think of Lionel Trilling, finally, his insistence upon literature's basic adversary intention, its "clear purpose of detaching the reader from the habits and thoughts and feelings that the larger culture imposes." If Delany's work could be characterized in a single phrase—and of course it can't—that phrase might be the very one, though certainly in ways Trilling never anticipated.

James Sallis
New Orleans

ASH
OF
STARS

The Languages of Science Fiction

Samuel R. Delany's *Babel-17*

CARL MALMGREN

> Science fiction is a literature of the Beyond, as well as a literature
> of the impact of change on Man. It deals with the Beyond in a
> historical sense: the Future, that is rapidly becoming the Present.
> It must also deal with the beyond of knowledge—without losing
> touch with a sense of the social basis of Man, whose knowledge
> this is. For, just as we are here making our world and our society,
> so in another sense we are engaged in the making of the universe
> through that which is at the root of our social being: our language.
> —Ian Watson, "Toward an Alien Linguistics"

In his essay on "Fiction about the Future," H. G. Wells
claims that the most significant "futurist" fiction, and the most difficult
to bring off, would be that sort which uses as its novum an estranged
social order—Wells uses the example of a world populated entirely by
women—and then focuses on the struggle of a few individuals to come to
terms with that social order. Kingsley Amis devotes much of his influential
book on science fiction to those fictions which dramatize "social inquiry,"
which serve as an "instrument of social diagnosis and warning" (NMOH
87). And Isaac Asimov baldly states that what he terms "social science
fiction" is the "most mature" and the "most socially significant" form that
SF can take (SF:TF 273). All three writers are privileging or valorizing one
particular SF form, alternate-society science fiction, the dominant novum
of which is an estranged or alternative social order.[1] The paradigm for this
fiction involves the visit to a utopic or dystopic society, during which the
visitor (in some cases the reader) is invited to compare that society with
his or her own. Alternate-society SF poses a wide assortment of questions,
including the following: What constitutes a good or bad society? What is

3

the proper relation between the individual and the community? To what extent are freedom and order mutually antagonistic? What are the main determinants of "social reality"? What is the function of particular social institutions? What is the relation between language and social order? These fictions, many of which figure as science fiction classics, mediate the proper relation between Self and Society, in general eliciting a normative reading, the establishment of a framework of value.

Dealing as it does with alien cultures and futuristic societies, alternate-society science fiction often refers to, calls upon, or plays with a spectrum of language novums—from neologistic forms to alien tongues to invented languages. Indeed, these linguistic novums, as both Katherine L. Spencer and Eric S. Rabkin have shown, serve to *real*-ize the imaginary SF world: "the items do more than denote the simple *thereness* of the world they belong to; they also tell us—again, usually in oblique ways—something about the *nature* of the world we find them in" (Spencer 43), a world whose linguistic norms call into question the norms of the originary society.[2]

Science fiction is a literature of otherness and change, and the most self-conscious alternate-society SF tries to take into account the inevitability of linguistic change and the possibility of linguistic otherness, if only by acknowledging that new and different societies presuppose new and different languages. Sorting through these linguistically self-conscious fictions, we can identify different levels of metalinguistic engagement. Some authors, such as Anthony Burgess in *A Clockwork Orange,* incorporate forms or examples of the new language into the discourse and dialogue of the fiction; in so doing, they are able to inject a degree of strangeness into that discourse (to "defamiliarize" it), while at the same time reinforcing the mimetic contract and adding another level of signification. Burgess's Russian/American patois at once underwrites the verisimilitude of his futuristic society and serves as an index to the idea of superpower domination. The metalinguistic function of "nadsat," Rabkin notes, is to make "a reality claim about the narrative world being a possible future state of our own world" (Rabkin 93). Other authors, such as Orwell in *Nineteen Eighty-Four,* more fully thematize language by incorporating episodes which foreground the form and function of the linguistic novum; in these fictions, language becomes a topic or theme highlighting the nature of the alternate society.

But, in a relatively few science fictions, an invented language becomes *the* narrative dominant, informing the plot, the themes, and the discourse of the fiction. These fictions necessarily investigate the nature of language, the relation of language and reality, and the possibilities of linguistic otherness. In *The Languages of Pao,* for example, Jack Vance imagines the transformation of an entire planet through the introduction of new language systems. The new languages—one militaristic, one mercantile, and one bureaucratic—are imposed from above on separate segments of the people of Pao, whose native tongue tends to render them passive, obedient, and communal. Once the languages are in place, Pao begins a metamorphosis from feudalism to industrial capitalism. Because "every language imposes a certain world-view upon the mind" (TLOP 115), Pao evolves into three separate language communities, each nurturing a certain outlook and each pursuing a corresponding activity. Ultimately, there appears Pastiche, an amalgam of the three tongues, a language which incorporates all three ways of looking at the world and is therefore more encompassing, less self-absorbed, less one-dimensional. The more languages one speaks, Vance suggests, the less self-centered one becomes and the more other-directed one is. Pastiche becomes "the language of service" on Pao, assuring that the planet will survive and evolve in a humanitarian way.

In a similar way, Ian Watson's *The Embedding* explores the possibility of using various languages, both artificial and natural, to discover "the plan for language," the "mind's idea of all possible languages" (TE 43). The linguists in the novel believe that such a plan will enable humans to find or invent a language that can "bespeak" reality—that is, totalize reality and then control it. Fictions such as these assume that language is not merely instrumental, that a person is to some extent spoken by the language he or she speaks. The most celebrated of such fictions is Samuel Delany's *Babel-17*. Although not a single word of the invented language Babel-17 appears in the novel, its centrality is indicated in the title itself. The novel systematically interrogates the function of alternate languages, the relation between language and reality, the problematics of communication, and the linguistic possibilities of SF in general.

At one level, that of form, *Babel-17* hardly seems worth close examination; it is, after all, action-packed, fast-paced, "Star Wars" space opera, involving intergalactic war, treacherous spies, exotic locales, strange aliens, dangerous missions, and rousing space battles (see Hardesty 63–69; Slusser 31ff). But Delany has worked a number of important transformations upon the simple space-opera formula. His protagonist, for example, is not a macho male roustabout, but rather a female poet. The most dangerous weapon in the work is not an SF gadget but a mysterious invented language. The real villain of the piece is not a mad scientist or an evil empire but rather the inability of one group of human beings to communicate with another group. The plot involves gaining control of the mysterious language and using it to overcome that villain. These transformations signal the fact that Delany has taken a marginal form—space opera—and tried to bring it to the center by reinventing it.

Language is not only the motor that drives the plot of the novel; it also dominates the text's thematics. The problematics of communication are frequently thematized explicitly. The novel opens with a scene in which a general meets with the poet Rydra Wong to discuss the problem of the new language of the enemy, Babel-17. On his way to the meeting he wonders about the needs of the city's inhabitants: "Take any of them, take any million. Who are they? What do they want? What would they say if given a chance to say anything?" (B 4). After he meets Rydra and falls in love with her, his feelings are mixed: "My god, he thought, as coolness struck his face, all that inside me and she doesn't know! I didn't communicate a thing! Somewhere in the depth the words, *not a thing, you're still safe*. But stronger on the surface was the outrage of his own silence. Didn't communicate a thing at all" (B 13). *Babel-17* is a novel in which strangers try desperately to learn how to communicate with one another, in which Rydra Wong searches for a language that will go to "the depth" of words.

In the course of her quest, Rydra discourses at length about languages in general and Babel-17 in particular, explaining to her comrades aspects of phonetics, syntax, and semantics, comparing languages and vocabularies, and discussing the limits of semiotic systems such as sign language and poetry. Throughout the novel, Rydra's crewmates testify to her ability to communicate with them, to cut through the separate worlds of isolated individuals, enabling them to converse and grow. The novel ends with a chorus of such testimony:

> "She managed to say so much to me in that one evening, so very simply." (B 172)

> "She told me flatly: No, I would have to tell her more. That's the first time anyone's told me I *had* to do something in fourteen years. I may not like it; I sure as hell respect it. . . . It's so easy to get caught in your fragment of the world. When a voice comes cutting through, it's important." (B 174)

> "She found a way to talk to us without [a discorporaphone]. She cut through worlds, and joined them—that's the important part—so that both became bigger." (B 81)

Indeed, at times it seems that the favorite topic of conversation is conversation itself:

> "Well, you . . . you come to us and immediately we start to learn things, things about you, and ultimately about ourselves."

"We're used to talking to each other."

"Yes, but you tell the important things. What you like, what you don't like, how you do things." (B 80)

In such a linguistically self-conscious text, even accidental or "noisy" references to the act of communication are partially foregrounded:

"Please, I've got to talk to you." (B 14)

"He seemed to know what he was talking about."
   "Talk, talk, talk." (B 26)

"You've got nothing to say to me." (B 37)

"Now, you talk to me, Calli, Ron." (B 44)

"I just wanted to say . . ." (B 50)

"Who can talk to people like that?" (B 176)

And the novel ends with Rydra's claim that she "can talk [her] way out of anything" (B 193). Despite its space-opera dressing, what *Babel-17* talks about is, in a very real sense, *talking* itself.

Language is central to the novel in large part because Delany's view of language is Whorfian; he sees language as constitutive of reality, not as reflective of reality. We see what our language enables us to see; we think according to the ways that language makes available to us. As Rydra Wong says at one point, "there are certain ideas which have words for them. If you don't have the words, you can't know the ideas" (B 132). Robert Scholes has suggested that the novel might well "have begun with Ludwig Wittgenstein's notion that our language is the limit of our world, or the Whorfian linguistic hypothesis that language shapes perception itself, so that people from different cultures actually 'see' different worlds around them" (qtd. in Meyers 178). Another critic, Walter Meyers, takes Delany to task for relying on "this questionable idea," claiming that Whorfianism is unidirectional and cannot account for ideational innovation (AAL 181). While we might acknowledge Meyers's objections, we could counter that Whorfianism supplies a valuable corrective to an instrumentalist view of language that underlies certain misconceptions, such as the ideas that the language of science is neutral and universal (see Sefler) or that perception is itself unmediated by language (see Eco). Perhaps we should see Delany's adoption of Whorfianism as a strategic move, one meant to foreground language, to stress its instrumentality in our perception of reality, while at the same time showcasing the possibilities of SF's invented languages.

At the very center of his novel, Delany places an episode that at once highlights his notion of the powers of language and serves as a paradigm for the larger plot. Rydra has been captured by a pirate spaceship, and she awakens strapped to a bed in the infirmary. She is thinking of language:

> Abstract thoughts in a blue room: Nominative, genitive, elative, accusative one, accusative two, ablative, partitive, illative, instructive, abessive, adessive, inessive, essive, allative, translative, comitative. Sixteen cases to the Finnish noun. Odd, some languages get by with only singular and plural. . . . The blue room was round and warm and smooth. No way to say *warm* in French. There was only *hot* and *tepid*. If there's no word for it, how do you think about it? (B 97)

Locked into English, Rydra awakens to certain reality—she is trapped in a strange restraining web. In desperation she switches in her thoughts to the language Babel-17, which she has partially mastered: "She looked down at the—not 'webbing,' but rather a three-particle vowel differential, each part of which defined one stress of the three-way tie, so that the weakest points in the mesh were identified when the total sound of the differential reached its lowest point." The perspective afforded by the new language enables her to see the weakness of the webbing: "By breaking the threads at these points, she realized, the whole web would unravel" (B 99). Switching to another language creates another reality: Rydra is able to free herself. In every key episode of the novel—the initial sabotage attempt, the assassination attempt, the battles in space—the formula is the same: Rydra moves from a language frame in which reality is constrictive or uncertain or exigent through the language frame of Babel-17 to a new reality in which obstacles are overcome, dangers neutralized, conflicts resolved. At the global level of macroplot, this structure informs the entire novel; ultimate mastery of Babel-17 means an end to the devastating intergalactic war.

An interpretive summary of the novel's five-part structure clarifies Delany's view on the relation between language and reality and the limits and powers of language in general. Each of the novel's five sections is named for a specific protagonist, and there is direct correspondence between the character and the thematic topos of the section. In the first section, titled "Rydra Wong," we are introduced to the "most famous poet in five explored galaxies" (B 5) and to her mission: the Alliance wants her to decode the language Babel-17 and to discover its role in acts of sabotage being perpetrated by the Invaders. In order to accomplish these ends, she requisitions a spaceship and recruits a crew for a flight to the Alliance War Yards where she feels the next act of sabotage will take place. The nature of this crew invites an allegorical reading, one which sets up the five-part structure of the novel. First Rydra enlists a pilot whose "nervous system [will be] connected directly with the controls" of the ship's "hyperstasis" faster-than-light drive (B 35). At the same time she finds a team of navigators to act as the computational "brain" for the journey. Later she makes a trip to the discorporate zone—the place where the energies of those that have discorporated but not died congregate—in order to recruit an "Eye," "Ear," and "Nose" to read the "hyperspace currents." It seems that there are some jobs on intergalactic flight that normal human beings just cannot perform; a "live human," one navigator explains, "scanning all that goes on in the hyperstasis frequencies would—well, die first, and go crazy second" (B 37). Once Rydra has signed up a platoon to do all the menial and mechanical jobs on the ship, her crew is complete. It should be clear that at a metaphorical level what has transpired is the assemblage of a composite human being, complete with brain, nervous system, senses, and body. Within this assembled totality, Rydra occupies the key position, her centrality having been signaled by the title of the section. She is that element which coordinates the disparate functions, which synthesizes the group by facilitating communication. Given her profession of poet, one might suggest that she serves as the Imagination of the assemblage; that is certainly one of her main roles in the adventures that follow. Describing to a friend how she went about selecting a crew, Rydra says that there was one basic criterion she applied: "they had to be people I could talk to" (B 49).

The mission of this crew, this composite being, is quite simple—to acquire control of the mysterious Babel-17, a language being used by the Invaders in acts of sabotage against the Alliance. But at the figurative level the crew must acquire a language with which to heal the breaches between alienated and isolated human beings. As one critic notes,

> The movement of *Babel-17* is directed by impulses towards more perfect communication: Rydra's psychological motivation, her unique talents, and the plot device of the mysterious language to be deciphered all point towards a climax of perfect communication. Delany emphasizes the need for it by repeatedly presenting gaps between people: between individuals, like the "triple" of Calli, Ron, and Molly; between groups, like the planet-bound and the spaceship crews; between "the Invaders" and "the Alliance" in the intergalactic war. (Stone-Blackburn 248)

The world of *Babel-17* is one of "isolated communities, each hardly touching its neighbor, each speaking, as it were, a different language" (B 64). That breach is figured most forcefully in the war itself, which pits not humans against aliens, but humans against humans from another galaxy. Indeed, Rydra is disturbed by the fact that her poems are immensely popular with both parties to the conflict, that her allegiance to the Alliance has been determined by an "accident of birth" (B 64). At the literal level mastering the new language will end the war; at the figurative level it will enable humanity to bridge the gap between Self and Other, healing the breach of isolation and alienation and clearing up the "misunderstandings that tie the world up and keep people apart" (B 19).

Part Two, titled "Ver Dorco," takes its name from the Baron who commands the Alliance War Yards. In this section, Rydra and her crew are exposed to the brutal reality of war minus a controlling language; they in effect experience the world "raw" (an appropriate metaphor given the food motif in this part.) Again the section begins with a paradigmatic episode. Rydra and her crew are preparing to eat; their preparations are interrupted by an act of treachery which jeopardizes their lives. Rydra resorts to her rapidly expanding knowledge of Babel-17 to analyze the problem and to effectuate a solution; she learns how "to go to another language in order to think about the problem clearly" (B 60). This formula is repeated several times in the novel, but its connection here with the act of eating is significant. The section culminates with a banquet that the Baron arranges for Rydra and her crew, a banquet disrupted by the assassination of the Baron and his key advisers by saboteurs responding to radio commands given in Babel-17. The banquet devolves into a madhouse scene of food, murder, and chaos. The ending of the section thus establishes a motif connecting food, language, and disorder; this motif suggests that the world untempered by language is at once murderous and carnivorous, that this kind of world will eat one alive.

The second section is littered with references to eating and with food imagery. The Baron is described as possessing a "disquieting appetite for [Rydra's] presence, a hunger for something she was or might be" (B 65). The "lean and hungry" Baron complains of being "starved" for intelligent conversation (a metaphor which links food and language) and interrupts a tour of the war yards because he is "famished" (B 65). When the Baroness refers to Rydra and her crew as "cool and pleasing, so fresh, so crisp," Rydra objects to being described as a salad. The Baroness responds, "I dare say if you stayed here long enough we would devour you. What you bring we are very hungry for" (B 80). Behind the veneer of a civilized conversation lies a carnivorous reality, something Rydra is figuratively unable to handle because she lacks the proper language. The section ends in murder and chaos.

Rydra and her crew are rescued from the debacle at the war yard by a passing pirate ship named "Jebel Tarik," which means "Tarik's Mountain" (B 101). The third section, taking its name from the ship, deals with Rydra's retreat from the world to a "mountainous" refuge. The epigraph for the section contains the line, "I would make a language we could all speak" (B 95), and that is the task that Rydra undertakes on Jebel Tarik. The pirate "shadow ship" represents a refuge from the carnivorous reality of the intergalactic war, a place where Rydra can perfect her understanding of Babel-17. During her stay on the pirate ship, she uses the language to foil an assassination attempt; her success here should be contrasted with her failure to prevent the death of the Baron in the previous section. She also demonstrates a growing mastery of the external world and its strife. Command of Babel-17 makes her into a formidable war general, and she wins two space battles with Invader fleets.

More important, in this section she meets another speaker of Babel-17 (though she doesn't realize it at the time), the dark other half that Rydra must link up with in order to make her language whole, the brutal ex-convict Butcher. At one point, the pirate leader, Tarik, suggests to Rydra that any whole person is "necessarily of two minds on any matter of moment" (B 108), thereby hinting at the central action of this section, the encounter between two minds, or better, the two parts of the mind which must connect for there to be wholeness; the conscious and informing mind of the poet must tap into the inarticulate and brute power of the unconscious. Butcher's mind is quite explicitly linked with the unconscious; his thoughts are "ego-less and inarticulate, magic, seductive, mythical" (B 159). During Rydra's stay on Jebel Tarik, he repeatedly shows himself capable of a "red bestiality" (B 128) that Rydra finds fascinating. Butcher's connection with the unconscious mind is underscored in the final section when he discovers, once his amnesia has been lifted, that he is Niles Ver Dorco and that he is responsible for his father's (the Baron's) death.

The meeting of the two minds in the fourth section, "The Butcher," is engineered through Rydra's power of teleplay. The poetic epigraph speaks of the birth and awakening of the dark "twin behind the eyes" (B 155), and the section represents an awakening to the power and amorality of the unconscious mind. The mind-link is at once sexual—"She had entered him in some bewildering reversed sexuality" (B 159)—and archetypal—

"the Criminal and artistic consciousness meeting in the same head with one language between them" (B 160). This experience is necessary for Rydra to become capable of doing what she has to, namely acting with the kind of ruthlessness it takes to put an end to the senseless and destructive intergalactic war. During the mind-link she says to Butcher:

> You're teaching me something, and it's shaking my whole picture of the world and myself. I thought I was afraid before because I couldn't do what you could do, Butcher . . . But I was afraid because I could do all those things, and for my own reasons, not your lack of reasons, because I am, and you are. I'm a lot bigger than I thought I was, Butcher, and I don't know whether to thank you or damn you for showing me. (B 162–63)

By tapping into the unconscious, by making ego go where id had been, Rydra has indeed become larger; she has, in effect, become whole.

In the fifth section—named after Rydra's doctor, Markus T'mwarba—Rydra, Butcher, and the crew make a final break from the Alliance and from the war altogether with full control of Babel-17. With a "language [they] could all speak," they will be able to heal single-handedly the illness that has infected the world: "This war will end within six months," Rydra confidently predicts (B 193). And thus a new language will create a new, more satisfactory reality.

At the beginning of the novel, no one can control the language Babel-17, in large part because it is an "impersonal language" (Weedman 41); it lacks the concepts "you" and "I." This lack is constitutive of more serious deficiencies or gaps. The lack of an "I" short-circuits the self-critical process; the speaker of Babel-17 is unable to stand apart from her or his linguistic formulations, to subject them to critical meta-commentary. As Rydra notes, the lack of an "I" "cuts out any awareness of the symbolic process at all—which is the way we distinguish between reality and our expression of reality" (B 189). Without the concept "I" we are unable to recognize language for what it is, a modeling system. And the concepts "you" and "I" are essential to the moral sense; without them, we cannot know that "for an *I* to kill a *you* without a lot of thought is a mistake" (B 139). Without these all-important concepts, the novel insists, we are blind to the idea of the Self and the Other; we exist apart from moral frameworks, are condemned to be both suicidal and sociopathic. Rydra is able to gain complete control over the language by creating personal pronouns for it. By adding an "I" she personalizes Babel-17 and converts it to Babel-18, the language with which she and Butcher will change the world. The language system *Babel-17*—the novel—also lacks a first person, in the form of the reader. Once that person has been added to the novel, once he or she has personalized it, then it too assumes a moral dimension, it too becomes self-critical. It becomes a language system that can affect reality.

One of Rydra's crewmates attributes to her the following quality: "She cut through worlds and joined them—that's the important part—so that both became bigger" (B 181). This same quality, of cutting through and joining worlds, is elsewhere attributed to science fiction as well: reading SF "you start thinking that maybe those people who live in other worlds . . . are real. If you believe in them, you're a little more ready to believe in yourself" (B 180). The reader of SF becomes, in effect, a little bit bigger. *Babel-17* also serves as a bridge between fragmented and isolated worlds, as a language system with the potential to make its "speakers" grow. Armed with this language system, we can, like Rydra Wong, begin to tell right from wrong, begin to right a wrong (Hardesty 69), indeed begin to change the world.

At one point early in the novel, Rydra complains to Markus T'mwarba that she feels dissatisfied as a poet because to this point she has simply been expressing the unarticulated ideas of others. "Now," she says, "I have things to say that are all my own. They're not what other people have said before, put in an original way. And they're not just contradictions of what other people have said, which amounts to the same thing. They're new" (B 17). At the end of the novel, she says that she may write a novel of her own, because she has "a lot to say" (B 193). Whether or not we conclude that *Babel-17* is her novel, we can still say that it has been author-ized by someone who shares her feelings and her ambitions. Samuel Delany has original things to say, and he needs a new language to say them in. The science fiction genre affords him the latitude within which to explore new domains, to express original propositions.

The most linguistically self-conscious alternate society SF frequently tries to do just that. In *Babel-17*, for example, the discorporate zone episode in part one, the awakening scene in part three, Rydra's foiling of the assassination attempt in part three, and the mental/sexual link-up in part four represent specific attempts on Delany's part to render new or extreme experiences in language. One critic has noted that Babel-17 works as well as it does because there is a direct connection between its words and the realities they define (Collings 64). The same could be said of the novel *Babel-17*: it undertakes a direct connection between its words and its realities. By enacting linguistic otherness, it tries to motivate the relation between signifier and signified. In so doing the novel aspires to the condition of Coleridge's Symbol, which "partakes of the Reality which it renders intelligible" (TCW 30).

Invented or alien languages, then, offer the fictionist specific venues in which to enact real otherness or to encode innovative semantic spaces. Suzette Haden Elgin, for example, takes on this kind of linguistic experiment in *Native Tongue*. She imagines a brutally patriarchical near-future society in which the 19th Amendment has been repealed and women have been relegated to the status of legal minors, well on the way to being reduced to chattel. The women are forced to invent a specifically female tongue, "Láadan," in order to subvert that social order: "And then, as more and more little girls acquire Láadan and begin to speak a language that expresses the perceptions of women rather than those of men, reality will begin to change" (NT 250). Láadan contains, among other things, distinctly feminist encodings, "the making of a name for a chunk of the world that so far as we know has never been chosen for naming before in any human language," "a chunk that has been around for a long time but has never impressed anyone as sufficiently important to *deserve* its own name" (NT 22). "Encoding consists," one critic says, "of assigning names and descriptions to female semantic perceptions" (Bray 51), of giving voice to a uniquely feminine perspective. With new languages like Láadan, we can speak the unknown or the unspoken; in so doing, we can bespeak new realities. In Ian Watson's *The Embedding,* one character notes that it is really almost impossible for one person "to imagine the otherness of another person" (TE 7). The most cognitively rewarding SF tries to enact that otherness, to *real*-ize it so that readers can experience it for themselves.

Postmodern writing is acutely aware that all systems of notation offer us models of reality rather than descriptions of it. Fiction, of course, is one such notational system; as Delany says, "fiction makes models of reality" (TJHJ 151). Science fiction's notational system presents us with a model at one remove from reality, a counterrealistic model. For Delany, however, SF is a privileged system, because in it, more than in any genre, one can legitimately undertake the search for new language models with which to construct or invent reality. In SF novels such as *Babel-17*, the fictionist can "use language in much the same way that Babel-17 is used: to . . . force the reader to think in new ways" (McEvoy 58). From this perspective, it is not at all surprising that most SF featuring an alien or invented tongue as its narrative dominant adopts a Whorfian view of the relation between language and reality. Such SF wants to emphasize the extent to which any new language system can affect our view of reality. As Jack Vance says in *The Languages of Pao,* "when people speak different languages, their minds work differently and they act differently" (TLOP 65). Delany would add that science fiction gives us many new and different languages to speak. Mastering these languages, we learn to think and act differently.

Notes

1. For a further discussion of alternate-society SF, see Malmgren, chap. 3.

2. Spencer deals at length with the way in which neologisms and other linguistic novums contribute to the real-ization of SF worlds. For a similar argument, see Delany, "Generic Protocols: Science Fiction and Mundane." Rabkin focuses on the way in which these novums underwrite the mimetic contract and interrogate contemporary value systems.

Works Cited

Amis, Kingsley. *New Maps of Hell: A Survey of Science Fiction.* New York: Harcourt, 1960.

Asimov, Isaac. "Social Science Fiction." Rpt. in *Science Fiction: The Future.* Ed. Dick Allen. New York: Harcourt, 1971. 263–99.

Bray, Mary Kay. "The Naming of Things: Men and Women, Language and Reality in Suzette Haden Elgin's *Native Tongue*." *Extrapolation* 27 (Spring 1986): 49–61.

Coleridge, Samuel Taylor. *The Collected Works of Samuel Taylor Coleridge.* Vol. 6, *Lay Sermons.* Ed. R. J. White. Princeton, NJ: Princeton UP, 1972.

Collings, Michael R. "Samuel R. Delany and John Wilkins: Artificial Languages, Science, and Science Fiction." *Reflections on the Fantastic: Selected Essays from the Fourth International Conference on the Fantastic in the Arts.* Ed. Michael R. Collings. New York: Greenwood Press, 1986. 61–68.

Delany, Samuel R. *Babel-17.* 1966. New York: Daw, 1984.

———. "Generic Protocols: Science Fiction and Mundane." *The Technological Imagination: Theories and Fictions.* Ed. Teresa DeLauretis et al. Madison, WI: Coda Press, 1980. 175–93.

———. *The Jewel-Hinged Jaw: Notes on the Languages of Science Fiction.* Elizabethtown, NY: Dragon Press, 1977.

Eco, Umberto. "How Culture Conditions the Colours We See." *On Signs.* Ed. Marshall Blonsky. Baltimore, MD: Johns Hopkins UP, 1985. 157–75.

Elgin, Suzette Haden. *Native Tongue.* New York: Daw, 1984.

Hardesty, William H., III. "Semiotics, Space Opera and *Babel-17*." *Mosaic* 13, 3–4 (1980): 63–69.

Malmgren, Carl D. *Worlds Apart: Narratology of Science Fiction.* Bloomington: Indiana UP, 1991.

McEvoy, Seth. *Samuel R. Delany.* New York: Frederick Ungar, 1984.

Meyers, Walter E. *Aliens and Linguistics: Language Study and Science Fiction.* Athens: U of Georgia P, 1980.

Rabkin, Eric S. "Metalinguistics and Science Fiction." *Critical Inquiry* 6 (1979): 79–97.

Seffler, George F. "Science, Science Fiction, and Possible World Semantics." *Aspects of Fantasy: Selected Essays from the Second International Conference on Fantasy in Film and Literature.* Ed. William Coyle. New York: Greenwood Press, 1986. 213–19.

Slusser, George. *The Delany Intersection: Samuel Delany Considered as a Writer of Semi-Precious Words.* San Bernardino, CA: Borgo Press, 1977.

Spencer, Katherine L. " 'The Red Sun is High, the Blue Low': Towards a Stylistic Description of Science Fiction." *Science Fiction Studies* 10 (1983): 35–49.

Stone-Blackburn, Susan. "Adult Telepathy: *Babel-17* and *The Left Hand of Darkness.*" *Extrapolation* 30 (Fall 1989): 243–53.

Vance, Jack. *The Languages of Pao.* 1958. New York: Ace, 1966.

Watson, Ian. *The Embedding.* London: Gollancz, 1973.

———. "Towards an Alien Linguistics." *Vector 71* 2 (December 1975): 14–23.

Weedman, Jane Branham. *Samuel R. Delany.* Starmount Reader's Guide 10. Mercer Island, WA: Starmount House, 1982.

Wells, H. G. *H. G. Wells's Literary Criticism.* Ed. Patrick Parrinder and Robert M. Philmus. Sussex: Harvester Press, 1980.

To See What Condition Our Condition Is In

Trial by Language in *Stars in My Pocket Like Grains of Sand*

MARY KAY BRAY

One of the definitive characteristics of Samuel R. Delany's fiction is its "consciousness-raising" function. The number of characters in his works who are marginal to their social contexts or outsiders to those contexts altogether calls attention to those social frameworks and what they offer or deny their inhabitants. Add to this awareness the dialogue between the givens of the present world and the givens created in an SF world which Delany suggests is evoked as part of the process of reading SF. To understand the social and artifactual givens created in an SF world, readers must conceive the changes from the present world which would be necessary for the fictional one to exist and, in so doing, become more aware of what exists or lacks in the present.[1] In Delany's fictions this heightened awareness of present reality typically comes through ironies and reversals played upon it by the text. Additionally, in *Stars in My Pocket Like Grains of Sand* (NY: Bantam Spectra, 1985), Delany gives the text itself an overtly directorial role in controlling and focusing readers' attention, this time upon—amidst a *richesse* of objects—the relationship between the shape taken by a society and the conditions of the lives of its individual members.

In *Stars in My Pocket*, the fictional organization which oversees the flow of information in the galaxy and seems also to oversee the evolution of galactic civilization is called the Web. As Delany has reminded his readers in an appendix to *Triton*, the word "web" comes from the Latin *textus*,

17

signing the fabric upon which text is imprinted as well as the fiber of which it is spun.[2] With both senses of that word at work in *Stars*, it is easy enough to see the activity of the fictional Web in controlling and modulating characters' awareness as also the activity of the textual web upon readers. An early signal of this necessarily dynamic relationship between text and reader comes during Rat Korga's first acts of conscious reading: "The new condition . . . was a web, a text weaving endlessly about him, erupting into and falling from consciousness, prompting memory and obliterating it" (37). The text of this novel seems devised similarly to modulate its readers' consciousness, directing their attention to moments which prompt key associations, then dissolving it to re-prompt it again in different frameworks, even at times speaking to them directly through asides.

Nor is a reader's attention allowed to remain passive. *Stars in My Pocket* is filled with resonances from the drama, a form meant to create direct and immediate responses. Readers are reminded frequently of the theater and of things being staged. Narrator Marq Dyeth's "Monologues" comprise the novel's central section. His "book" of Vondramach Okk's poetry projects a holographic stage with her image displayed upon it. He also reminds readers that most of what they see as details of setting is "spectacle" (342) projected by sophisticated media technologies. In the theatric sense, a spectacle is a staged display meant to evoke a response as much affective as intellectual, and, in fact, many of the key scenes in *Stars* have the additional affective dimension of taking place upon or near the stage of the Dyethshome amphitheatre.

Unique to the text of *Stars in My Pocket* in its evocation and control of its readers' attention, however, is its shift in the semantic registers of their own language, standard English. Standard English, with its implicit sociocultural rankings of individual worth, privileges males over females in its supposedly generic "he" and is limited in semantic application to a single sentient species consisting of two sexes. In that semantic frame, English is too limited a system not only for the two human sexes on contemporary Earth but also for the many worlds created in the galaxy of *Stars in My Pocket*, a galaxy which is home to many intelligent species, each possibly comprising more or fewer than two sexes. Societies and characters in *Stars*, with occasional exceptions, use the more inclusive and egalitarian Arachnia standard, a semantically expanded version of the language brought by the Web. "She" has become the generic pronoun and "woman" the generic noun for all individuals of sentient species. "He" is reserved for use only when an individual, regardless of sex or species, is the object of sexual interest. This shifted language, in which over four-fifths of the novel is narrated, becomes a primary means through which the text directs and controls readers' perceptions.

Characters called "women" in *Stars* are most often not females and frequently not humans. Nor can readers automatically envision human males in picturing scenes which use the word "he." Both new categories of perception and increased attention to text are demanded. Without habitual linguistic cues, descriptive details provided are not always sufficient for readers to picture a character as alien or human, for instance. Sometimes human characters are clearly males or females, but sometimes not. Is Japril male or female? Is that certain? Most importantly, unless sexual interest is involved, does it matter? Now, readers are forced to stop at the onset of each new scene, new action, new set of characters, and with conscious effort depart from automatic responses and reconfigure what they are picturing to accord with whatever details the text is (or is not) providing.

Denied the possibility of advancing through the text swiftly and linearly, readers are required to reread each scene, each moment highlighted by that text, and to pay attention in new ways. This *recursive* reading pattern, mirroring Marq Dyeth's pattern as narrator in Arachnia standard, modulates readers' attention so that they retrace each textual moment and experience intratextual resonances that grow through accretion.3 With such returns made a necessity, readers eventually experience resonances that expand beyond Marq Dyeth's sections as narrator to encompass the whole novel, including its third-person prologue narrated in standard English. By then that prologue on Rhyonon, significantly titled "A World Apart," can be seen as an opening spectacle displaying a failed society, setting the stage for what follows.

From that expanded perspective, reader attention is directed to sets of contrasting societies that frame the experiences of two main characters, Marq Dyeth and Rat Korga. It is through these characters' experiences that readers might most readily compare their own societies to those set on stage by the novel. The degree to which the shape taken by a society in *Stars in My Pocket* matches the non-hierarchical and inclusive potentials implicit in the language Arachnia standard becomes a measure for readers' judgment, first of that society and then of their own. Both Rat Korga's home society on the planet Rhyonon and Marq Dyeth's at Dyethshome and Morgre on the planet Velm, are displayed fully enough to be seen in terms of their effects on their members. The fate of a third planet, Nepiy, with a society at the outset more resembling Morgre's than Rhyonon's, seems about to be determined to its population's detriment by a fourth group, the Thants from the planet Zetzor.

Each of the two main characters comes from a society which has chosen or leans toward either Family or Sygn, the two contrasting models for social structure at play in the novel. The Family model generates closed, hierarchical, exclusionary systems that try to freeze social structures to fit "a classic past as pictured on a world [Old Earth] that may never have existed" (86). This system leans toward stasis, the end of dynamic possibility, ultimately death. The Sygn model, by contrast, is "committed to the living interaction and difference between each woman and each world" (86). It generates open systems that are inclusive, dynamic, flexible, and life sustaining.

On Rhyonon, Rat Korga's society is a closed system that has cut itself off from the rest of the galaxy in several ways. It uses the "archaic" (216) language that retains the pronouns and gender hierarchy of standard English; it has refused connection with the Web's General Information system that links most societies in the galaxy. Its sole population is human so that it lacks the range of social perspectives and possibilities that would come with interspecies interaction. Closed off from outward contact, Rhyonon has made the worst of itself. The practice of slavery there, under the ironic guise of social concern, gives objective form to an extreme capacity for dehumanization. Slaves like Rat Korga are created by means of "Radical Anxiety Termination" in a process banned elsewhere in the galaxy. Also dehumanizing is Rhyonon's maintenance of the gender inequities implicit in its citizens' use of the old language. Females are secondary to males and disparaged by them. The woman who outlaws herself in buying Rat Korga to satisfy private desires is testament to the effects of these inequities.

Involution and repressiveness permeate both custom and law in life on Rhyonon. Individuals must wear "faces," masks that actually *cover* their faces. Wearing a bare face, like going naked, indicates one's social insignificance. Another involution renders physical height a negative index of social worth, with those shortest in stature being highest in status. Equally absurd are laws about sexual behavior forbidding sexual contact between the very tall and the very short and between males under twenty-seven years old. On Rhyonon, such absurd repression seems to be connected to various forms of sadomasochism practiced by those who have power upon those who have none, like the Rats.

At its deepest substratum, fear underlies Rhyonon's society, fear that evokes research projects on killer viruses and ongoing struggles for power among political factions. Ironically, this society ultimately seeks to find safety by freezing its social forms into the Family pattern of "strong powers, mediating powers, and subordinate powers" (129) not long before the

Cultural Fugue it has feared actually occurs and obliterates it. The universe in *Stars* is not one in which form can be frozen and the dynamism of life maintained. The only solid form that remains after Rhyonon has undergone the meltdown-like Cultural Fugue and had its traces erased from history by the Web is the ball of slag to which it has been reduced.

From the life experience embodied in Rat Korga, it is not difficult for readers to see the effects of Rhyonon's society on its members. Rat Korga has been enslaved essentially because a learning disability has kept him illiterate, unable to protect himself with or from words although he has longed for the knowledge and understanding that the ability to use them would bring. The only choice—if it can be called that—readers see him make is his decision to undergo the RAT process, a decision into which his inability with language has caused him to be duped. Even after the destruction of Rhyonon, Rat Korga is not a free man. By the time he comes into Marq Dyeth's life, he has been "reborn" at the hands of and educated by the Web. He sees, literally and figuratively, with Web-installed eyes which symbolically go dark or disappear depending on the light in the same way that information's flow or erasure in the galaxy depends on the Web's plans. His desire for knowledge and understanding has been fulfilled through his use of the Rings of Vondramach Okk. However, those rings have been provided by the Web, and his actions are subject to the Web's bidding. Ultimately when a Web agent tells him to leave Velm and Marq Dyeth, his perfect (to within a few decimal points) mate, he leaves. Growing up on Rhyonon has apparently shaped him only for a life of being controlled.

When considering the ways in which the present and known world would have to be different for a society like Rhyonon's to exist, readers might well surmise that except for its alternative placement in time and space, Rhyonon already exists. Contemporary life is riddled with sexual and social taboos and functions according to embedded power hierarchies that privilege a select few. Just as the social structure on Rhyonon closely matches the disparities in individual empowerments implicit in contemporary standard English and manifest in contemporary societies that speak it, so the egalitarian, accepting, and nurturant society embodied at Morgre and Dyethshome most closely manifests the potentials suggested by Arachnia standard, potentials that are furthest from contemporary social practice.

The fundament of Morgran society—and of Marq Dyeth's Morgran life at Dyethshome where Arachnia standard is the common tongue—is *eros*, not *phobos*. Of the several societies displayed in *Stars in My Pocket*, this Sygn-based society is the one that offers its members the fullest opportunity to realize their own potentials. It is one of several societies in the galaxy rooted in an interrelationship between two sentient species. Many of the values and practices embedded in the culture of the one species have been absorbed by the other, and the whole society has grown therefrom. At Morgre the interrelationship between species sustains itself by fostering fulfillment rather than repression of desires.

Morgran life is grounded in bonding and union. On the sexual level, Morgran society recognizes the free play of its members' desire natures, inter- and intra-species and inter- and intra-gender, to be natural. It incorporates that play of desires into the material shape of urban life by providing, along with parks and other recreational areas, a variety of "runs" where a full spectrum of physical desires can be fulfilled. In enabling that full play of desires, Morgran society avoids generating sadomasochistic behaviors like the ones on Rhyonon. In addition, the free play of desires in Morgre apparently fosters the full play of creativity. Sculptures are present in the runs; decorations and embellishments adorn bare surfaces everywhere.

The Morgran desire for union takes other literal and metaphorical forms. Literally, Morgrans unite with one another by eating cloned human and evelm flesh. They have also joined flesh in the biogenetic addition of some evelm substance to Marq Dyeth's human sister Little Maxa. Dragon "hunts" for specimens of a non-sentient trisaurian species on Velm are done in pursuit of a technologically assisted perceptual union. Songs sung afterward by humans and evelmi become emblematic of the "multiplicity, richness, and beauty" (276) that come from the Morgran joining of species and cultures. Among Morgrans, a habitual greeting or leave-taking is "I love you" (238).

This relish of multilayered diversity is also signaled in Morgre's having adopted the evelmian nurture stream as a structure for propagation, kinship. Streams contain parents and children of both species and are not structured according to bloodline or authority hierarchies. It is from an early "unfettered experience of alien life" (356) provided by his stream parents that Marq Dyeth's life work as an Industrial Diplomat has grown. From his society he has learned to seek contact, to relish moments of communication achieved through layers of possible semantic misunderstandings. He embodies Morgran trust and openness, entering experience literally and metaphorically naked both as a guide on his own planet and as a diplomat on others. The self he presents, unlike the masked faces on Rhyonon, is genuine, not veiled.

On the whole, it is the basically loving nature instilled by his society that sustains Marq Dyeth through his experience of extreme loss when Rat Korga is taken from him and he loses the ability to feel desire. In the scene that ends his narrative, readers see that he retains his basic generosity of spirit even so. One of his actions in that scene is to reposition the dangling arm of an unconscious fellow passenger suspended in transport webbing. Then, during an exercise period, he is struck by a joy at the wonder of experience, at "the play of the infinite universe . . . and the dazzle of its totality" (374), the kind of joy that has been his at moments of communication achieved throughout his life as a diplomat. In that sense, his life work, the one that his society has enabled him to find, is what keeps him whole.

By contrast, the behavior of the Thants when they visit Dyethshome becomes a spectacle in the negative sense, a visible reminder to readers of how far current social reality is removed from the possibilities either latent in Arachnia standard or manifest in Morgran society. The Thants of Zetzor, even though for the most part they speak the newer language, manifest in their actions—like Rhyononians—more the value systems embedded in standard English. Unlike Marq Dyeth who goes openly and nakedly into experience, the Thants, members of an all-human, species-exclusive society like Rhyonon's, frequently conceal themselves behind projected privacy screens or use projections to augment and mask their actual physical appearances. The negative connotations associated with masks on Rhyonon apply as well to the Thants and their screens, especially in their dehumanizing treatment of their hosts. On Rhyonon masked supervisors talk about Rat Korga in front of him as though he were invisible to them as a human being. Similarly, at Dyethshome the Thants screen themselves at a dinner party held in their honor and, in front of their human and evelm hosts, talk about them with dehumanizing contempt and disdain as "animals who copulate with animals" (326).

The motives of the Thants have not been entirely clear to Marq Dyeth by this point, in part because he shares his own society's good-heartedness. The Dyeths tend to be confused by but tolerant of strangers' ways, but for readers, earlier clues about the Thants are likely to resonate with this scene. Readers will have noticed clear signs of the Thants' nature—contempt for other species, love of power and prestige, desire for renown, and even a clear leaning toward the hierarchical Family model for shaping society. Like Rhyononians, they want to freeze and maintain structures they control. They appear regimented to an almost military degree, laughing in unison, "swaying with . . . precision" (119), standing in line toe-to-toe. Although they represent their "reproductive commune," the Thants' ethos is far removed from the communal spirit which underlies Morgre. They more resemble the nuclear family recognizable by twentieth-century readers, being structured in a strict hierarchy headed by a dominant male, with a senior son on the ascendancy and a traditional mother standing to one side, a "jeweled extravaganza" (119) who plays no active role. Readers might notice too that the Thants have not altogether abandoned the older language spoken on Rhyonon. Offspring are called "sons" (204), even female ones.

What makes the Thants' decision to be a Focus Family on Nepiy—"when we leave, we're going to Nepiy. And we're going to take it over" (341)— particularly ominous is that they are heading for one of the worlds which, like Velm, home planet to Morgre and Dyethshome, houses two species and has the potential of becoming the sort of open society where interspecies love is one of the enablers of creativity and growth. But Nepiy, like Rhyonon, is more and more driven by fear. Having experienced botanical plague and widespread starvation, Nepiyans are frightened of Cultural Fugue. In turning to the Thants in pursuit of stability, they are choosing to align with Family. That structure is the one the species-exclusive Thants will bring to Nepiy, ending the possibility of Nepiy's developing a society like Morgre's.

In the end, of the societies displayed for readers' view in *Stars in My Pocket*, one has been obliterated, another has made a self-destructive choice, and only one sustains its potential to foster its members' growth and wholeness. Ironically that one, Morgre's, closest in form to the possibilities implicit in the Web-brought Arachnia standard, seems furthest from the actualities of contemporary life. For Morgran society to be possible, contemporary distrust of differences among individuals, including differences in race and sexual orientation, would have to have vanished.[4] Inequitable distribution of social empowerment among individuals would have to have vanished. Social repression of natural desires would have to have vanished. Openness would have to have replaced fear, and desire for contact would have to have replaced desire for domination. However, contemporary societies show little sign of these changes being imminent.

In the ongoing resonances which accrete in this novel, readers will have noticed a repeated refrain in variations on the line, "the world is a big place/small place," a refrain that takes on the function of a dramatic chorus, stepping in and directing reader attention to significances. This particular line, sounded repeatedly by Marq Dyeth in his monologues, culminates in his epilogue, "Morning," with his perception of Aurigae, the stellar supergiant, as large enough to encompass "all the possibilities that, in their shadings and subtleties, must be as varied as the . . . variegations on that star itself" (360). This notice reminds readers that reality is dynamic, malleable, that anything can happen, that the shape of the human future is not fixed.

To use the metaphor suggested in Marq Dyeth's final scene, readers are wrapped in textual *web*bing, making a transit in which motion is given and destination is infinitely variable. They have been set to exercise in response to social spectacles staged by the text. Perhaps they should take the advice that JoBonnot—a sometime agent of the Web and thus also an agent of the text—gives Marq Dyeth in her final appearance (advice spoken, not insignificantly, from the center of the Dyethshome stage): " 'Look up' ". . . . " 'Look at the real stars in the real sky that you can't see from here because the damned lights are too bright' " (347). Perhaps here readers are being told to look beyond the spectacles lit in the fictional world and see the actualities that surround their own lives. For that view, the lens of the Web's Arachnia standard, imaging the fictional while registering the actual, suffices. Like the transit webbing holding passengers in *Stars in My Pocket*'s final scene, ultimately the textual webbing of which the novel is spun might have been designed to prepare readers for a "proper waking" (374).

Notes

1. See Samuel R. Delany, "Generic Protocols: Science Fiction and Mundane," *The Technological Imagination*, ed. Teresa DeLauretis (Madison: U of Wisconsin P, 1980) 178, 193. Delany returns to this idea in several essays included in *Starboard Wine* (Pleasantville, New York: Dragon Press, 1984).

2. Samuel R. Delany, *Triton* (New York: Bantam, 1976) 133.

3. See Martha A. Bartter, "The (SF) Reader and the Quantum Paradigm: Problems in Delany's *Stars in My Pocket Like Grains of Sand*," *Science Fiction Studies* 17 (1990): 325–340. Bartter argues that since each act of reading is an act of co-creation of text, re-reading as such is not possible. In the recursive reading pattern I am suggesting here, *re*reading is a dynamic process in which layers of perception both shift *and* accrete upon each return to a text.

4. The different human races have blended by the time of the future described in *Stars*. Interspecies distrust and avoidance remain in some cases—witness the single-species planets like Rhyonon—but not in Morgre.

Debased and Lascivious?

Samuel R. Delany's *Stars in My Pocket Like Grains of Sand*

RUSSELL BLACKFORD

I.

Samuel R. Delany has been a prolific writer in recent years, having just completed the trilogy that began with *Tales of Nevèrÿon*, as well as working on a far-future diptych that begins with *Stars in My Pocket Like Grains of Sand*. The Nevèrÿon books deserve a separate extended discussion.

Stars in My Pocket has its own internal structural complexities: it is actually two stories, or perhaps three counting its Epilogue, as well as forming the first half of a diptych, the second half of which is still awaited. This is to be entitled *The Splendor and Misery of Bodies, of Cities*, a suggestive title when read against the subject matter of *Stars in My Pocket*.

The two stories which make up *Stars in My Pocket* are a virtually self-contained novella, actually listed as the Prologue and entitled "A World Apart," and a notably ragged-ended set of "Monologues," with a final "Epilogue." Presumably the ragged or open-ended nature of this whole sequence, and hence of the novel itself, will be tidied up when the second half of the diptych becomes available. From the shape of the first book, it appears that the two volumes might be going to form a genuinely unified work, and not just a novel with a sequel to keep readers and the publisher going. I say this because the overall shape of *Stars in My Pocket* is somewhat peculiar, with a major unresolved crisis taking place at the end, and with a number of major elements left unexplained. Most obviously, the full roles of a universal information-distributing organization called "the Web" are left quite unclear, even though it is the conspiratorial force driving many of the events. Even more unclear is the role of a species of aliens known as the Xlv. It may well be that the second book of the diptych will be written in such a way as to be virtually inaccessible to anyone who has not read the first book, while *Stars in My Pocket* itself appears to end prematurely unless we go on to tackle *The Splendor and Misery*–but that the frayed edges of the two novels will be sewn neatly together. It may also well be that the manner in which the Prologue is injected into a larger political and imaginative context in the first book will provide the pattern for the entire two-volume work, in which case I would be unwilling to criticize the first book for having loose ends; in fact, if Delany is able to develop the pattern he has established within the first book, I for one will consider this to be a refreshing and courageous development in sf—he will have my applause.

This is not to say that every difficulty I will be drawing attention to in the plotting of *Stars in My Pocket* can be given the benefit of the doubt on the ground that the sequel will make all clear: some of the difficulties would appear to be endemic to Delany's fundamental approach in this novel. But I am suggesting that the unexpected overall shape of the book is not necessarily to be considered a fault, depending on what Delany is going to come up with next.

In trying to analyze the aesthetic and thematic characteristics of *Stars in My Pocket*, I have found myself thinking about how typical the book is of Delany's work in general, and how much it illuminates what Delany has been doing in his other more recent books. I am very aware that such critics as George Turner and Bruce Gillespie, among other skeptics in this country, have been unwilling to accept that Delany is saying anything profound or worthwhile behind the often difficult surfaces of his narratives. While I have not taken the opportunity to refresh my reading of the whole Delany oeuvre at this stage, it does seem to me that Delany has been saying important and potentially explosive things in his recent novels. I am not going to attempt to explore the extent to which the same themes and attitudes found in *Stars in My Pocket* also appear in Delany's earlier work, but I would suggest that many of the same tropes are present and should probably be given the same significances. It also seems to me that the strengths and weaknesses which I have found in Delany over the years, and which have been commented on by George Turner and others (particularly the weaknesses in Turner's case), are exemplified very well in this latest book.

The Prologue, which I have referred to as a virtually self-contained novella, tells the story of an (initially) unnamed slave on an unnamed world. Later on, we find out that the slave's name is "Korga"—he comes to be called "Rat Korga"—and his planet is Rhyonon. Korga is a misfit on a very backward planet. On the first page (all my page references are to the hardback Bantam edition), we are introduced to him at an Institute which practices a process called "Radical Anxiety Termination." This consists of destroying certain neural pathways in the brain so as to turn off the capacity for aggression, anxiety, and original thought. It is a kind of far-future lobotomy with more drastic results: once subjected to the RAT treatment, a "rat" is apparently completely tractable, even to the extent of being willing to sleep in his own excrement. The social practices on Rhyonon declare that rats should be made the slaves of institutions which have need for the cheap but menial labour they can provide. Individuals are not entrusted with owning human lives, and the institutions which use rats are supposed to be screened to ensure that they are humane—but this is treated as a great, if bitter, joke by Delany, since the institution where Rat Korga spends most of his time withholds even the most universal and fundamental dignities. It is difficult to imagine how a society such as this would work, or how any pretensions to humanity could be found in a society which contains people who think like this, but so Delany has stipulated. As soon as I start to describe what is going on here, it seems to me that I am unmasking something of the kind of inconsistency in Delany that has rightly worried George Turner, though alleged practices in this country's mental institutions make me wonder whether Delany is not, against expectation, right.

At the polar research institution where Rat Korga spends most of his time working, he lives a life which appears fantastically debased and humiliating, and there is nothing in the book to compel us to see it in any other way. However, the book goes on to present us with a series of apparently degraded lifestyles, actions, and desires, and leaves us to sort out which are which in terms of morality and value. The conditions under which Korga lives in slavery on Rhyonon provide one version of degradation, or one touchstone for it, but that is all.

The main action in this first part of the novel concerns a woman who seeks the company of her own slave; she is a sadist who wants someone for sexual use and abuse. In a key episode, the woman demands that Korga make love to her (he is not interested since he is entirely homosexual, but his RAT treatment does not allow him to refuse), to allow her to whip him bloodily, to allow her, also, to spit upon him without defending himself. But she also gives him a glove-like device which plugs into his neural circuits with the effect of healing his mind, while, at the same time, she grants him the release of knowledge. It transpires that under certain conditions a rat can absorb information many hundreds of times faster than a human being who has not had the RAT treatment. The woman wishes to be able to spit upon a man who has read all the books she has not, so she sets him to read a sequence of major works through direct neural input, scoffing down the equivalent of tens of thousands of pages within seconds. It appears that the effect of the RAT treatment is not only to eliminate anxiety and so on but also to eliminate certain filtering mechanisms that limit or retard the processing of input information by our brains. The glove which the woman sadist provides compensates for the RAT treatment rather than undoing it, so Korga is able to retain his enhanced information-processing potential even while enjoying his return to something like a state of creativity and initiative. Once again, Delany has so stipulated the technology, though it is all suspiciously convenient to his thematic purpose.

The description of Korga's first experience of reading—and, with it, the exponential expansion in his consciousness as he starts wolfing down books—is very impressive as a straight sf rendering of experience beyond the edges of anything which we could ever encounter. It is also full of successful tricks, some of which I shall return to. Preeminently, Delany provides a sensitive depiction of a feeling of splendor, the exploration of new realms of consciousness, completeness, and joy. This is the other side to *Stars in My Pocket*: it presents forms of degradation and misery, even versions of what might be the definitive forms of degradation; but, at the same time, it shows startling forms of splendor and joy, once again verging upon the extremes or the definitive versions of these things. Throughout, Delany's emphasis is that the obvious question, "which is which?", is either a wrong question even to ask or, at least, the assumptions which our own society might make in answering it are so parochial and problematical that we may as well start over again and dismiss what our society assumes. *Stars in My Pocket* is very much an attack on notions that there is an accumulated traditional wisdom about these things. The premise is radically constructivist: meaning, significance, value, and the social organization of relevant behavior are not inherent in brute physical/biological fact, but are more or less arbitrarily constructed for and by societies.

In the case of Rat Korga, the woman who inflicts what we might consider the most degrading experiences of all upon him is also the woman who makes available to him the vistas and the splendor of thought and intellect. When Korga is "rescued" from her, we feel immediately—some might say that Delany has tricked us into feeling—that he has suffered an overall loss.

Indeed, in a kind of coda to this section we get a poignant description of what Korga is like afterwards, wistfully and pathetically teaching his fellow rats to wear one work glove, in memory of the device which gave him his mind and a mental world—before it was literally torn from him, and both mind and world rushed away.

At the end of the Prologue, Korga's world is destroyed, and with it, apparently, Korga himself. In this context, all questions of moral judgement or disgust seem to be held in abeyance, and we are aware only of pathos, futility, and a splendor which has been lost. The Prologue, however, is injected into the larger story, wherein it becomes clear that Korga is possibly the only survivor of a cataclysm which destroyed Rhyonon. The larger story is narrated by one Marq Dyeth, a small bearded male human (within the larger Universe where Marq roams, the word "man" is an archaism seldom encountered). Rat Korga and Marq Dyeth are spectacularly sexually attracted to each other, and the larger novel is mainly concerned with their relationship in the context of staggering political conspiracies that are impacting upon the lives of humans and other intelligent beings (generically known as "women" in this Universal meta-culture) on 6000 planets: the backdrop is grand space opera in the inimitably baroque Delany mode, while the foreground is a kind of love story which could have been produced by Robert A. Heinlein revising *Stranger in a Strange Land* with the aid of a manual of (supposed) perversions and fetishes, or perhaps a manual of safe sexual practices and a determination to exemplify the *don'ts*. Of course, our cultural definitions of what constitutes a perversion or fetish are very much at stake here.

II.

As I have already described, the RAT treatment undergone by Rat Korga has the effect of destroying the will, despite sophistical assurances to the contrary which Korga is given early in the narrative. But it also makes possible a super-accelerated expansion of knowledge under particular circumstances. Accordingly, the RAT treatment, while destructive in itself, or perhaps by itself, contains within it a potential for experiences of splendor as well as degradation. Thus it provides an example of how degradation and splendor can be conjoined, can be inextricable within a set of experiences, can even be aspects of the same identical experience, a point to which Delany returns again and again. Note that Delany here has simply stipulated that this is how the technology works. He is able to gain a very poignant effect in the Prologue, and one which challenges our own deepest cultural revulsions, but it is worth asking whether he has not gained part of his effect by cheating.

The answer to this question is not simple. Delany is certainly entitled to use whatever thematic images he likes and to set up his technology how he likes—but only in the context of the larger world which he is creating. The trouble with the RAT treatment and the way it works is that it is just too thematically convenient, since we are not given any detailed information about a larger technological context in which it might function: when it is revealed that RAT has a splendid as well as a degrading side this looks more as if Delany is trying to pull a rabbit out of his hat—it was up his sleeve all the time, of course—than as if the logical outcome of the information we have been given has been reached. This does not mean that Delany is a slipshod writer, at least not entirely: within the super-speed-reading sequence, Delany is brilliant. The description of what it is like for Korga to build up a world of vicarious experience for the first time is sensitive, vivid and moving, and this reader, for one, did not care whether it would or could really work that way or not. Delany launches forth on a rich and seemingly inexhaustible account of the books Korga reads; they are luxuriantly and precisely named and described; more profound is the manner in which Delany describes the patterns which the different books form in Korga's mind, each throwing the ones before into a different series of relationships and significances, each enriched by the patterns which Korga has already built up. This is a very acceptable sf technique, extrapolating from the process of literary growth that we all know so well, but presenting a version of the experience far beyond the edges of what we can ever go through—but not what can be imagined. The scene also contains some wholly successful trickery, and even jokes. It turns out that Korga has dipped into a pile of women's literature by mistake, and he has failed to realize that what he has taken to be the literary canon of his world is actually a literary ghetto. There is even a note of self-deprecation here, since Delany is one of those writers whom we would expect to champion such alternative literary canons. There is a surprising amount of humor in the novel, but some of the other jokes are at the expense of the reader rather than the writer.

The joke on the reader in this "books" sequence is that Delany provides some clues that he is actually writing about a women's literary ghetto, but the reader misses them: in the development of this joke there is a sense that Delany is concerned with narrative logic rather than with mere stipulation and contrivance. Every time the sex of one of the writers of the material Korga is reading is revealed, it turns out that the writer is female. Yet, we find ourselves assuming automatically that the other writers are male. So strong is our cultural heritage that we do not even notice that only feminine pronouns are ever used, when pronouns *are* used, until the trap is finally sprung on us (I wonder whether women tend to fall so readily into the trap . . .). So Delany is able to have a laugh at himself, at Korga, and at *us*, too, all with perfect narrative logic, and in an extended scene which works too powerfully when read "straight" to be dismissed as just a cheap narratorial trick. Yet, though the scene works well internally, and follows a logic which is very satisfying, it appears in the context of a quite unsatisfying technological stipulation, which, in turn, is in the context of a stipulated society that is vague and problematic. It seems to me that this unsatisfactoriness at the contextual levels of the societies and technologies which Delany works out, combined with a satisfying development of symbols and of narratorial direction within sequences, is part of the reason why some critics such as George Turner remain so skeptical about the value of Delany's work, while other critics and readers find a great deal to read with admiration and delight, even awe.

I am one of the readers who feel some of the abovementioned awe, admiration, and delight when reading Delany, but I must admit that I do not find his novels entirely satisfying. A related difficulty in *Stars in My Pocket* to what I have been describing is that much of the impetus behind the plot is provided by vast powers of universal scope, particularly the Web and the Xlv. The result is that there are no clearly scrutable rules by which the logic of the events may be assessed: almost any coincidence has a chance of being justified as really manifesting conspiracy; almost any sequence of events can be shaped by powers which have no clearly defined restraints. Accordingly, the book loses some of its appearance of accountability to the reader, and to the reader's sense of narrative logic and the characters' psychology. This is a very common fault (or at least cause of dissatisfaction) in sf, but this book seems to take it to extremes—particularly because it does rely, extravagantly, on coincidences, which presumably we have to interpret as conspiracy, without any ground rules being established to test the workings of the conspiracy. At the same time, there are occasions where we have a sense that what Delany is stipulating about this universe is very unlikely, even nonsensical. For example, there is a great deal of discussion and argument about the nature of "fuzzy-edged" concepts, some of it logical: the total population of the Universe can never be given exactly because it continually fluctuates by a billion—fair enough, though the only reason why this could be so is that the Universe's population is so vast that an approximation to the nearest billion, or five, or ten billion would be highly precise in percentage terms. The idea of fuzzy-edged concepts is used to equivocate about whether Rat Korga was or was not the only survivor of the destruction of Rhyonon. The simple answer seems to be not that the concept is particularly fuzzy but that the question is ambiguous. Delany tries to pretend that there is a difference in principle between being the only survivor when a world is destroyed and being the only survivor when, say, a town is destroyed. But the very same ambiguities arise: what about people on the way out? the way in? normal residents who were not home?

While the fuzzy-edged concept is a respectable philosophical animal, Delany appears to deploy it in such a way as to suggest that he is prepared to try to dazzle the reader with the first bit of old rubbish he thinks of—in this case, apparently, just to avoid admitting that there is a meaningful sense in which Rat Korga does seem to be that melodramatic phenomenon, the sole survivor of a planetary cataclysm (a conclusion which he appears to want to fob off on to his characters, disowning it himself while still getting mileage out of it). Another such piece of old rubbish is the odd assertion made by Marq that "You may assume, about absolutely any fact . . . that nine hundred and ninety-nine people out of a thousand do *not* know it—which goes for the working assumption too" (139). This is really used as a piece of humorous hyperbole, yet Delany appears to wish us to take it seriously as an explanation of the otherwise mysterious state of affairs wherein nobody much in the Universe he has created is aware of the existence of the Xlv, despite the fact that this is the only alien species capable of space flight. Delany tries to persuade us that there is no area of common knowledge in his far future Universe at all—and is completely unconvincing. Despite anything he has Marq tell us, it is impossible to shake off the feeling that there would be plenty of knowledge of such general interest that virtually anybody would be acquainted with it.

Part of the difficulty in reading this novel is that it takes away many of the codes which we are used to in constructing pictures of characters and actions from black marks on paper. In doing so, it draws attention (by their absence) to some of the most basic codes which are involved in the process. Most obviously, *Stars in My Pocket* dispenses with the simple distinction in language between male and female people. In this novel the word "man" for "male human being" is said to be an archaism seldom encountered, while the pronouns "he," "she" and their cognates are not used to denote gender; rather, these words are used to distinguish only between the mass of humanity (together with other species) and those by whom the speaker is sexually excited. Intelligent life-forms are called "women," and the pronouns "she" and "her" are used; the pronouns "he" and "him," by contrast, indicate that the speaker refers to someone who sexually excites her. The result is that we have difficulty visualizing characters as Delany presents them, because in our culture the first vital piece of information we need in attempting to visualize someone is knowledge of his or her sex. Because of the roles and values traditionally assigned to males and females in our own society, we tend to assume that characters in books and human agents in general are male unless we have evidence to the contrary, and this is reinforced by our language, which traditionally uses the masculine gender in many contexts to include the feminine. In Delany's novel, however, we find ourselves routinely encountering what strike us, though not Delany's characters, as feminine pronouns. We come to assume that characters are female as the default option, even though we know that the "feminine" pronouns do not have the same meaning as in our own culture. This effect seems to corroborate the hypothesis that language does actually shape assumptions (it is an interesting experiment in the area on Delany's part). However, we are able to go beyond the effect I have described so far, to some extent, to get used to the idea that "masculine" pronouns indicate not the male sex but the excitement produced as a sexual object by the person spoken of.

This whole effect is very disorienting, and we sometimes balk at being unable to use our normal basic clues in attempting to visualize characters. On the other hand, we also learn to take some pride in picking up the new cues Delany provides and responding with upraised eyebrows at the occasional use of the pronoun "he" and its cousins. Another point demonstrated here is that language, as well as shaping, or at least reinforcing, cultural attitudes also manifests them. In the highly permissive universal meta-culture which Delany has created, it is obviously not only acceptable to reveal openly when one is sexually excited and by whom—such revelation is actually demanded by the language itself, and it seems scarcely less "natural" for these people to distinguish in the course of speech by whom they are excited than it is for us to distinguish whether the person spoken about is male or female.

Apart from the level of language, *Stars in My Pocket* also challenges our assumptions as to what sort of details will be selected to evoke the nature of people when they are described. In particular, Marq Dyeth does not automatically tell us whether a character is male or female, so the information we look for in pronouns is not supplemented by his descriptions. Moreover, in selecting evocative details, Marq will often point to veins, scars, calluses, and fingertips, rather than hair, breasts, facial features and other characteristics which we are more used to when visualizing people. As a result, the narration seems to be very vivid; yet we end up with many aspects not properly visualized because they do not fit in with our normal codes. Delany provides at least as much sensory detail as the average writer, and he thus draws our attention to the way we are dependent upon being told certain kinds of detail in constructing pictures and identities out of the black-on-blanks that make up a novel. However, as with the point about the use of pronouns, the violation of normal descriptive conventions also works in direct ways, creating a strong cumulative sense that we are in someone else's mental world. Different readers will probably find different levels of disorientation in Delany's various techniques. For myself, I found it very difficult to understand some of the array of new concepts which Delany expects us to absorb, often with no simple discursive explanation. At the end of the book I decided I did not really understand the distinction made between $work_1$, $work_2$, and $work_3$, despite the concept appearing at times to be perfectly simple. We need to cope with a range of high-powered sf concepts: the Web, the Xlv, Cultural Fugue (the state reached by a planet before it destroys itself), the Web's officers, who are called "spiders." Also Marq does not explain anything more than is necessary for someone in his own culture, as a result of which we never get sustained descriptions of the things he is familiar with. At the end of the book I am still not precisely sure what the evelmi, a race of six-legged reptiloid aliens who live in symbiosis and sexual interrelationship with human beings on their home world, look like. Yet, as with the humans of whose sex I remain unsure, the evelmi are treated as individuals, and some sharp individual distinctions are made by Marq on coloration, the shape of talons, and so on.

A final question which should be raised about these various new codes of language and description is how much they can simply be stipulated, and how much they should be placed in some historical context to allow the reader to understand how they could have evolved. George Turner has placed great emphasis on his view that anything new about a future world should be explicable as having evolved from our own culture. Delany obviously prefers a "black box" technique: we are to assume that the intervening time represents whatever "box" is required to have produced the necessary transformations of our own experience; if the passage of time is great enough, it can be envisaged that almost any sort of "box" could have been there, given that human nature is considered to be plastic rather than fixed. On this point, I am inclined to agree with Delany, provided that what we are shown does not violate our (admittedly problematic and vulnerable) sense of the most basic human needs, interests and capacities, and provided that the individual elements of future society, language, technology, etc. are mutually consistent and exist in some sort of shaping context that we can understand, rather than merely providing an arbitrary and convenient set of symbols. Delany does sometimes merely stipulate stuff which is symbolically convenient, but he is also able to develop sequences and far-future changes with great rigor, even while plundering them for all the poetic effects that they are worth. These are his fiction's strengths and weaknesses.

III.

The thematic centre of *Stars in My Pocket* is the idea of degradation or debasement. This takes many forms: a great deal of emphasis is placed upon nudity—which can signify a lowering of status combined with great vulnerability, or can signify a situation where clothes are seen as unnecessary. Stripping a victim or enemy is a well-known method of humiliating him or her, making the enemy vulnerable, demeaned, attacking some of the sources of identity and pride. At the polar station where Rat Korga works in the early part of the book, he is treated negligently and demeaningly in that he is not fed enough meals, is not provided with toilet facilities, is forced to work naked—his clothes are never replaced but are allowed to wear out. However, this is not the only context in which nudity is presented in the book, since the characters are also shown as going naked at Dyethshome, where Marq and his fellows live in an innocent symbiosis with the evelmi. Here the emphasis is upon the lack of need for clothes. Nakedness is a sign, in other words, both of shame and degradation and of innocence and transcendence; Delany is able to exploit this widely-recognized ambiguity.

As already touched upon, many elements of the book simultaneously convey ideas of degradation or shame and splendor or transcendence. *Stars in My Pocket* seems to have little to do with the concepts of good and evil as such. Such concepts are largely abstract and intellectually-based ones; more visceral feelings than those of moral condemnation are horror and disgust, and it is at the concepts associated with these feelings that Delany appears to direct his analysis. An attempt to hold together the disparate elements of the novel by relating them directly to moral approval or disapproval would fail, since many of the experiences described, though emotionally potent, would probably be considered to be morally neutral upon dispassionate analysis. For example, it is hard to believe that anyone would be morally concerned one way or the other about Marq's sexual interest in calluses and bitten fingernails rather than the conventional bums and tits—but the feeling could easily be that such sexual interests are nasty, debased, and unfortunate, comic rather than wicked, with the comedy based upon a mild form of disgust. Other aspects, such as Marq's sexual relations with reptiloid aliens, would be both disgusting and wicked according to conventional wisdom. However, Delany challenges our assumptions of what experiences should strike us as degrading, should disgust or repel us, or make us feel vicarious shame. In doing so, he also challenges much of the basis for conventional morality. Delany goes to the core of what is natural or acceptable experience for a human being, and to the question of the limits of tolerance for behavior which his own society constructs as degraded or disgusting; he stretches the boundaries of what can seem acceptable or even, in the right circumstances, delightful. As far as Marq's relationships with evelmi go, the view that interspecies sexuality might be shameful is made to appear mistaken, parochial and itself comic.

Towards the end of the book, the Dyeths' friends, the Thants, attempt to make a statement distancing themselves from and denouncing the Dyeths. Their way of doing this is to avoid coming to dinner, instead huddling about, wrapped in privacy clouds, and saying scornful and insulting things about "lizard lovers" (earlier we have been introduced to other insulting terms, such as "front-face" for heterosexual). The Dyeths, both human and evelm, find the whole display incomprehensible but are most perturbed that their carefully prepared meal is being left uneaten. Under the circumstances, the Thants appear to be rude and narrow-minded, while we identify with the Dyeths. It all seems like a humorous clash of a more generous and a meaner culture—in which the upholders of what we might normally consider the most basic assumptions of sexual morality are simply ridiculous.

Delany places in the foreground the whole idea of cultural difference and the social construction of meaning and value that goes with it. Marq's job is that of an industrial diplomat, someone who has to deal in trading relationships between many cultures and even species. For him, it is second nature to assume that responses to situations, together with the very concepts which are employed in those situations, will vary fundamentally from culture to culture. He has internalized this assumption so much that, ironically, he sometimes appears bemused when not all others share it but are sometimes locked into their own cultural assumptions. Marq is very aware that he lives in a Universe of 6000 inhabited planets, each with cultural variations of its own.

The outer limit of acceptable behavior seems to be marked when Marq encounters the proclivities of a male sadist, Clym, early in his narrative. Clym is a professional psychopathic killer, as well as being sexually excited by torture:

> " . . . I am going to take you by force, chain you in a special chamber I have
> already equipped for the purpose, and do some very painful things to your

body that will possibly—the chances are four out of five—result in your death, and certainly in your permanent disfigurement, mental and physical." (We live in a medically sophisticated age. You have to work very hard to permanently disfigure any body.) (96)

Marq responds coolly enough by our standards; Delany employs a mixture of conventional humor and his own far-future codes to show us how his protagonist feels. Marq says: "Just tell me, is this part of your job₁ or just your way of being friendly?" (97) At the same time, he suddenly refers to Clym as "she" and adds "from then on 'she' was the only way I could think of her"—Marq's sexual distaste is emphasized more than any familiar moral reaction! However, he takes the opportunity to warn a more innocent-seeming acquaintance to beware of Clym before moving "sixty million kilometers away" and adding "And I wished it were sixty million light years and in another sun system" (98). The tone here is comic self-deprecation at being unable to cope with such an experience as meeting Clym, rather than of disgust or moral outrage. Marq refers to Clym as one of the "odd creations of our epoch," but does not judge him any more harshly than that, and does not denounce him to anyone.

The initial implication, and not a trivial one, seems to be that here is a variety of nastiness beyond the pale of cultural relativism or sexual permissiveness, but that even Clym merits some respect and consideration in that he gave his potential victim fair warning. In this book's terms, Clym seems to be just about at the far limits of tolerance. We may contrast the woman who wished to treat Rat Korga sadistically—the two scenes, both occurring fairly early in the book, are obviously to be read against each other. The woman seems harmless compared with Clym, even though her desires are selfish and spoilt. She is unable to do Korga any real physical harm, and she begins to do him a great deal of good. Even within the ambit of sadism, it is possible to make distinctions as to what is tolerable and what is not tolerable behavior: there is no attempt to apply conventional blanket judgements. Here, then, is perhaps the further implication of such scenes: as the feminist anthropologist Gayle Rubin has emphasized in another context, we tend to construct less privileged forms of sexual activities in our own culture's moral hierarchy as uniformly repulsive—without grace, consideration, or individual complexity. Delany is prepared to create and juxtapose scenes which include a range of intelligent interaction and a degree of complexity that subvert the popular cultural assumptions.

Degradation is frequently associated with both sex and sin in our own culture, and the equation is shown as not forgotten in *Stars in My Pocket*, though it is much attenuated in the ultra-sophisticated culture in which Marq Dyeth moves. When the woman who buys Korga does so, she underlines the equation by asking whether he is willing to obey her every whim and caprice, "no matter how debased or lascivious?" (19). He responds simply "Yeah . . . ?" The desires which she wishes to articulate are both lascivious and debased by the standards of our culture—debased in part because they are lascivious. But the concept of what should count as "lascivious," a value-word if there ever was one, is just one more which is very much up for grabs.

Accordingly, in reassessing what debased behavior might be, Delany is looking mainly at various kinds of less mainstream sexual activities. In some cases, these are somewhat comic, even for Marq, such as when one of his encounters is with a fetishist interested in high-tech paraphernalia; Marq's friend ends up described as "a-crackle with sparks from the low-amperage high-voltage electrodes that he had me play across his handsome, lithe body in its various manacles and restraints" (76). Other behaviors shown, however, would normally strike most of us as ugly, off-putting, even disgusting. Marq is attracted to people whom we would conventionally think of as ugly, and to bits of their bodies which we would consider blemishes: calluses, severely bitten fingernails, acne scars. All this is apart from the fact that Marq, a male human, has sex both with other male humans and with the lizardish evelmi. Throughout, Delany builds up ideas of what it would be like to be sexually attracted by things which are usually thought of as ugly or disgusting in a sexual context. In doing so he manages to create a romance of ugliness, deformity, and mutilation.

Science fiction has tackled the question of cultural relativity as it applies to sexual behavior before. The most celebrated example, prior to Delany's work on the theme, would be Heinlein's *Stranger in a Strange Land*; Delany, the "left-wing" constructivist, and Heinlein, the "right-wing" libertarian, agree on the parochialism of our cultural taboos on sexuality, and on much else. But the most obvious difference between Heinlein and Delany, leaving aside their underlying politics (as interpreted by a society which defines political difference in terms of certain concepts rather than others), is that Heinlein's characters are all the stuff that wish-fulfillment is made of. His supermen and superwoman display a transcendent morality, which includes the area of their sex lives—in fact especially the area of their sex lives—but they are basically folks who can be recognized as the fantasies of well-heeled types brought up on the symbols offered in *Playboy*, *Cosmopolitan* and their ilk. While Heinlein usually has at least one character of advanced years in each novel, the familiar Jubal Harshaw-Robert Heinlein figure, his characters would never be shown as in any way ugly or even plain: the men are handsome, clean, heterosexual, usually dashing; the women are beautiful in standard Western terms, ultra-smart, perhaps with a trace of fashionable male-fantasy bisexuality. It is easy to scorn Heinlein, and possibly more relevant to praise him for the success he has had in the area he has mapped out. But Delany has gone far beyond Heinlein's justification of a narrow form of sexual radicalism in terms of the other values of his culture, and has suggested that the most intense assumptions within that culture of what is nice and what is nasty might be without foundation. (Perhaps the most obvious example of libertarian thought generally falling short of true radicalism is in its complacent or rationalized acceptance of socially-constructed property concepts; Heinlein, with his millionaire heroes, is not an exception to the rule.)

The point has already been labored: degradation and splendor are not necessarily separated in *Stars in My Pocket*. Many things which would normally be considered ugly or sordid are actually splendid to those involved, and the two kinds of experience often seem to go together. A notable example is the dragon hunt on which Marq embarks with Korga: this is not actually a quest to slay a dragon (a larger biological relative of the evelmi) but to capture its thoughts and momentarily be a dragon. The feelings in this state are wonderfully rich, exhilarating, and a monument to the goal of understanding rather than destroying—but also explicitly sexual. In addition, Korga and Marq make love during the dragon hunt, apparently exploring each other in intimate physical ways which our culture conventionally and automatically considers degrading. Without bothering even to provide any explanation, Marq tells us: "He came twice, I, once, and we joked about it. Later, both our hands wet with his urine, we lifted our bows . . ." (260). The title of the book is a reference to the idea of personal splendor, and is picked up in such a context within the book, and it also links with the description of a particular star, Aurigae, the largest star in the Universe, which appears like a vast sunset. Though the woman who tries to own Korga identifies lasciviousness and debasement, the book as a whole more identifies splendor and degradation, or perhaps splendor and misery.

It should not be thought that Delany attempts in this book to redeem notions of sexuality by equating sex with love. At times, the question is raised as to whether Marq and Korga love each other; the question is not ultimately answered, because, as Marq tells the spider, Japril, who originally brought them together, they were able to know each other for only a day. Delany does not attempt to sentimentalize lust as equating with love, but neither does he deny the splendor in lust itself. Rather, *Stars in My Pocket* seems to be ordered consistent with a viewpoint most often articulated in our society by the male gay community, but now being taken up by at least some radical feminists and others, that the ideals of fidelity and permanency are not necessary to give value to sexual relationships, and nor is it necessary that the physicality of sex should be subordinated to deep emotional experiences for sex to be in itself a splendid experience. Any idea that the sexual experience stands in need of redemption by particular emotions and ongoing relationships, emotions and relationships which might accompany the experience but are not demanded by it, is parasitic upon a socially constructed fear of sex in itself as somehow debased or degrading. If this insight is followed through, it becomes, for example, false and sentimental to defend gays by claiming that their relationships can be as faithful, profound and "spiritual" as those of traditional couples—for, in the process of developing such a defence, one accepts an unnecessary and repressive construction of the nature of sexual experience.

Towards the end of the book, Marq defends his particular sexual makeup in a powerhouse speech worthy of Shakespeare's Shylock reminding us that Jews bleed. This speech is a kind of manifesto, though elsewhere Marq cannot be precisely identified with the implied author, suffering as he does from his own failings of understanding—we often see him bemused by what is going on around him, but only in contexts where we are led to understand that bemusement is a civilized, even if not a totally comprehending, reaction. Civilization is another possible opposite of degradation, and no matter how degraded Marq's tastes and actions would appear in our own society, Marq always strikes us as preeminently civilized, a true diplomat. Despite this, Delany sometimes attempts to make aspects of Marq's life take on poignancy—and here he fails where elsewhere he succeeds. It may be that the apparent failure is based on an inability to win us over from our own cultural assumption that a relationship needs to be based upon more than sexual attraction and even wonder before it can affect us as poignant.

In conclusion, *Stars in My Pocket* is a courageous attempt to dramatize explosive themes in the teeth of traditional social attitudes and the recent anti-sex attitudes that have been having such a successful run, encouraged by social elements as disparate as cultural feminism and the New Right. By creating whole new cultural/linguistic codes and forcing us to live with them, Delany tackles his theme more radically than any other sf writer before him. Much of what is given dramatic expression in *Stars in My Pocket* was already latent in the earlier books. It was there in *Dhalgren*, which explored the taboo areas of sexuality—kinky, flaunted, polymorphous, and sudden—in such a way as to show interaction, complexity, and humanity;

it is in the Nevèrÿon books where, for example, Gorgik the Liberator's interpretation of his slave collar makes it both an emblem of servitude and a sexual statement or focus. But Delany is writing closer to the bone than ever in his new diptych, and using far-future sf tropes with a radicalism and ruthlessness that justifies the far-future sub-genre itself. If his work is uneven and not entirely satisfying, it is nonetheless pointing the way for the rest of sf, including the works of less audacious but more conventionally perfect writers. Once what Delany is doing, or attempting to do, is understood, it is difficult to be satisfied with the ambitions of any other sf writer, much less the overwhelming bulk of mainstream fiction.

Still a young man in his early forties, Delany has many years of pioneering sf and fantasy ahead of him. We can only await with enthusiasm what he is going to do, first of all in the second half of his present diptych, and then in greater things to come.

Author's Note: This review was based upon a talk presented to the Nova Mob, a science-fiction interest group in Melbourne, Australia, in 1985. It was first published in the following year. Some stylistic changes have been made for republication.

The Politics of Desire in Delany's *Triton* and *Tides of Lust*

ROBERT ELLIOT FOX

In the breakdown of repression, the artists do their part by first
dreaming the forbidden thoughts, assuming the forbidden stances,
and struggling to make sense. They cannot do otherwise, for they
bring the social conflicts in their souls to public expression.
—Paul Goodman[1]

"And I assure you, as one who is also a fair performer, desire *is*
something else again."
—The Spike, in Samuel R. Delany's *Triton*[2]

Speculative sexuality may be the final frontier for science-
fiction writers, and Samuel R. Delany, while not the only extrapolator to
cross into this particular territory of the imagination, has probably gone
as far as anybody in penetrating it. In his story "Aye, and Gomorrah,"
he tells of the "frelks," individuals who are sexually drawn to neutered
spacemen; in *Babel-17*, starship navigators form sexual as well as func-
tional/psychological triads[3]; in *The Einstein Intersection*, there are three
sexes; while in *Triton*, there are "forty or fifty basic sexes, falling loosely
into nine categories," four homophilic and five heterophilic (*T* 117), and
individuals can, if they so choose, alter their race, gender, and sexual
preferences through surgery.[4]

Still, as one commentator has noted, Delany is careful "to maintain the
distance of artifice; we never, for example, see just exactly what goes on
when a frelk manages to 'land' a spaceman."[5] This circumstance alters
drastically in *Dhalgren*, Delany's most experimental work, which contains
what is perhaps the most graphic sexuality to be found in any science-
fiction novel. For this reason, among others (having to do with questions of

43

coherence, charges of willful obscurity, etc.), it is often considered Delany's most controversial work—in my opinion, an erroneous judgment based on the fact that the text which truly merits that designation, a pornographic novel entitled *Tides of Lust*,[6] is largely unknown to the majority of Delany's readers and difficult to obtain.[7] In both of these novels, it is precisely the *lack* of distance in handling sexual matters which constitutes an important aspect of the artifice.

Since *Dhalgren* has already commanded so much attention, I intend, in the discussion which follows, to focus primarily on *Tides of Lust* and *Triton*, novels which immediately preceded and followed *Dhalgren*, and in which matters of sexual politics seem to be most prominent. The limits of this essay prevent me from undertaking a thoroughgoing examination of either book, each of which could easily sustain a full-fledged critical analysis.[8] Furthermore, I shall begin my examination with *Triton*, which, although it is the more recent, is nevertheless the less problematical of the two novels.

Triton is set in the year 2112, when human beings inhabit two worlds (Earth and Mars) and a score of moons. The satellites are far more libertarian societies than the planets, and a state of tension exists between the two groups, ultimately resulting in a horrendous war which nearly destroys the planets. This conflict, an interplanetary extrapolation of the present-day neocolonial struggle between the center and the periphery, provides the background to the story of Bron Hellstrom, the novel's protagonist and, given the extent to which he is (unwittingly) a self-antagonist, its antihero. One of *Triton*'s persistent themes, in fact, is the torment that confusion may generate amid a plenitude of possibilities. Bron hates those who know what they want, because anyone can have his/her desire (which marks him as an elitist, as does his insistent portrayal of himself as a unique individual in a society in which he is constantly reminded there are only types). The problem is, Bron doesn't know what *he* wants, only what he has (often too easily) decided he doesn't like. The point seems to be that you have to be properly prepared to find freedom, rather than chaos, in a realm of endless choice. (A major message of *Tides of Lust*, on the other hand, concerns the self-entrapment which results when one form of license—in this case, sexual—is mistaken for freedom.)

In Triton society, three out of every five people are bisexual; one out of five is gay; one out of nine, into S & M; one out of eight, a fetishist. Women bear only 70% of the children; men can suckle infants, if they so choose; and multiple parenting is common (Bron, born on Mars, had only two parents;

Gene Trimbell—alias the Spike—born in the Satellites, had nine). Both prostitution and marriage are illegal on Triton. On Earth, marriage is legal, female prostitution is legal, male prostitution is prohibited (but exists); on Mars, female prostitution is illegal, but male prostitution was legalized by a woman president named Brian.

Bron, before leaving Mars, had spent several years as a male prostitute, his "specialties" being women with physical deformities, older women, and sadism. Lawrence (a septuagenarian homosexual who proves to be Bron's most steadfast friend) at one point tells Bron that he is a "logical pervert," something now quite rare, but previously (in our own time, perhaps?) very common: " 'You're a logical sadist looking for a logical masochist' " (*T* 253–254). It is this judgment that is partially responsible for Bron's decision to turn himself into a woman. He has previously acknowledged that " 'Perhaps I never had much of a bent for relationships, even as a kid; which is why I went into prostitution in the first place' " (*T* 84–85). Bron seems to have trouble relating to people nonsexually, but even his sexualizationships are more performances than feeling unions, a carryover from his days as a professional. The wealthy older women who paid for his services seem to have done a great deal to shape him socially, but in a superficial and egotistical manner. Yet he still looks to others (sometimes desperately) for self-fulfillment, even self-definition. Coming from a world with a rhetorical but actually illusory freedom, Bron is sadly unprepared to deal with the implications of a more concrete and demanding freedom.

In Africa, as one scholar has demonstrated, style "is another word for the perception of relationships, a dynamic . . . attitude which focuses . . . on the occasion." It is precisely style, in an identical sense, which Bron lacks. His problem is his failure to recognize that "balance through dialogue is essential for the avoidance of overstatement and isolation." Like the African musician who loses aesthetic command through imbalance and a lack of coolness in his performance, Bron's behavior is habitually "hot, intense, limited, pretentious, overly personal, boring, irrelevant, and ultimately alienating."9

One of metalogician Ashima Slade's notes, quoted in Appendix B, has a great deal of relevance for Bron's personal dilemma:

"Our society in the Satellites extends to its Earth and Mars emigrants, at the same time it extends instruction on how to conform, the materials with which to destroy themselves, both psychologically and physically—all under the same label: Freedom. To the extent they will not conform to our ways, there is a subtle swing: the materials of instruction are pulled further away and the materials of destruction are pushed correspondingly closer. Since the ways of instruction and the ways of destruction are *not* the same, but only subtly and secretly tied by language, we have simply, here, overdetermined yet another way for the rest of us to remain oblivious to other peoples' pain. In a net of tiny worlds like ours, that professes an ideal of the primacy of the subjective reality of all its citizens, this is an appalling political crime." (357–58)

"To understand and translate the meaning of words like 'freedom,'" John Miller Chernoff has observed, "it is necessary to examine the social context of their use, to look at what someone who talks of freedom does."[10] The fact that Slade, after the "holocaust" which devastates the commune of gifted people (including the Spike) in which (s)he had lived, "was found, unconscious, in an alley two units from the house, blinded, severely lacerated, and otherwise maimed—most of the injuries, apparently, self-inflicted" (*T* 354–55)—certainly points to personal experience of the possible confusion between instruction and destruction. This may explain Slade's aphorism that madness and obsession are the "gates" to contemporary philosophy (356). In any event, what separates characters like Slade and the Spike from someone like Bron is that they are able to bridge the instruction/destruction dynamic via *con*struction: in the Spike's case, through scintillating moments of micro-theatre; in Slade's, through the logico-political formulations of the modular calculus. They have, in other words, the refuge of art, whereas Bron's refuge is a perverted logic, and his "only steady reference is his own image,"[11] which, unfortunately for him, is a regressive and distorted one. He claims to be concerned, not with history, but with " 'the here and now' " (14), yet he is too confused simply to live in the moment, and he persists in using his personal past as judgmental reference point. A perfect example is his behavior during his night out on Earth with the Spike: he acts as if he were involved in a reversed-role replay of his Bellona days as a prostitute and assesses everything accordingly (and for the most part negatively). He is more concerned with ego and artificial decorum than he is in relating naturally to the woman with whom he professes himself so much in love. Typically, he pushes too hard and then reacts like a hurt child when the world refuses to conform to his demands or expectations. He then stigmatizes the individual or situation, thereafter assimilating this subjective linguistic summary into his future actions as if it were objective fact. Hence, Miriamne, who spurns his obvious advances because she is uninterested in men, becomes "that crazed lesbian" (*T* 76, 115); the Spike, when she emphatically rejects him because she doesn't like the kind of person he is, is then considered "some dumb actress" who is "crazy *and* vicious," or later, simply "that crazed bitch" (231, 257).

Bron, whom one critic has described as "a misfit in utopia, an unregenerate male chauvinist,"[12] longs for a "simpler" past in terms of sex roles. And, despite his own training as a metalogician, he fails to incorporate his intellectual understanding of the fact that " 'language is parametal, not perimetal,' " that " 'the significance of "white," like the significance of any other word, is a *range* of possibilities' " (*T* 59, 57–58); he behaves as if things were *merely* black and white, qualified only by his personal interpretations (Miriamne isn't into men, therefore she's a lesbian; she doesn't like *him*, therefore she's crazed).

The reactionary nature of Bron's grasp of categories of race (black/white) and gender (male/female) is particularly underscored in his relationship with Sam, a tall, powerful (both physically and politically) black male who used to be a blonde, blue-eyed woman desirous of other white women who themselves were attracted to black men. While still a man, Bron had thought of Sam as a "black bastard" (*T* 34); he dislikes Sam because he is not " 'oppressed by the system,' " but is, instead, in a position of considerable power and privilege (31). Bron begins to change his attitude towards Sam as a result of their trip to Earth shortly before the war breaks out, during which Bron is subjected to the humiliations of arrest and assault at the hands of the Earth authorities, and rejection by the Spike, and at the same time becomes aware of the extent of both Sam's responsibilities and capacities. When Bron becomes a woman, it is Sam whom she really desires and seeks out, putting herself at his mercy in the role of a helpless female, an ironic posture when one recalls that one of Bron's justifications for his sex change was to "preserve the species," for he imagined he would be bringing the courage of manhood to the feminine with its (as he sees it) failure of understanding. But although Bron has become a woman very much like the one Sam used to be, the type that Sam desires, Sam, too, is unwilling to take Bron as a partner: " . . . she lay her head against his neck, held on to him. Had he been a column of black metal one degree below white-heat, he would not have been harder to grasp" (*T* 308). This is beautifully succinct and suggestive: the old black male/white female taboo/desire, here complicated by the fact that the black male in this instance used to be a white woman, and that the white woman clinging to him now was formerly a white male! White-heat indeed, through a transformational prism. What is persistently revealed is Bron's essential emotional weakness, despite his "logical" view of himself as a strong individual waging a lonely crusade, someone who is dominating and possessive who nevertheless desperately desires to be possessed.

Delany shows us Bron on the brink of his operation, then jump-cuts, signaling that the procedure is complete by shifting to the use of the feminine

The Politics of Desire in *Triton* and *Tides of Lust*   **47** pronoun: "The drugs they gave her made her feel like hell" (*T* 243). He handles this matter even more deftly in Appendix B, switching pronouns *within the same sentence* to accommodate Ashima Slade's own sex change: "Two months after his arrival he became a woman, moved again to Lux . . . : it was here she first met Blondel . . ." (350). Later, Slade reverses the situation, and Delany alters his usage accordingly: " . . . she had again become a man . . . he emerged . . . frail, blind . . ." (355)—like Tiresias.

This careful attention to language is partly demanded by the complex situations Delany creates for his characters, the challenges he sets for himself as an artist, but it is also due in part to the progressive nature of his understanding. Delany believes, for example, that "there *are* no sexist decisions to be made," for sexist attitudes are ingrained and hence unconsciously operative. "There are anti-sexist decisions to be made. And they require tremendous energy and self-scrutiny."[13] Delany has also condemned D. H. Lawrence as "an absolute prig" for his "institutionally rigid" concept of sex, wherein men and women must remain in their "divinely ordained" roles.[14] Delany transcends this kind of limitation by his tendency to, in the words of one critic, make "fluid" what is "normally static"; or, as another has stated, "Blurring of distinctions is both a technique and a theme. . . ."[15] One of Ashima Slade's own precepts, that "there is no class, race, nationality, or sex that it does not help to be only half" (*T* 356), reinforces the attack on an ideology of absolute categories and "pure" identities, positing instead the need for (minimally, at least) an acceptance of dualism, of fusions rather than separations.

The desirability of maximizing opportunities for *difference* is reflected in Delany's projection, alongside "the redundant formality of the orderly, licensed world" (*T* 10), of an area of each city known as the unlicensed sector where "no law officially held," and where "anything may happen,"[16] but where "the interface between official law and official lawlessness produced some remarkably stable *un*official laws . . ." (9, 11). It is in the unlicensed sector that Bron meets the Spike, although he himself lives in the licensed sector. It is significant that the unlicensed sector is the venue for the Spike's micro-theater performances, which are designed to inspire new instances of perception and (self-) recognition. The u-l also has analogues in Bellona in Delany's previous novel *Dhalgren*, in which everything is possible and allowable, and in the port where the action of *Tides of Lust* is situated, where law and order seem designed only to uphold the recurrent possibilities of sensual fulfillment.[17]

Triton begins with an epigraph from Mary Douglas' *Natural Symbols* which states, in part, "The social body constrains the way the physical body is perceived." Douglas goes on to explain that the interaction between the social and the physical makes the "body itself a highly restricted medium of expression." But this is only true in societies in which the social body is oppressive/repressive. In traditional societies, for example— in contrast with the West (which would seem to be the universe described by Douglas)—the dance is a medium in which the physical self gives articulate expression to the social. In societies such as our own, however, in the conscious struggle against constraint, the body becomes a kind of weapon, even (especially) in a sexual context. In *Tides of Lust*, in which the body is free to assert its basic drives but not much more, Douglas' strictures apply very well: the expression *is* highly restricted, to various permutations of aggression and penetration—a case of "radical skin, reactionary imagination."[18] There is revolt here, perhaps, but there has clearly been no real revolution. As Antonio Gramsci wrote in his *Prison Notebooks*, "The old is dying and the new cannot be born; in this interregnum there arises a great diversity of morbid symptoms."[19] The necrophilia, cannibalism, and other forms of aberrant behavior depicted in *Tides* would clearly seem to support this insight.

In *Triton*, Delany castigates "overdetermined systems"— e.g., governmental bureaucracy—but it strikes me that the compulsive polymorphousness of the sexual relationships he depicts, not only in *Tides of Lust* but also in *Dhalgren*, is itself overdetermined, like the more extreme varieties of Gay Liberation and Feminism, or the fundamentalism of the so-called Moral Majority.

Gregory Renault has also remarked on the polymorphous sexuality of *Tides* in his insightful article on the novel, and argues that while this exists on the "immediate, sensuous level of the text," "consideration of the structure and character figures at the formal level takes us from the totally perverse to the totally unjust, from voyeurism to complicity/revulsion. The issue that then emerges is that of forbidden knowledge."[20] This, of course, is where the Faust myth comes in, and I will have something further to say on this point shortly. Here, however, I wish to note that, like the sensory shield on Triton that "merely shields us from the reality of night" (*T* 9), the erotic engagements in *Tides of Lust*, while certainly associated with the nightside of the psyche, also function as a means of shielding the participants from reality. For as Proctor, the principal Faust-figure in that novel, explains, "Man has devised three systems for effecting the oblivion necessary for sanity." They are, first, the bourgeois work ethic; second, religion; and third, eroticism (*TL* 61). The novel focuses on the third alternative, but it is nonetheless repetitive, like work, and often mystical like religion.

The Politics of Desire in *Triton* and *Tides of Lust*   **49**

In *Triton*, Delany depicts a sect known as The Rampant Order of Dumb Beasts who are committed to putting an end to meaningless—or meaning-ful—communication (the text, quite deliberately, never specifies which), and the characters in *Tides of Lust* often seem like dumb beasts themselves, furiously fucking and sucking under a dispensation that cannot, finally, be clarified as either totally meaningless *or* meaningful. Like *Triton*, the world portrayed in *Tides* is "an ambiguous heterotopia," which, according to Foucault, as quoted by Delany, exists to "dissolve our myths and sterilize the lyricism of our sentences" (*T* 345).

It has been observed that the effect of Delany's use of space opera ele-ments ("entertaining, predictable, and essentially conservative"), combined with "extrapolative or thought-provoking" concepts and a linguistically sophisticated style, makes *Babel-17* "an ironic commentary on itself." "Rydra's discovery of the need to break down barriers in thought is also the reader's need: to perceive this fiction in appropriate terms, one must discover a new way of thinking about fictions of the sort which it appears to be."[21] I think these observations have relevance as well for *Tides of Lust*. As Peter Michelson notes, "Unlike either 'hard' or 'soft-core' pornography, complex pornography is structured according to its own demands rather than those of its audience."[22] Although Gregory Renault insists that the novel "should be read as a significant attempt by Delany to explore further the artistic possibilities of contemporary mass culture,"[23] it seems to me that Michelson's conception is more to the point, since the intellectual level of discourse in *Tides*, with its Faustian metaphysics, and the pornographic plane, which has its analogues in hard-core films, "Tijuana bibles," or the underground comic art of someone like S. Clay Wilson,[24] are not properly situated in "mass culture" in the way that the soft-core bestsellers of the Harold Robbins variety are.

The dual level of discourse ("idealist" and "pragmatic") to which I have just referred has its counterpart in such things as the dichotomy in American experience between the stated idea ("all men are created equal") and the actual (slavery, discrimination), the double consciousness of the Black American (as delineated by Du Bois), and the bidialectal nature of Black linguistic usage (ebonics and white English in the United States, pidgin and "standard" English or French—apart from indigenous languages—in, for example, West Africa); it is also paralleled by the literary/philosophical defense of pornography (specifically that lacking any real literary/philosophical content or even pretense), where "respectable" arguments by prominent people are marshaled in the name of "freedom of speech" to protect what is essentially nothing more than the cash nexus of wet dreams. Censorship is bad, but so is "kiddie porn." The Faust motif is mythic, but compulsive buggery is not. There are inevitable tensions between these different extremes, which are *not* equal. These tensions and seeming disparities will be explored in greater depth as I proceed.

One very revealing fact which Renault reports in his essay on *Tides* is that, "Ironically, the most extensive discussion [of the novel] may be by Delany himself, in an unpublished 'critical analysis' written under the pseudonym 'K. Leslie Steiner' in 1973, 'A Note on the Anti-Pornography of Samuel R. Delany.' (Delany has used the Steiner persona for other unpublished pieces on *Dhalgren* and *Triton* . . .)."25 Steiner, "a young, black, American scholar," putative translator of, and commentator on, the Culhar' Fragment ("sometimes, the Missilonghi Codex"), also figures prominently in the appendices to *Tales of Nevèrÿon* and *Neveryóna* (the preceding quotations are from the latter volume [New York: Bantam Books, 1983], p. 367), works avowedly based on that very (fictitious) ancient text. That Delany would label his own book anti-pornography, and that he would do so in a critique that is supposed to be the work of a black woman, gives us, I believe, some vital clues to his real strategy in creating what is, in various ways, a problematic text. (The fact that Delany's analysis of *Tides* remains unpublished helps, of course, to maintain the problematic, and the existence of "Steiner" articles on *Dhalgren* and *Triton*, which form a kind of sequence with *Tides of Lust*, likewise points to the complex manner in which Delany has extended the fictionality of his novels beyond the specific texts back into the *textus* [see *Triton*, pp. 333ff.] from which they have been scripted.)

The first thing which needs emphasis is the etymology of the word *pornography*, which comes into English "through the French *pornographie*, based on the Greek roots *porne* ('whore,' 'purchased slave') plus *graph* ('writing,' 'painting')."26 Pornography, in other words, is the depiction of whores and, at the same time, the portrayal of slaves. History being what it is, and what it has been, this conjunction of slavery and sexuality should come as no surprise. Instances of it come up in Delany's work frequently—for example, in *Triton*, when the Spike takes Fred (one of the Rampant Beasts, who had earlier assaulted her as she initially approached Bron, and who has since become her lover) to one of her university classes on a chain and has her students toss him raw meat for, as she claims, the theatrical sense of it all.27 There is also the leather collar which Bron wears, and a similar collar which Bull (a white character in *Tides of Lust*) wears; these, however, should be considered in the light of the disquisitions on the meanings of the slave collar in *Neveryóna*, Delany's most recent novel, wherein it is stated that to wear the collar involuntarily is a sign of oppression, whereas to wear it willingly is an emblem of desire. One of the things which is so thoroughly repulsive about the master/slave relationship in sado-masochism is that it is a psychosexual parody of a relationship (which, to be sure, had its own psychosexual aspect) involving large masses of people, not just individuals, under conditions of the most overt compulsion. And although the spirit was sometimes able to soar, if not merely survive, in adversity in ways that lent strength to the oppressed under actual slavery, the voluntary slavery of sado-masochism betrays a lapse of the spiritual into the demonic, a deliberate rejection of freedom, a testimony on the one hand to the seemingly unquenchable desire in man to have (absolute) power over others (a transformation of human beings into things) on the part of the "masters," and at the same time a shuddering revelation of the willingness to forego control of their own lives, a desperate will to be dominated, on the part of "slaves." The strong affinity between sadism and masochism forms an interface between the two extreme forms of human behavior generating a tension, a vicious dynamic, that feeds the whirlpools of history. To seek power, and to feed power—there is no more dangerous symbiosis than that created when these two drives come together.

Delany may have chosen to write pornography because it is a form in which, within a certain plane of discourse, all things are possible. Pornography, like science fiction, is outside the realm of the "mundane" (a word Delany accepts as indicative of "mainstream" writing), but it can be brutally boring nonetheless. On the other hand, Roland Barthes, writing of the "divine marquis," claims that "Sade is boring only if we fix our gaze on the crimes being reported and not on the performances of the discourse."[28] Since Delany is, like Sade, far above the ordinary pornographer-as-panderer, I shall keep this admonition in mind with respect to my judgment of *Tides of Lust.*

Delany seems to accept the conventional acts and obscenities of pornographic discourse as a given, but he transcends the limitations inherent therein by superimposing both a philosophical framework (as Sade did in *Philosophy in the Bedroom*) and allowing himself a good deal of literary/metaphoric license, as in the opening scene, in which the Captain is masturbating, which has the quality of an impressionistic screenplay.

Words like *nigger* are tossed about in the novel without evoking any angry response from those to whom they are addressed. There seem to be several reasons for this; first, such terms are often used referentially and presumably habitually, simply to describe rather than to stigmatize. Geneva Smitherman notes that, among blacks, the word *nigger* is often void of meaning and merely supplies a sentence with its subject.[29] In such a context, the word is part of what Randolph Quirk calls *Umgangssprache*—that is, the speech of familiars (which is also, presumably, speech among equals).[30] Even though the word is not used exclusively by blacks in Delany's novel, it is "balanced" by the use of analogous forms of racial reference by black characters directed toward whites ("little white pig," etc.). There is no sense of racial inferiority manifested by any of the characters in *Tides of Lust*; sexual prowess seems to be the measure of "superiority," and that prowess is abundant everywhere. Often, in Delany, apparently derogatory epithets are part of what Quirk calls *Gangbangsprache,* the speech of the gang; but it is important to note that the term "gangbang" implies rape, and this leads me to my second point, which is that, when there *is* a kind of violence implicit in this sort of epithetical usage, it is a violence that is subsumed in a sexual act and hence rendered erotic. (In fact, in Delany's novel there is really a double edge to such words, which function as interchangeable terms between the *Umgang* and the *Gangbang*.) Purely psychological violence—as opposed to the psychosexual—seems to be generally nonexistent in this book, but there *is* physical violence, without justification on any level the reader can properly accept. Robby and Peggy-Ann, for example, who both die violently (and needlessly) in the novel, are, not coincidentally, two characters who cannot go along unquestioningly with the relentless hyper-sexual activity of the others. They seem to be the only ones who set limits to their behavior, and this makes them victims, because they thereby put themselves in the role of "outsiders." In an erotic universe of this totality, no one ever says "no" or "enough," or if they do, it is only to have these protestations overridden. Here, lust is all, and the time is always ripe.[31]

Desire has no limits, as the Faust myth demonstrates. Uncontained, desire easily transforms itself into need, and in the words of Peter Michelson, "The face of 'evil' is always the face of total need."[32] Perhaps this is the reason that Delany combines the anarchic energy of unfettered sexuality with the artistic requirement for order and symmetry: to structure need and lend it meaning. Wittgenstein claimed that the limits of one's language are the limits of one's world; in the novel it is language which both limits and lends coherence to desire.

Henry Louis Gates, Jr., has discussed Charles Davis' sense of the importance of the trope of blackness as absence in Afro-American literature[33]; in *Tides of Lust* it is the trope of *love* as absence which is crucial in defining the negative aspects of compulsive eroticism and of pornography in its cruder forms. Black and white in Delany's novel are equal in their obsessions: either fantasies of the Other (in terms of race, sex, or both), or engagement in incest, bisexuality, etc. The sexual plane becomes the level on which opposites literally come together.

Chapter Two of *Triton*, "Solvable Games," has an epigraph from Robin Blaser's *The Practice of the Outside*, which states, "The death at the center of such discourse is extraordinary and begins to let us see our own condition." This is very pertinent for the world of discourse of *Tides of Lust*, in which the death in question, apart from actual killing, is an emotional one, all feeling having been reduced to sensations of either pleasure or pain. Is there a message here for a society based to such an overwhelming degree upon endless consumption and self-gratification? Does the concern in the novel with "order," "symmetry," "balance" have anything to do with legislated attempts in this country to rationalize problems of race and gender, after generations of institutional complicity in discrimination followed by malign neglect—both forms of "order" operating on the basis of an almost complete failure to come to grips with the complex *human* consequences of such engineering? Does it have anything to do with persistent irruptions of the irrational in societies monumentally dedicated to reason? We must always keep in mind that, as Joel Kovel asserts, "men are creatures of conflicts, of seams and splits and dialectically opposed beliefs: creatures of impossible contradictions, of whom it might be said that the higher one part of them reaches, the lower another part must stoop."[34]

One apparently glaring *a*symmetry in the novel is the absence of a foregrounded black woman. Gregory Renault mistakenly asserts that "there are no black *women* in the novel. . . ."[35] Therese, the Captain's sugar-mama while he was a young man in New Orleans, and Nig's mother are two black women referred to in the text, but they are in the past, a part of history. In terms of the present action, there are "two black women in the back of the crowd" in one scene (*TL* 134), and two "colored women" are seen momentarily toward the end of the novel, kissing (157), but they are little more than "extras" in this sexual extravaganza. Indeed, the only *major* female character in the novel is Catherine, who is white, and who is overpowering more through her absence than through her presence.

In the words of Terry Eagleton, "The ideology of the text lies in the distance between these two discourses—in the fact that the 'phenomenal' text is able to 'show,' but not *speak of*, the covert coherence which sustains it."[36] In *Tides*, the sexual scenes constitute the "phenomenal" text—what we might term, for our purposes here, the sub-text—while the philosophical/mythical level—or super-text—speaks directly to the justificatory relevance, beginning with Delany's own Author's Introduction, which advises us that "these pages bear the most circumscribed reverence for sanity. They concern form—which saves no one, but is icily instructive" (*TL* 5). (The word *icily* underscores the distancing which Eagleton is speaking of. It is comparable to the "chilling grace" with which Mordecai, in the epigraph to Chapter One, taken from Thomas Disch's *Camp Concentration*, delivers Mephistopheles' lines beginning, " 'Why this is hell, nor am I out of it. . . .' ") It is instanced also by Proctor, when he says, in response to the Captain's request for details about Catherine, " 'They are private, and not for this book. Because they entail love. . . . But this must be an evil story' " (77–78), a judgment echoed towards the end of the novel in the Captain's log: "Perhaps this is a bad book" (167). During his address to the gathered orgiasts,[37] which is a major key to the novel's intentionality, Proctor again refers to "this book." His speech is conscious of itself as a text (oral) within a text (written); as a character, he is aware of the artifice of which he is a part.

There are additional examples of this reflexive self-consciousness: " . . . a strange, big-bellied black (spades cannot smile in this story) grinned . . ." (84); " 'Yeah, nigger, you better grin. Niggers can't smile in this book' " (88). In the first instance, it is the narrator, speaking parenthetically; in the second, it is a (white) character called Nazi. Keeping in mind that this story takes place in a Gulf Coast port, ironic passages such as those above, in which the super-text "penetrates" the sub-text, seem to turn *Tides* into a kind of pornographic minstrel show. Whites and blacks both act out roles for one another which are mutually stereotypical. It is worth noting here that Delany's original title for the novel was *Equinox*.[38] Because an equinox provides a "balance" of light and darkness, the original title may have been intended to express a rough equality between black and white, as well as to emphasize the book's concern with symmetry. (*Tides of Lust* itself suggests a pattern as well as movement; tides, after all, are influenced by the lunar cycle.)

I write "rough equality" deliberately, because it is black potency with its "implication of mythic chaos" (*TL* 124) which is called upon to overturn order. Speaking to the Captain, Proctor declares, " ' . . . you black devil! I have you! I'll squeeze the juices from your black fruit into that sphinx' monstrous hole yet. . . . You'll defile the equalized altars of day and night, and this world will come tumbling around us!' " (134–35). Although Catherine ("that sphinx") later claims that the Captain will not do as a proper devil, she concurs that " ' . . . it *is* the mystic black devil who must be satisfied for a new age to begin . . .' " (150).[39] The context of these statements is satanic, but the underlying sociopolitical implications are nonetheless obvious: for a true, rather than a rhetorical, equality to come into being, the thwarted aspirations and energies of black people must be allowed fulfillment. That apparently racist terminology can be given a reading on another level is supported by Delany himself in his own usage in a quite different context, when he describes the classic works of twentieth-century science fiction as "great, mysterious shapes of mind, lit here and there with the coalescing energies of our new technology, but, for the most part, *black and unholy* with mythic resonances."[40] "Black and unholy," though innately encoded with atavistic bias, is, in this instance, intended to be decoded with positive metaphysical import: as provocative, unsettling, deeply imaginative. For if revolution is the concrete crumbling before the fantastic, as Catherine proclaims (150), then all of these various meanings—positive *and* negative—must come into play, in "the rounded and rich rendering of the interface between the actual and the ideal" (149; Catherine again) where chaos can be "contained in ritual" (171; Proctor).

With regard to the need for a black as primum mobile in the overthrow of established order, one might profitably refer to the difference between Western aesthetics, with its emphasis on harmony, and African aesthetics, with its emphasis on rhythm and recurrence. African art, for example, is often asymmetrical. In African music, the notes fall on the off beat; off-beat phrasing is also a stylistic feature of Afro-American jazz. Furthermore, "In African music *there are always at least two rhythms going on.*"[41] One is tempted to compare this with the two levels of discourse which Delany employs in *Tides*, which reflect the mind/body separation underscored in the novel, and which appear to work at cross-purposes but in fact serve to highlight one another. There is also the principle of repetition in African music and oral literature, which serves to clarify the meaning, and which could explain both the repetitions in *Tides* and the principle espoused in *Triton* of mentioning everything at least twice in different contexts. Faust, the Western magician par excellence, needs, it seems, a non-Western ally.

Ultimately, there is a tension in *Tides* between the symbolic (the Greek *symballein* means "drawing together") and the diabolic (*dia-ballein* means "pulling apart"). Proctor's invented belief that a new age will be ushered in if the devil "comes seven times between noon and midnight" (56) demonstrates this quite clearly, for the devil is, in the Christian tradition, *diabolus* per se, whose *symbolic* act (copulation, in which two are drawn together), performed seven times (a magical number), is supposed to bring forth a different world, which, since it will personify chaos, is really a *de*creation of already-existing order (itself based on a symbolic symmetry, upset by *seven*, an odd number, and therefore "unbalanced"). This may help to explain Delany's persistent concern with the criminal-artist figure, a conjunction of the symbolic and the diabolic within a single individual. Proctor himself, indeed, is such a person—Faustian artist and Mephistophelean provocateur[42]—who lies frequently, " . . . for I am a man whose interest in the truth is only its aesthetic fascination in a landscape of lies" (122), and who is " 'transported by the idea of using the material in such a way that all the relations remain unreal' " (170). Keeping in mind that another word for *lie* is *fiction*, one cannot help feeling that this is Delany himself speaking, for, despite the occasional grotesqueness of the ruthlessly clinical sex, there *is* aesthetic fascination in this landscape of fiction and falsehood—remembering, too, the political implications inhering in *landscape*, evidenced in Appendix B to *Triton*. All the relations between characters in *Tides* do remain unreal, though they do not lack intensity for all that, whether it be a tragic or a trivial intensity. The dual qualification here is necessitated by, and points to, Delany's deliberately duplicitous practice in the novel, in which everything is Janus-faced: the linking of the symbolic with the diabolic; Faust as speculator and manipulator, mage and fakir, tempter and tempted; scurrility coupled with sophistication in both word and deed; pornography indicting itself as anti-pornography. Delany, much more successfully than Faust (since he does not need to contend with the requirement of damnation imposed by Christian theology and morality), is able to overreach himself, indulging his fantasies (and perhaps a few of our own as well) by means of an aesthetic vehicle—a text—which conveys an intimacy it simultaneously sanitizes. "Language," writes Roland Barthes, "has this property of denying, ignoring, dissociating reality: when written, shit does not have an odor. . . ."[43] Through pornography's "transparent body may be seen a dialectic of reality and unreality"[44]—a dialectic, I might add, that transcends the text.

Notes

1. Quoted by Hayden Carruth, in "Paul Goodman and the Grand Community," *The American Poetry Review*, 12, No. 5 (1983), 25.

2. New York: Bantam Books, 1976, p. 91. All subsequent references to this work, abbreviated *T*, will be situated in parentheses in the text.

3. Triads in various forms are pervasive in Delany's writings, as I have previously observed in "The Mirrors of Caliban: A Study of the Fiction of LeRoi Jones (Imamu Amiri Baraka), Ishmael Reed and Samuel R. Delany," diss. State Univ. of New York at Buffalo, 1976, p. 216 and elsewhere.

4. Total body transformation—e.g., male to female—is considered merely cosmetic; genetic changes are classified as radical.

5. Adam J. Frisch, "The Landscape of Sex in Recent Speculative Fiction," mimeographed ms., 1978, p. 4.

6. New York: Lancer Books, 1973. All subsequent references to this novel, abbreviated *TL*, will be found in parentheses in the text.

7. A recent article by Gregory Renault, "Speculative Porn: Aesthetic Form in Samuel R. Delany's *Tides of Lust*," *Extrapolation*, 24 (1983), 116–29, may serve to bring this novel wider attention. Renault notes that *Tides of Lust* was written in 1968 and was immediately followed by another, still unpublished, erotic novel entitled *Hogg* (pp. 126–27, fn. 4).

8. Delany has not only afforded us this degree of textual density as a writer of fiction, he has also provided an explicational counterpoint in *The American Shore* (Elizabethtown, NY: Dragon Press, 1978), a book-length critical meditation on "Angouleme," a tale by Thomas Disch. In his introduction to this work, Delany argues that criticism "(assuming it is done with passion and precision) has an autonomous value in itself" (p. 40).

9. John Miller Chernoff, *African Rhythm and African Sensibility: Aesthetics and Social Action in African Musical Idioms* (Chicago: Univ. of Chicago Press, 1979), pp. 125–26, 140.

10. Ibid., p. 21.

11. Karen L. Shuldner, "On *Dhalgren* and *Triton*," *Riverside Quarterly*, 7, No. 1 (1980), 11.

12. Tom Moylan, "Beyond Negation: The Critical Utopias of Ursula K. LeGuin and Samuel R. Delany," *Extrapolation*, 21 (1980), 248. Moylan calls the society of *Triton* "a utopia of the streets," where other forms of politics "give way to the politics of everyday life" (pp. 243, 244), which is the level on which most of the characters function; but there are constant allusions to a much vaster political frame of reference that culminates, as previously stated, in a catastrophic interplanetary war. Politics may intrude very subtly, as for example, in the notation in Appendix B, which informs us that the language of eighty percent of Earth, and of Mars and the Satellites, is a "Magyar-Cantonese dialect" (*T* 352) or in the mention of a People's Capitalist China (189)—both of which provoke speculations in the reader's mind as to what kinds of historical changes Delany's twenty-second century has inherited— or it may arise more straightforwardly, as when Lawrence tells Bron that because women have only been treated as human begins for the past sixty-five years, and then only on the moons, they are far less willing to put up with shit; but the political is always present.

Similarly, Delany "is more than tangentially interested in racial themes," despite the fact that he is "assuredly not a one-dimensional 'black writer,' that is to say, a writer concerned only with racial identity . . ." (Emerson Littlefield, "The Mythologies of Race and Science in Samuel Delany's *The Einstein Intersection* and *Nova*," *Extrapolation*, 23 [1982], 236, 238). In Delany's own words, "To be black in this country is simply too pervasive an experience for any writer to omit from his or her work. It *has* to be there in one form or another" (quoted by Michael W. Peplow, in "Meet Samuel R. Delany, Black Science Fiction Writer," *The Crisis*, 86 [Apr. 1979], 119). This, too, of course, has political implications.

13. "Shadows—Part Two," *Foundation: The Review of Science Fiction,* Nos. 7–8 (1975), p. 129. The first part of "Shadows" appeared in issue number six of the same journal, and the entire work was reprinted as part of Delany's first collection of critical pieces, *The Jewel-Hinged Jaw: Notes on the Language of Science Fiction* (Elizabethtown, NY: Dragon Press, 1977). As one example of the almost mischievous manner in which Delany "fictionalizes" his own life while at the same time "actualizing" his fiction, the woman "editor" of Appendix B to *Triton* informs us that Slade's first important lecture, *Shadows,* appeared in issues six and seven/eight of the journal *Foundation,* and that (s)he took the title "from a non-fiction piece written in the twentieth century by a writer of light, popular fictions" (*T* 357).

14. *The Jewel-Hinged Jaw,* pp. 44-45.

15. Peter S. Alterman, "The Surreal Translations of Samuel R. Delany," *Science Fiction Studies,* 5 (1978), 28; Gregory Renault, "Speculative Porn," p. 124. Renault is addressing himself specifically to *Tides of Lust,* but in my own estimation the comment has a much more general significance for Delany's overall canon.

16. Similarly, science fiction was, for a long time, "unlicensed" in the sense that it was generally considered non- or para-literature by the professional literary establishment.

17. The do-your-own-thing ethos of the u-l sector in *Triton* and of Bellona in *Dhalgren* are clearly rooted in the "free love" philosophy, the let-it-all-hang-out attitude of the countercultural movement of the 1960s—which was both a circus and a transcendence—and in Delany's own personal experience, as the autobiographical *Heavenly Breakfast* reveals. Ironically, we are informed in *Triton* that although, in the year 2112, the 1960s are "very *in*" on Earth, the "audience" is the most conservative in the solar system (172).

18. This phrase is taken from Marilyn Hacker's poem "Peterborough," in *Taking Notice* (New York: Knopf, 1980), p. 88.

19. Quoted as the epigraph to Nadine Gordimer's novel *July's People* (New York: Viking Press, 1981).

20. "Speculative Porn," pp. 122–23.

21. William H. Hardesty, III, "Space Opera, Semiotics, and *Babel-17,*" mimeographed ms., 1978, p. 11.

22. *The Aesthetics of Pornography* (New York: Herder and Herder, 1971), pp. 59–60.

23. "Speculative Porn," p. 117. Is this what Proctor means when he declares that " . . . Faust seeks to gather to him a greater public; one who, by definition, will participate" (*TL* 123)?

24. Proctor: " 'Is it such a terrible thing to content yourself with only visiting places like this in sleazy books or in . . . what do they call them—underground comics?' " (*TL* 110).

25. "Speculative Porn," p. 126, fn. 3.

26. Gary Kern, "The Search for Fantasy: From Primitive Man to Pornography,"

in *Bridges to Fantasy*, ed. George E. Slusser, Eric S. Rabkin, and Robert Scholes (Carbondale: Southern Illinois Univ. Press, 1982), p. 218, notes.

27. I am reminded here of the photographs of singer Grace Jones, caged and "vicious," which have been displayed as avant-garde art but which exploit (and it is in this that the true viciousness lies) the most pernicious stereotypes and anti-black, anti-woman fantasies.

28. *Sade/Fourier/Loyola,* trans. Richard Miller (New York: Hill and Wang, 1976), p. 36.

29. "White English in Blackface, or Who Do I Be?," in *The State of the Language,* ed. Leonard Michaels and Christopher Ricks (Berkeley: Univ. of California Press, 1980), p. 163.

30. "Sound Barriers and *Gangbangsprache,*" in *The State of the Language,* ed. Michaels and Ricks, p. 10.

31. At the end of the novel, it is true, Kirsten and Gunner want to know if it was necessary for Robby and Peggy-Ann to die, and the Captain tells them, " 'That's the law. . . . their law. Not ours' " (*TL* 173), but it is not at all clear how these three, despite the fact that they are only visitors in this port, conform to a law that is radically different. The Captain confides to his log that he didn't feel sorry for Robby at all, even though he was "afraid of what was on his face" (167), and we know from his earlier log entries that he has committed a number of murders himself, though he has "more babies than deaths" (35). In other words, although the Captain rhetorically situates himself and his two "companions" outside the ethical universe of the other characters, there is really nothing other than his *words* to give evidence of the truth of this.

32. *The Aesthetics of Pornography,* p. 75.

33. "Charles T. Davis and the Critical Imperative in Afro-American Literature," introduction to *Black is the Color of the Cosmos: Essays on Afro-American Literature and Culture, 1942–1981* by Charles T. Davis, ed. Henry Louis Gates, Jr. (New York: Garland, 1982).

34. *White Racism: A Psychohistory* (New York: Vintage Books, 1970), p. 90.

35. "Speculative Porn," p. 118.

36. *Criticism and Ideology* (London: Verso Editions, 1978), p. 150.

37. Peter Michelson, *The Aesthetics of Pornography,* p. 163, quotes Mircea Eliade to the effect that "the orgy destroys creation while at the same time regenerating it; man hopes, by identifying himself with formless, pre-cosmic existence, to return to himself restored and regenerated, in a word, 'a new man.' "

38. "Speculative Porn," p. 126, fn. 4.

39. This insistent identification of the black man with the devil is so pervasive that it has been adopted in an inverted, *positive* manner in a good deal of black literature. Two examples: (1) In Toni Morrison's *The Bluest Eye* (1970; rpt. New York: Pocket Books, 1972) one of the characters imagines the devil "holding the world in his hands, ready to dash it to the ground and spill the red guts so niggers could eat the sweet, warm insides. If the devil did look like that, Cholly preferred

him. He never felt anything thinking about God, but just the idea of the devil excited him. And now the strong, black devil was blotting out the sun and getting ready to split open the world" (pp. 106–107). (2) In John A. Williams' novel *!Click Song* (Boston: Houghton Mifflin, 1982), the protagonist, Cato Caldwell Douglass, an Afro-American novelist, narrates a dream he has of playing pool with God, in which the deity explains, "You're probably wondering, my boy . . . why the eight ball is the black ball and the last to go, the ball you must not get behind. And the cue ball, white like the sun, is the contact ball. . . . The black ball is the stranger hidden in the heavens, a threat. . . . The Dark Prince hides behind galaxies, constellations, and nebulae. . . . The black ball demands more, is more, than we can imagine" (p. 325). In *Tides of Lust,* Proctor wants the Captain to spill the old world's guts; he is the cue ball, trying to finally "pocket" the Captain as eight ball and "rack up" a new game.

40. "Letter to a Critic: Popular Culture, High Art, and the S-F Landscape," in *The Jewel-Hinged Jaw,* p. 17 (italics mine).

41. John Miller Chernoff, *African Rhythm and African Sensibility,* p. 42. Emphasis in the original.

42. Proctor himself declares that "In the public imagination, Faust and Mephistopheles become confused," and that Faust is "a magician (and a charlatan)" (*TL* 122–23).

43. *Sade/Fourier/Loyola,* p. 137.

44. Kern, pp. 193–94.

Editor's Note: Under its original title *Equinox, Tides of Lust* is again available as a paperback from Masquerade Books (NY: 1994). *Hogg* finally saw publication last year as a hardback from Black Ice Books.

On *Dhalgren*

JEAN MARK GAWRON

On the brown desk in the brown-paneled study in which I am sitting, there is a hexagonal container composed of six trapezoidal compartments surrounding a seventh hexagonal. Each compartment is covered by a padded flap embossed with a word or words in gold letters. The words on the six outer flaps are *clips*, *rubber bands*, *stamps*, *coins*, *matches*, and *keys*. Under *clips* there are two lengths of plastic left over from a package of nylons, a price tag for $9.44, a curtain hook, a mysterious blue pill, a safety pin, and two screws; under *rubber bands*, washers, a suspender clip, a molly nut, and a tie pin; under *stamps*, two cuff links and a tie clip; under *coins*, screws, a button, and, at last, a paper clip; under *matches*, a discarded electric shaver head, some nails, a hat pin, and a rubber band; under *keys*, several blocks of staples and a fistful of paper clips.

The central compartment bears the trademark of the drug company that manufactured this container for promotional purposes. It is empty, but there is a funny groove and a hole in the plastic, apparently left from a time when the container served as an ashtray.

One aspect of this container that may immediately strike readers of *Dhalgren*, even before they lift the flap to find its purpose, is its playful juggling of expectation, the manner in which it creates a growing sense of pattern which, ultimately, is never realized. The patterns, of course, are there to be found, but we began by looking for them in the wrong place. A

62

second time round the hexagon will change the game drastically, and will reveal more about what is outside the container than what is inside.

Another reader, cognizant of *Dhalgren's* intense concern with language, might observe what a neat linguistic illustration the container makes, demonstrating what is known as the inmixing of the signified, the way meaning smudges, metonymically distributing throughout the surrounding structure, and changing its very nature. One might, of course, expand to a dodecagon, adding compartments for buttons, pills, electric shaver heads and so on. But the completion of such a container is a hopeless cause. The compartments are close together and easily accessible to one another. There must always be more things than compartments, or we would have to turn matters around and begin storing compartments with things. In order for it to function, the actual organization of the container will have to be far more flexible than its labeling.

In any case, whatever speculations readers make regarding the nature of the above container, they will doubtless be influenced by the label heading this text, and by the label on the outside of this volume. Such expectation is essential if containers are to exist at all, and cements knowledge together. The next time I hunt for a paper clip, I will immediately know which compartment *not* to look in.

But, in an introduction to a work that is really about the mechanics of expectation, let me shy from the expected topic a little longer and address myself to the curious objects which sometimes are and sometimes are not found *in* the container: clips, rubber bands, stamps, coins, matches, and keys. A little reflection will show that they are all mechanisms, of one kind or another, for making specific correspondences in the world, for imposing order. Stamps calibrate a certain payment with a certain service. Coins sharpen the contours of value so that they will exactly match—after myriad arcane transformations—those of production. Rubber bands and paper clips keep the right sorts of things together; keys keep the right sorts of people and the right sorts of things together. Matches package fire, a prime commodity, into discrete quanta. Each of these tiny artifacts may be called an instrument of order.

But the paper clip found while hunting a cigarette invariably recalls the time ransacking the den turned up only loose credit card invoices. These objects are subject to the same mechanics of muddle as everything else, perhaps more so because of the precision demanded of them. The fact that they dispense order makes their muddle the more memorable; that muddle may even launch us on an examination of the nature of order. Note that the container we began by considering is an instrument for ordering the instruments of order. The fact that such a container exists at all shows how quickly the instruments of order become the emblems of disorder.

In *Dhalgren*, in what is really a very similar process, the emblems of disorder are made instruments of order. The chaotic landscape of Bellona, with its leather queens, quasi-bikers, ex-pimps, hustlers, drifters, and deserters, all embroiled in the occasional Apocalypse, is subject to a powerful force that regulates the minds and actions of its inhabitants. As Tak tells Jack, the latest of many newcomers he introduces to Bellona: "It's a strange place, maybe stranger than any you've ever been. But it still has its rules. You just have to find them out" (97). The emblems of disorder are as subject to the forces of organization as any emblems, and may become, as leather freak Tak does with this assertion, an instrument of order.

The container for this process, the novel itself, sometimes ordering, sometimes assigning emblems, is the instrument for ordering such emblems. Ultimately, like our real world container, it proves subject to the same forces it wields.

Order, of course, is a function of the grid we put to it, of expecting to see certain things in certain boxes. Being entirely a creature of thought, it is fair game for the dialectical games we have been playing. On the social plane, as well as on the "absolute" plain of the technical, the very specification of the emblems of disorder is a powerful ordering act. Because the Pope excommunicated Michael Cerularius in 1504, the Orthodox Schism was created and the Church redefined. Because we have specified randomness, computers call up random numbers by rigorous laws. We develop sets of expectation for order and disorder alike, and there is no procedure for determining either set the more complex.

Let us begin, then, with expectation, the binding force of the grid. When we expect, we work within a field of relative probabilities; some things seem more likely than others. As we open to *Dhalgren's* first page, we do not begin with an empty field. We have, at the very least, the trained fictional expectations of those who have read novels before, perhaps of those who have read science fiction novels. We have the title, perhaps some hearsay knowledge of the work, perhaps a familiarity with Delany's previous books; in the paperback edition we have the cover and the covermatter (both are elegant and misleading).

Traditionally, the basic thrust of the novel has not been towards order. What is desirable is the improbable, the incongruous, the unexpected, because that gives the most information in the shortest space. But at the same time it is necessary to establish a rich field of events in which expectation can flourish, so that the *conditions* for surprise are there.

From the first word, *Dhalgren* plays off against that initial set of expectations we bring to any reading. It begins mid-paragraph, mid-sentence, marked off by no indentation, and no upper-case letter: "to wound the autumnal city." Many will instantly suspect an experimental work, and a reading of the next two paragraphs will seem to uphold that suspicion. To some, such a beginning will instantly suggest circularity; a quick flip to the last page will again result in confirmation. It is curious that all these expectations are structural. In place of the usual fictive signals of setting, voice, or situation, we have certain structural signs that bid us be wary of the purely fictive. Throughout the novel to follow, signals that *seem* fictive, and seem to be further elaborations on the fictive world, will prove to be structural, elaborating only on the fiction. This does not reduce Bellona to a series of empty compartments. In fact we are given an enormous amount of information about the city, and that particular *kind* of information, the textural, the language of color and smell and feel, we will learn to trust.

The second paragraph of *Dhalgren* is also one line long and moves towards grammatical completeness: "So howled out for the world to give him a name." We have a sentence fragment with a third person dative which will not be given true rhetorical direction until we fix its missing subject. "I," "he," or "she" howled? Or even "you"? The bulk of the novel that follows tends to make us supply the masculine third person, but before backreading we have only the dative pronoun for our orientation, a suspended "him," both nameless and sourceless, a being-there with little more than tense and grammatical position.

The third paragraph, beginning with the intriguing line, "All you know I know"—adding a suspended second and first person to our already suspended third (first, second, and third, a dischord)—follows with a series of scattered sensory impressions. The sense of a single, dominating identity emerges. The "you" resolves into the general you of informal prose, the "I" into the thinking I of récit.

We are further reassured in the fourth paragraph when, on the pick-up note of "a full minute" we move into more or less standard, heavily foregrounded prose. We are definitely in the third person now. A man and woman meet, make love, talk. He does not know his name. Lulled, we may begin to forget our early warnings.

That the protagonist does not know his name is a fact we may look at as our first textual surprise (if we have skipped reading the cover flap of the paperback edition), at least in the sense that it gives us more information than the conventional fact it replaces. (To know that our hero's name is Ishmael tells us less, fictively speaking, than to know he has no name at all.) The motivating force of the novel, and of information in general, is that a surprising datum correspondingly narrows the field of expectation with its informative impact, thus increasing the chance for further surprises.

Our next surprise is a straight-out foray into magic heavily laced with myth. The woman of this first sequence goes hamadryad and turns into a tree. The mysterious yet relatively mundane tone of her encounter with our protagonist is shattered, and we are now prepared to weight the incidents that follow with all the significance that accrues to details in a myth. The shadows of madman and god have fallen across our nameless drifter. He enters a city in the aftermath of a disaster as nameless as he is, hazy, aflame, largely abandoned.

We have begun by now to develop a whole matrix of what and what not to expect: this book is about a nameless drifter who enters a strange city seeking his name. After a number of events of great import (enough to fill all the pages we have in hand), perhaps he finds it.

In fact these expectations are met; and in fact most (if not all) of the expectations raised in *Dhalgren* are met, as long as they are put in the form: more information about X. Yet somewhere along the line, for some readers, at least for many of *Dhalgren's* reviewers, something in the game goes wrong. The general analysis goes something like: there are too many disordering events. The field of expectation is thrown open so far that there can be no more surprises. The game stops.

It is worth pausing a moment in our consideration of expectation to take note of some of the real-world expectations *Dhalgren* has confounded. For a novel so obviously ambitious and difficult, one carrying about it the "taint" of the experimental, for a science fiction paperback published with little fanfare, which opened to a storm of critical displeasure, *Dhalgren* has done astoundingly well on the marketplace, selling upwards of half a million copies in its first two years of existence, still far short of the hallowed land of the best seller, but enough to fall comfortably within the ranks of the top ten best selling science fiction novels of all time. Why?

And here we have blundered near one of those mysteries which completely transcends our container, like the drug company trademark. Because, obviously, people liked it. As to why they liked it, those reasons were doubtless as multifaceted and various as the novel is rich. As to why so many critics should speak so vituperatively against the book (and, in all fairness, there were a number of favorable critical reactions as well), that is equally a mystery. If we were, however, to hazard a guess, it might be: because they knew what they were looking for. Most of *Dhalgren's* bad press has come from within the science fiction world (and again, there *were* highly favorable reactions), both fan and professional; and much of its audience, to judge by its unusual numbers, has been drawn from outside that world. It may simply be a question of certain fixed expectations not being met.

Let us return to the game with which we began this essay. Someone only interested in finding clips under *clips* and stamps under *stamps* could only be frustrated once they reached the sixth flap. They would know in advance that, underneath, there were no keys. Even if the slim hope of finding a key were rewarded, the response would have to be: "so what's wrong with the other five?" Our hypothetical spoilsport takes all signals as signals about the container. He sees it as utterly cut off from the world around it, and believes that if the labels are not "true" labels, then they are superfluous.

We alluded above to the central flap, which bears the trademark of the drug company that made the container. Obviously the nature of the relation between the word on the flap and what is inside (always problematic) has radically changed. The drug company trademark is the emblem of a vast and essentially unfixable world beyond the bounds of our immediate evidence. Much as the trademark "explained" the box itself, so the world "explains" the trademark. This explanatory outside world, completely beyond the bounds of any experience we may apprehend, is a concept every bit as remote as Berkeley's God, who integrates the scattered illusions of individual perception as the underlying consciousness of the world. The world, as an explanation for things in general, has in its turn demanded explanations of the most intricate sort from philosophy. The central compartment, then, is the compartment of explanation; it is empty. Its position in the container is far more important than anything that may be found inside it. Syntax outweighs semantics. Our clearest emblem of this sort of naming in *Dhalgren* is the title, but we shall postpone consideration of that until the very end of this essay. For the moment let us simply note that, in a reading of *Dhalgren* as in our reading of the container, the positions of things in the network may be far more important than what they are.

There is, of course, another point to the parable. All our considerations of the container have taught us about what we have come to expect of containers. Likewise, *Dhalgren* teaches us about what we expect of novels.

Dhalgren is, first of all, a self-referent work. Traditionally, self-referent works have essayed some sort of commentary on their own form. André Gide's *The Counterfeiters*, in which Edouard is writing a novel entitled *The Counterfeiters*, ends with a journal just as *Dhalgren* does—ends, in fact, with three journals, Edouard's, Gide's and Lafcadio's (Lafcadio being a character from another novel entirely). Gide's is an author's journal which openly discusses problems of fiction. So does *Dhalgren's* journal, but its embedding in the text is of a completely different nature than Gide's journal, and, if we are to heed our own warning about position and syntax, we must examine that embedding for new properties.

To begin with, the authorship of the notebook is ambiguous. Shortly after our drifter's arrival in Bellona a notebook, many of its pages already written in, is found and given to him. In some ways this notebook resembles Edouard's novel more than Gide's journal, for it is the most openly self-referent of the texts in *Dhalgren* (the others being the drifter's poetry, which we never see, and the Bellona *Times*); the opening of the novel is transplanted into this notebook in the first passage we read from it; "to wound the autumnal city." (36) (But the notebook soon diverges from the text as we know it.) It is tempting, in a novel by the same man who wrought the author's journal of *The Einstein Intersection*, to read this notebook as the author's, somehow dropped, through the magic of Bellona, into the text of the novel itself, to read the passage just alluded to as a first draft. This notion may persist with us for six chapters; by the seventh, when the notebook has moved into the foreground and become the text, it becomes apparent that the relation between notebook and novel is far more complex (and we shall later examine that relation). Yet it is certainly suggested, regardless of who wrote it, that the notebook reflects many of the concerns of the novel at hand:

> Poetry, fiction, drama—I am interested in the arts of incident only so far as fiction touches life; oh no, not in any vulgar, autobiographical sense, rather at the level of the most crystalline correspondence. (401)

And because this is a statement not only *about* the novel we are reading, but also *in* it, we may conclude that one of *Dhalgren's* subjects is the relation of fiction to reality.

Yet *Dhalgren* is more than a self-referent work. It is a self-conscious work as well; the fictive structuring forces may, from time to time, be perceived as such by the characters:

> "Then be glad you're not a character scrawled in the margins of somebody else's lost notebook." (5)

> My life here more and more resembles a book whose opening chapters, whose title even, suggests mysteries to be resolved only at closing. But as one reads along, one becomes more and more suspicious that the author has lost the thread of his argument, that the questions will never be resolved, or, more upsetting, that the positions of the characters will have so changed by the book's end, that the answers to the initial questions will have become trivial. (831–32)

This last is a straightforward capsuling of *Dhalgren*; one reason some readers may have been unhappy with the book is that, for them, those initial questions never became trivial, either because they never read far enough for the necessary shift of perspective to take effect, or simply because they ignored that shift, preferring to focus on matters which grew smaller and smaller in the Bellonean glass, their positions in the network radically changed.

In this self-conscious mode, we may read the "you's" at the beginning and ending of the novel as, respectively, author and character:

I want to know but I can't see are you up there. (878)

All you know I know. (1)

And the "I's" are, respectively, character and author. There is the suggestion of another confrontation between the two in the Emboriky department store much later, or earlier, when the protagonist (by then named Kid) looks into a mirror and sees a complete stranger (376). Further on, we read in the journal:

"Consider: if an author, passing a mirror, were to see one day not himself but some character of his invention, though he might be surprised, might even question his sanity, he would still have something by which to relate. But suppose, passing on the inside, the character should glance at his mirror and see, not himself, but the author, a complete stranger, staring in at him, to whom he has no relation at all, what is this poor creature left . . . ?" (401)

"All you know I know," then, as a vertical statement, may only move downwards, from author to character; the character is constrained to a pitiful "I want to know." The task of the novel is to effect this epistemological transfer from author to character. He begins a drifter with no purpose and no name, his face too young for his years, his years, in any case, frozen like those of a character in a novel: "Well, if you were born in nineteen forty-eight, you've got to be older than twenty-seven" (5). The text we read gives him movement, purpose, name, informs him as it informs us.

Dhalgren is a coming to consciousness, an exploration of the constitution of knowledge. "I have come to," (879) the novel ends—"coming to" signalling consciousness regained—"to wound the autumnal city" (1). It is this act of consciousness, the constitution of the text we read, that effects Bellona's apocalyptic limbo.

And what of Bellona? Before coming to grips with the structural problems of *Dhalgren*, we must encounter its texture. Thus far we have spoken only of the novel's dispositions, its beginning and ending, its edges. What of the inside, the city coextensive with its book, this city of words, Bellona?

It is easy to see how *Dhalgren* could have been made a far more conventional science fiction novel (and we shall presently argue that it *is* science fiction). With only a few alterations here and there, a panel of lights, a constellation out of whack, a paragraph placed in the mouth of a passing physicist, Bellona could have been made the center of some bizarre dimensional warp. With perhaps a few more changes, it could have been set in a depopulated future, its visitors flocking from a more conventional part of the landscape. Instead it is left to coruscate weirdly in our own 1970s America, in the perilous immanent present, where it becomes deniable (no such thing is likely to happen) and immanently dated. One reason, of course, is inherent in *Dhalgren's* self-consciousness. The "cause" of Bellona's predicament is that it is in a novel, and novels, ultimately, mine their material from the eras in which they are written (even a historical novel is bound to the latest histories). They are cut off from the "real" present the way Bellona is cut off from the world. As our "real" world ages, Bellona becomes more and more impossible, if only because of that "nineteen-forty-eight" line cited above, which locates the characters, and Bellona, within a lifetime of that date. This positioning in the real world does not invalidate *Dhalgren* as science fiction (which, after all, is dated all the time and still remains science fiction), but does lend it a different sort of fictional suspension from that of most science fiction, or that of most fiction, period.

Each miracle in such a Bellona demands a corresponding miracle in our outside world. The modern-day megalithic republic is a vast organism which would inevitably mobilize powerful defensive mechanisms should some part manifest as great a disorder as Bellona's. These mechanisms are briefly alluded to in *Dhalgren* (there *was* at one time television coverage; there *were* at one point National Guardsmen), but are quickly allowed to fade away. This is plainly miraculous. A real-life Bellona would be proscribed, investigated, destroyed. It would never be ignored. Bellona's miraculous inevidence to the outside is no more unbelievable than much of its *inside*, but it is significant that the fictional suspension must cover our real world entirely, that *Dhalgren* is a science fiction novel literally set now. The net result is to shade every event in Bellona with doubt. As long as there is some chance of error in the report, some hint of refraction in the seeing, some whiff of swamp gas, some hint of translucence, then what we call the real world is still the real world. After two moons have shown up one night in Bellona's cloudy sky we read, in the Bellona *Times*:

" . . . *any* 'agreement,' 'certainty,' or 'definiteness' about these moons are cast into serious doubt—unless we are prepared to make even *more* preposterous speculations about the rest of the cosmos?" (132)

Thus Bellona remains in the most delicate of fictive suspensions, a bubble, already fragile because it is fiction, then set to quivering with doubt. We have already suggested a model with similar properties; this is the "world" to which we were led through the central compartment of our container, at once explanatory and emblematic of the inexplicable. Just as the unfixed, abstract "world" of everyday speech is a fiction which may, in fact, be incoherent by the usual laws, so is Bellona, to its inhabitants, intractable to any logical laws, a fiction on which they suspend judgement, a "world" in itself. The only difference is that Bellona is something they immediately experience. For Calkins, writing in the Bellona *Times* above, the moorings of the immediate city have had to be loosened so that "the rest of the cosmos," the world outside Bellona, may remain fixed. For Calkins Bellona is a fiction of that cosmos. For us, who must, as we have argued above, regard that cosmos dubiously, it is a fiction of a fiction. And if that cosmos is, literally, a "world," a fiction of the fictional entities outside Bellona, then Bellona is a fiction twice removed, removed entirely through our efforts to keep other fictions intact.

Dhalgren is a novel that deals with the relationship of fiction to reality— one of Chinese boxes. Truth, as Calkins realizes, is a function of a given system. We call certain things false because we want others to remain true. It will become apparent in our exploration of *Dhalgren* that all the phenomena of Bellona can not be encompassed in a single system, that there must be different fictive levels, fictions within fictions without end, a construction reminiscent of Gide's two mirrors effecting their *mise en abîme*, but with the added complication that our real world, and not just the novel, also consists of such mirrors.

In a rare breach of his usual reticence concerning his work, Delany has written:

> Anyone who finds it helpful may approach *Dhalgren* . . . as (and in) an attempt to explore and respond to the deep structure (to use a deceptively topical phrase) of the language of human signs. It tries to focus on the deep structure of that language by dramatic stripping of these signs' surface coherence.[1]

We must not, of course, be too trusting of this declaration. Bellona's the poet Ernest Newboy eloquently outlines the enigmatic nature of the artist's relation to his or her work. The easy equations authors give us for their books often bear only the most fragmentary relations to the long process of creation or the finished product itself. "One does not finish a work of art, one abandons it," Valery tells us. There is a world of anxiety connected with this abandonment. Nevertheless, this suggestion, however suspect its source, provides an interesting prospect from which to launch another consideration of Bellona.

Deep structure, then, may provisionally define the relationship of Bellona's signs to those of the real world, and explain why that relation is not a linear one. Deep structures in linguistics provide a new grid on which to map sentences, hopefully the same grid which generates them. The classic examples:

John is easy to please.
John is eager to please.

Here we have two sentences whose surface structures are perfectly identical, which, because their meanings are so different, must derive from entirely different deep representations to be interpreted. The elements of these representations are called kernel structures.

The sign relationships of Bellona, then, may be seen as transformations of sign relationships in our real world. Because these transformations operate within a different grid, their final configurations may first be perceived as chaotic, particularly when applied, as Delany has applied them here, to real world emblems of disorder. Just as the kernel structure of a simple sentence will be incomprehensible without a formal key to kernel structures, so will Bellona's signs seem confused if not read by its special laws. This is why Kid, in his first introduction to those laws, is beaten up outside Calkins' estate. Entering a city in which all the traditional boundaries of privilege and property are inevident, he has yet to learn that, nevertheless, such boundaries *do* exist; they have merely changed form radically.

Having invoked the words "deep structure," however, we are not obliged to assume that Delany has penetrated to the core of language. Willard Van Orman Quine, in his essay, "Methodological Reflections of Current Linguistic Theory,"[2] makes the useful distinction between fitting and guiding grammars, pointing out that we may have two sets of rules, both accounting for every sentence in the language, only one of which is actually used by speakers to guide their speech. Quine goes on seriously to question whether there can be such a thing as a guiding grammar in the Chomskyan sense. We shall echo Quine's note of caution in our consideration of whatever deep structures *Dhalgren* may reveal, and acknowledge the grammar that exhibits them only as fitting. (Some may object here that the very term "deep structure" implies some pre-existent truth which has been uncovered; this is undoubtedly so, but we shall take the deep structures as belonging, not to the sentence under consideration, but to the grammar we are employing to consider it; the "truth," then, is entirely grammatical.) Whether or not they actually reflect the generation of social surfaces, kernel structures are bound to illuminate new relationships in the surfaces themselves. They may also highlight differences analogous to those between "easy to please" and "eager to please," or the similarities in the relations of sentence parts in active and passive voice—comparisons that may be far less apparent on the social plane, where sign and sense are by nature far less distinct.

The mechanisms for such transformations in Bellona are evidently tied up in that peculiar illusionary quality that we have already noted. With no fixed reality, there are no fixed entities arbitrarily defined as signs. All relations become associative as the laws of the signified become dominant; things are freed to mix in the endless alchemy of metonymy and name. Let us examine some of these names, and their associations, within the informing field of Bellona.

The city has somewhere near a thousand inhabitants who, by and large, have taken up lodging in whatever abandoned homes they find convenient. There is a largely black band of outcasts and lowlifes called the Scorpions, led jointly by a black woman named Dragon Lady and a white ex-pimp named Nightmare. When Kid joins, Nightmare willingly concedes him his position and moves to Dragon Lady's Nest. The traditional black ghetto area, Jackson, still houses a relatively large population of blacks, and the roughest section, Cumberland Park, is the home of both Dragon Lady's nest and a large group of blacks who have rallied round George, Bellona's resident folk-hero/demi-god. In the city's spacious park, under the leadership of an earnest organizer named John, a number of more wholesome, sixties-vintage freebooters have banded into a commune which forever embarks on long, never-to-be-finished, work projects. The social center of Bellona is *Teddy's*, a leather bar through which every visitor to Bellona must at some time pass. *Teddy's* is owned by an Eastern Aristocrat *manqué* named Roger Calkins, who continues to publish the city newspaper (authoring, as we have noted, some of its articles) and lives on a sprawling estate up on Brisbain Avenue.

Calkins is the nearest thing Bellona has to a central government, but he has relatively little direct influence on the lives of its inhabitants. He remains behind the scenes except for a single dialogue with Kid in the last chapter which, even then, is conducted from behind the screen of a confessional. By means of his newspaper, his bar, and his parties, he is, to some extent, able to concentrate the attention of Bellona where he wishes (and this seems at least partly the reason for his retiring presence, for he seems *not* to wish to draw that attention to himself). His role is somewhat that of a lighting man, a not inconsiderable power in this city of illusion; he is Bellona's social artist.

Both Kid the poet and Calkins the politician wonder, at different times, whether one must be a good man to pursue their respective paths with any real success. The question is, of course, unanswerable, and though it would be unanswerable in any world, its suggestion of a correspondence between Kid's and Calkins' roles is particularly resonant in the compressed world of Bellona. Here, with all social constraints and conscriptions dissolved (there are no immediate pressures *making* people do things, no state to serve), politics and art are equally a set of conventions and a game. The politics of any artistic endeavor and the aesthetics of any political act are signs of the same order. Indeed, this is probably the single aspect of the Bellonean condition that most deeply distresses Kid. His political roles of Scorpion and hero become obstacles to his work as an artist. At Calkins' party, and particularly during his interview with Bill, we glimpse the enormous distortion his other roles wreak on Kid the artist:

"Do your friends in the nest like your book?"
"I don't think most of the guys read too much."
"Hey, man!" Nightmare called out. "I ain't even *in* his fuckin' nest and I read every fuckin' one!" Which caused someone else to call: "Yeah, they're great! The kid writes great," and someone else: "Sure, ain't you got this party for him?" (708)

Clearly, there is no way that anyone in Bellona can read his book of poems purely as "poetry," even, considering the vast associative matrix through which art may escape being itself.

We may occasionally view the drawing on the cave wall as a unified exercise in art, religion, and politics, but in fact art as such does not yet exist for the cave dwellers. To impute all three kinds of responses yields a quantity quite different from what we began considering, a drawing associated with a specific complex of responses in the cave dwellers who view it. It would be difficult to sift from that complex any one response that we could call aesthetic, religious, *or* political. The parallel is that Bellona, because of its smallness, because of its distortive nature, tends to blur and sometimes to eliminate the distinctions between the political, religious, and aesthetic spheres. All we have said noting correspondences between Kid and Calkins might just as easily apply to Kid and George; all *three*—Kid, George, and Calkins—have large entourages, mass-produced artifacts lending presence to their public persona (printed poems, posters, and newspapers), and an impact that definitely crosses over from the social plane on which they are most comfortable; but to exhaust all the resonances of this particular trinity is to reexamine *Dhalgren* from an entirely different perspective, one beyond the bounds of this introduction. Let us simply note that the fields of influence of Kid, of George, and of Calkins interpenetrate extensively, that each in some way does his bit to extend or sustain the influences of the others (Calkins' paper rockets George to stardom; George makes Kid the hero when he and Kid save five children from a fire; Kid gives June Richards, George's rape victim, one of George's posters and keeps that all-important interaction alive). In sum, were we given a glimpse of Kid's poems we, as readers of a real work of prose in a real world, would render more or less "purely aesthetic judgements," whatever that phrase may mean. But that peculiarly mixed system of responses of the native Bellonean— in which Kid must to some extent have participated when he wrote the poems—would be inaccessible.

It is not that the Bellonean's response is non-aesthetic. It is rather that aesthetic responses themselves may be more complicated than we have until now supposed. Perhaps the *only* thing peculiar to such responses is that they can at once be called many things—moral, political, religious, philosophical, scientific, and playful. The inhabitants of Bellona exhibit each of these various responses. The aesthetic may in fact be some function of differentiation itself, of the interplay of a whole complex of internal responses, an endlessly rearranged collage that mirrors (constitutes?) our own endlessly shifting internal state. And what of our cave dweller, with no theogony, no schooling, no politics, who *cannot* share in all the above responses? Does she, staring fixedly at the cave wall, experience stirrings we might call aesthetic? We shall assume here that the word is a generous one. Whatever unknown map of the world she carries about inside her, traced with shapes we can never name and boundaries we cross daily without thought must—at the instant the drawing forever alters her conception of bison and drawings—be reformed and recolored. Her response is as inaccessible to us as a real Bellona, and so, ultimately, is her bison.

We have argued that the aesthetic response requires some extensive, perhaps even holistic, reference to a conceptual map of the real world. That lands us once again in the central compartment of our container, which is where Kid's poetry ultimately must fall—with the nameless and misplaced, the abstract and explaining, the unattainable "world." We may see its antecedents, its referents, even hear it moving towards utterance, but we may not see it as such. We shall presently extend this notion of inaccessibility, but for the moment let us continue with our brief overview of Bellona, armed with the knowledge that certain of its compressions may make vast differences.

Another notable such transformation may be observed in the social role enjoyed by the Scorpions, the closest thing Bellona has to a police force. As Bunny, *Teddy's* resident male go-go dancer comments:

> "You Scorpions do more to keep law and order in the city than anyone else. Only the good and pure in heart dare to go out on the street after dark. But that's the way, I suppose, the law has always worked. The good people are the ones who live their lives so that they don't have anything to do with whatever law there is anyway. The bad ones are the ones unfortunate enough to become involved, I rather like the way it works here, because, since you *are* the law, the law is far more violent, makes much more noise and isn't everywhere at once: so it's easier for us good people to avoid." (359)

Here, stripping the surface channels of power from the social edifice has created the context for a statement about power's underlying patterns: Power is something that accrues to social entities merely because of their position in the network. Of course Bellona's portioning of power has completely redesigned the role in question. Bellona has no laws, apart from those discoverable by hard experience (such as Kid's when he is beaten up outside Calkins' wall). Yet the Scorpions, privileged by their numbers, their coherence, and their potential of violence, are clearly granted the same powers granted the police. The park commune pays "taxes" in care packages filled with food. Calkins hires Scorpions for "protection."

All this, again, is done by convention rather than constraint. Thus the relations between certain signs prove recognizable, although the signs themselves have changed: the relations between Calkins (the state) and the Scorpions (the police) is one of mutual mistrust and ignorance. The *Times* frequently misreports Scorpion escapades. The Scorpions have, until the occasion of Kid's publication party, never been inside Calkins' estate. This matches much of what we know, historically, of the capricious relations between the state and its armed enforcement agencies. What such correspondences show is merely what the invention of a science of semiology presupposes, that we "read" the relations between signs rather than their references; but the fact that such relations are shaped within the fluid society of Bellona, where traditional mechanisms of constraint are inoperative, suggests they are the results of "deeper" forces. This reading is, of course, supported by Delany's suggestion regarding deep structures, and it is a highly persuasive one. But to avoid the appearance of seeking ultimate truths in a novel so highly ambivalent about the relation between the true and the real (its epigraph, "You have confused the true and the real"), we shall note that the surfaces of Bellona do not necessarily claim any fixed, privileged relation with those deeper forces. In other words, a different set of outcasts might have assumed new configurations, in which a different set of contouring relations would be familiar. This is in line with what we have supposed about Bellona's being only a fitting grammar.

What seems to emerge now is that under Bellona's transformations and compressions, the same social spaces, no matter how radically changed in shape, exercise about the same amount of power. (Kid's power, of course, proceeds not from his status of artist, but from that of enforcer, and as artist he struggles to remain aloof from it: "I do not tell how I gain or maintain it (power). I only record the ginger stroll through the vaguely fetid garden of its rewards" [753]).

The single glaring exception to the constancy of power is on the racial plane, where the high percentage of blacks left in Bellona has given them majority rule. Nevertheless, because Bellona *does* still sit in the real world, blacks as a group in Bellona continue to act like blacks, a people severed by history from the lines of power. Asked why Nightmare, a white man, and then Kid, a half-Indian, were chosen leaders of the primarily black Scorpions, Glass (black) replies:

" . . . I think more or less everybody has got it in their head that after one of these runs or other, the shit is gonna come down. Hard. When it does you gonna see niggers fade in the night like nobody's business. But the chief scorpion, maybe, ain't gonna be able to fade quite so fast." (844)

We earlier promised to argue that *Dhalgren* was a science fiction novel. Hopefully, that argument has been taking shape throughout the course of this essay. We have been making of Bellona a society which, though some parts of it may be inaccessible, still bears correspondences enough with our own to allow an understanding of its peculiar why's and how's. The particular informative suspensions employed here are native to science fiction. To present an oversimple model: In the mundane novel we are given events with the understanding that we know the rules they follow; the novelist then shows that, given these rules, here is what must *really* happen. In a certain kind of science fiction novel, we are given events in order to induce or deduce the rules; the novelist shows that, given these events, these rules must apply. There is frequently the further implication that these rules are in turn the consequences or metaphorical extensions of real world events now in progress, but this is generally a vertical process. The capsule account of this type of science fiction novel is, simply: We are given a peculiar society, and shown why and how it works. In practice, of course, the distinction between rules and events is not as clear-cut as we have made it. Mundane novelists are perfectly capable of concatenating events so as to imply a rule that, although imbedded in a perfectly familiar situation, is not at all evident; we may, for the sake of argument, claim that the events are based on more familiar rules, and that the inevident rule is only an heuristic reduction of what "really" happens, but it is clear that the boundary line is already growing fuzzy. This should cause us no great distress since it is the general fate of boundary lines between literary genres; they may serve one specific purpose but, turned to another, they quickly fall apart. Ours was drawn in hopes of showing that the rhetorical thrust of *Dhalgren* parallels that of a whole class of science fiction novels.

Science fiction is a literature of edges. Often knowledge of the why's and how's of a science fictional world is gained by experiencing the edges of a society, by tracing its contours through its outcasts or its elite, those who have the most at stake because of its fundamental assumptions. Bellona is composed almost entirely of outcasts and aristocrats structured round the ghost of the old society; it is practically a pattern case.

The fact that Bellona is practically all contour seems just one more aspect of its illusory nature; yet there are still survivors of the old social center in the city, and these Belloneans are perhaps the most deeply wrapped in illusion of them all. These are the remnants of Bellona's once-powerful middle class like the Richards, acting out a fantasy bourgeois existence amidst the ruins of the city. June Richards, the family's only daughter, has been tied in with the center of the apocalypse because of her rape by a "hulking, sadistic, buck nigger" (278), which may have been one of the triggering events of Bellona's peculiar retribution. It is also the event which, thanks to the publicity given it in Bellona *Times*, has elevated George to demi-godhood. June's parents, however, although they are shown June's front page picture *in flagrante*, fail to recognize George's blond partner. Obviously to do so would be to bring Apocalypse within their thin apartment walls, shattering their rigorously constructed retreat. The fragility of that retreat emerges with almost agonizing clarity in one of the novel's major high comic scenes, Kid's first dinner with the family. Mr. and Mrs. Richards blithely discuss June's plans for college, although she is really "daddy's little girl," and not really the college sort, although, outside, Bellona's mist churns round mayhem and anarchy. Mrs. Richards gushes over Kid's poetry and Mr. Richards, in response, maunders on about a friend of his who has written an engineering instruction manual (an allusion to John Ashbery's early poem, "The Instruction Manual"?).

Witty, pathetic, exhaustive, the scene is a ghastly study in social forms drained of all content (Bellona again: all edges). It reads like a sitcom by Proust.

What is left of the middle class in Bellona is diseased or dying. In a second dinner party with the Richards, we are treated to a generous sampling—three couples whose male halves Arthur seems to have met through "his work." Participants in this affair later make appearances, armed and dangerous, at the Emboriky, a department store from which a number of white snipers conduct an informal war on all those (mostly black) who approach, and at a religious meeting at George's where, stripped of their "surface coherence," they discuss shooting niggers. Mr. and Mrs. Richards host a strange evening in which all the usual pleasantries of place and occupation have become taboo, while, two floors down, emblematic of the disease that has struck down his city and his social class, the body of their teen-age son rots in his old bedroom.

To find the living personality of Bellona, one must leave the partial vacuum of the social center and move outwards. What emerges, of course, is the collection of outcasts we have been examining all along—thieves, pimps, hustlers, punks, drifters, deserters, the human flotsam of Bellona. "What is the simplest way to say to someone like Kamp or Denny or Lanya," Kid wonders at one point, "that all their days have rendered ludicrous their judgement of the night?" (573). Like the city itself, the days and nights of Bellona have been turned inside out. Those who rule Bellona's misty days are the very same creatures of night who once made Denny's, Kamp's, and Lanya's afterhours so fearsome. They have filled Bellona's sky with cosmological wonders and proven *all* judgements, social and scientific, inadequate. And in the circular text of *Dhalgren*, in a world where all the traditional landmarks, down to the basic fixing of night and day, have been toppled, it is impossible to read either of these phenomena as controlling the other.

The basic pattern of Bellona is curiously reminiscent of that ascribed by the young R. D. Laing in *The Divided Self* to the schizophrenic personality. The pre-schizophrenic, faced by continuous double binds, retreats behind a series of shells which may then suffer the inevitable consequences, turning paradox to paralogism and freeing the self. These masks the pre-schizophrenic regards as divorced from the self, as demands made by the other and thus surrendered to it. But in time more and more of the self is invested in these masks, leaving the interior hollow, marked only by an elaborate boundary, a self whose inside is no different from its outside. The schizophrenic may either treat everything as external, making of himself a machine, or a catatonic, or everything as internal, becoming that supremely sensitive organism, the paranoid.

Kid's description of his own bout with madness leans towards the paranoid, but it is curious how his picture also calls up Bellona, where, as we have seen, once invisible forces may become screamingly evident:

> " . . . the real mind is invisible; you're less aware of it while you think than you are of your eye while you see . . . until something goes wrong with it. *Then* you become aware of it, with all its dislocated pieces and its rackety functioning, the same way you become aware of your eye when you get a cinder in it. Because it *hurts* . . . Sure, it distorts things. But the strange thing, the thing you can never explain to anyone, except another nut, or, if you're lucky, a doctor who has an unusual amount of sense—stranger than the hallucinations, or the voices, or the anxiety—is the *way* you begin to experience the edges of the mind *itself*." (53, 54)

In the city of edges, it would be monstrous paranoia to claim every illusion as your own, and pure catatonia to deny them all. Bellona *forces* recognition of its contours, and makes its presence, its process, keenly felt. Like Laing's schizophrenic, a society under stress invests more and more of its energy in its edges, then denies them more vehemently than ever. Bellona is the image of those edges freed from their empty center; it is an optative madness, a form for illusion, a consciousness.

The "real" Bellona is invisible to the world ("the electric nation") just as the "real" schizophrenic self is. It has, by redesigning "knowledge and perception" (15, 16), eluded all real world consequences. But in so doing it has freed certain forces of anxiety and terror; it has become a city of "inner discordances and retinal distortion" (16). The result is a dreamlike apocalypse, always in progress but never progressing, a strange amalgam of fears found only in the mind, a projection of social terrors, fire, earthquake, lightning, assassination, the rape of a white woman by a black man, all events that, in our modern myth cycle, may bring on the crumbling of the social order.

Meditating on the death of the Richards' teenage son, who is "accidentally" pushed down an elevator shaft by his sister June, Kid wonders at one point if it was murder. Bobby had, not long before that, threatened to tell their parents about the poster (of George) Kid had brought. But then a far more horrifying possibility strikes Kid. Suppose it was an accident; suppose it just happened:

> " . . . that means it's the city. That means it's the landscape: the bricks, and the girders, and the faulty wiring and the shot elevator machinery, all conspiring together to *make* these myths true. And that's crazy." (278)

We are left with the grim possibility that in Bellona it really does bring down death and destruction for a black man to have sex with a white woman. In Bellona it really *is* wrong.

Whatever the myth may be in this case, the outcast of Bellona has no trouble distinguishing the forces behind it. Kid writes (and in the passage following "they" are those at the social center, the well-adjusted):

> . . . they are sure that any social structures that arise, grow out of patterns innate to The Sex Act—whatever that is; while we have seen, again and again, that the psychology, structures, and accoutrements that define *any* sex act are always internalized from social structures that already exist, that have been created, that can be changed. All right: let me ask the terrible question: could it be that all those perfectly straight, content-with-their-sexual-orientation-in-the-world, exclusive-heterosexuals really *are* (in some ill-defined, psychological way that will ultimately garner a better world) more healthy than (gulp . . . !) us? Let me answer: *No way!* . . . any madness is preferable to *that*. And madness is *not* preferable! (794–95)

The myth of George, that sex between a black man and a white woman is rape, and the myth that homosexuals are sick really belong to the same cycle; they are both fictions founded on the assumption that there are "normal" sexual patterns anterior to the social patterns that cast them. That the city should function to make myths such as these true is, as Kid tells us, madness.

Thus the city's madness is evident on a number of different planes, while Kid's madness, his forgotten days, his fractured internal monologues, his queasiness at certain passages in the notebook, occupies much of the novel's foreground. Ultimately the two reflect one another indistinguishably, neither signifying the other, joined at the juncture of mirror and mirrored into a single whole. It is this specific lack of definition which makes knowledge of his internal state so difficult for Kid. If Bellona, with its capricious cosmology, its fantasy apocalypse, its gray sky, is some vast solipsistic projection, then it is true, as Kid thinks at one point that: "I am traveling my own optic nerve" (94). But he leaps to the complementary hypothesis in the very next sentence: "Limping in a city without source, searching a day without shadow, am I deluded by the inconstant emblem?"

Have the names of things changed so that he can no longer make sense of them? The names and emblems of Bellona, as we have seen, *have* changed, just as its street signs do from day to day. The reason given us for this, extending at once over Kid and all the other things without name in the city, other Scorpions whose appellations are as new as his, the gigantic sun which one day covers one quarter of the sky, is: " . . . certain images lose their freedom and resonance if, when we regard them with a straight face, we do so through the diffraction of a name" (549). Names, even as they mythify and exalt, draw inviolable limits; and, extended, they may become immobilizing constraints. Can anything fix George's position in the Bellonean mythos more completely than the extension of his name to cover the second moon that rises over Bellona? And though that moon quickly surrenders its place in Bellona's night, the nature of the name, though it again refers only to a mortal man, has been irrevocably transformed.

We are of course given our closest look at Bellona's inconstant emblems in connection with the name Kid; the nameless drifter who enters the city is variously called kid, Kid, and Kidd (the first "calling" made by Tak, the guardian of the gate who seems to greet all of Bellona's newcomers), but acceptance of some form of the name is universal. It is pointedly the special gift of Bellona itself: "So howled out for the world to give him a name" (1). The gift, however, is not completely validated until he has committed himself to the city. On page 156, after he has eaten of his first food there, after he emerges from his first bath—after, in other words, ritual gestures of Eucharist and Baptism—Kid is for the first time referred to as Kidd by the narrator, who has until then kept entirely to "he." Kid's name, then, sits uneasily within the web of the conspiring city's myths, associated both with rites of naming and of sacrifice. At first, within the warped field of the Richards' home, it is written Kidd, but as soon as he moves into the more authentic Bellonean world of the Scorpions, it reverts to its original (but now capitalized) form. Kid's novelistic name is, indeed, Kid—Kidd, with two d's, represents a corruption of that name that only adheres to him while he is with the Richards, i.e., while his vision of his own priorities is doubled, distorted, and rendered a stuttering parody of that same vision, once it is freed from the Richards' set of anapocalyptic blindnesses.[3]

Kid is a specifically Bellonean name, both monicker and common noun (like those of many of the Scorpions), at once associated with false appearances (his seeming youth), and with deeper truth (through its ritual antecedents). It is both truth and fiction, more and less than a name. As Kid puts it: "To find who I am I've had to give up my name and who knows what part of my life" (802). Kid, then, may not be a name, but it may be who he is.

But the inconstant emblems of Bellona are only capable of capturing essences within the web of Bellona's other emblems. Bit by bit, the whole network of associations has become unique. Kid tells us:

> In any house here, movement from room to room is a journey from a place
> where twin moons have cast double shadows of the windowsill upon the floor

to a place where once, because the sun had grown so immense, no shadow was cast at all. We speak another language here. (830)

There is hint of Eden in this state of inconstant reference and continual naming; yet Bellona is unquestionably a landscape over which apocalypse has burst forth. How, then, are we to tell the post-apocalyptic from the pre-lapsarian? Bellona has its share of plenitude, food, companionship, shelter, spiritual comfort; but it also has its share of want, of sickness and violence. Every surfeit of light sheeting the sky as if by celestial fiat also has its obliterating mist, its dissolving night. Which way does Bellona's arrow point, towards or away from entropy, towards constitution and creation, the mooring down of things, the closure of signifier and signified, or towards apocalypse, the complete rupture of sense, the all-consuming fire?

We have called *Dhalgren* a coming to consciousness. Implicit in that, because of the novel's circularity, is a leaving-of-consciousness. Apocalypse and Genesis, in Bellona, are co-extensive terms with different meanings, like Russell's morning and evening star, like George before a second moon rose, and George after. Bellona is the act of consciousness through which we perceive it, and consciousness is fluid, an endless exercise in Adamic magic, like our readerly constitution of the text before us, the naming of the fiction. Yet *omnis determinatio est negatio*, to resurrect a motto of Spinoza's. Consciousness is an equally fluid deconstruction. Each designation of order strikes out another emblem of chaos over previous designations, assuring the continuous coincidence of naming and named. To constitute the miracle of order is to reconstitute equally miraculous disorder—and Bellona belongs among these "cities of reconstituted disorder" (716)—not merely in the act of drawing boundaries between them, but in necessarily obliterating others, in creating a great field claimed by both, the field where Bellona is located, in the emptiness of the mid-American plain, an utter plenitude, a barren form, a being and a nothingness. We evoke here the first two terms of Hegel's famous dialectical triad in *The Logic*, so that we may turn instantly to the third, becoming, which is the truth of Bellona. Bellona is inconstant boundaries; and the man of many backgrounds who makes our only interface with it—whose consciousness constructs it for us—is equally unfixable, is half-Indian, half-white, half-mad, half-named, bisexual, one-shoed, ambidextrous, willful, labile, poet, and hero. He is a model of dialectical progression, and his very loss of memory, his emptiness of content, is a model of its adherence to form. Kid is the consciousness the text fills, and the emptiness with which it begins is only made the more emphatic by the novel's violent, mid-sentence opening. Ultimately it must end the same way, all the same questions unanswered, brought up short against the same violent emptiness, unpunctuated, its boundary incomplete. Neither knowledge nor consciousness can be completed any more than the container with which we began this exploration can, because each must deconstruct itself in order to continue; the container must open and close to function.

We have from time to time made reference to *Dhalgren's* solipsistic undertones, prompted by the novel's persistent reference to illusion and distortion. In fact, illusion and distortion prop up some of the strongest empiricist arguments for sense data and against idealism, in its simplest form of *esse est percipe*. If anything, *Dhalgren* shows traces of a later, more fashionable, phenomenological sensibility:

> On the dismal air I sketch my own restraint, waking, reflexively, instant to instant. The sensed center, the moment of definition, the point under such pressure it extrudes a future and a past I apprehend only as a chill, extends the overlay of injury with some retentive, tenuous disease, the refuse of a brick-and-mortar-grinding violence. (297)

The "sensed center" here is of course consciousness, interpenetration is between the awareness and the thing in its phenomenological aspect. But it is important to note that this passage, and others like it scattered throughout, written in a difficult, splintered diction in the first person, are those which most closely approach the *feel* of madness. In *The Phenomenology*, once he has proven that all categories derive from consciousness (Geist), and that things and their attributes can only be constituted by a consciousness, Hegel goes on to assert the mutual dependence of thing and consciousness, thus identifying the true with the real, and consciousness with self-consciousness. It is this very identification, of the edges of the world with the edges of the mind, that Kid has equated with madness in the passage already cited (53). In *Dhalgren*, the world of pure thought, where the true and the real blend indistinguishably, is a nightmare.

Knowledge is the mind's mooring to reality. It is specifically uncertainties regarding what he *knows* that most distress Kid, because these are the uncertainties that may leave him trapped in the nightmare world of the purely mental. When a giant sun blots out Bellona's sky, Kid is panic-stricken until he knows that his friends also see it. Truth, as we have noted, is a function of what other things one wishes to keep true. To affirm the giant sun does not entail denying his friends, and thus, for the moment, Kid's system of knowledge is safe. He grows calm, then ecstatic. The edges of the world have been pushed back out; the boundary of the self has held.

But for how long? In Bellona, the act of observation has broken down, "the miracle of order has run out" (108). At times what Kid knows is inaccessible to him simply because words fail him, because the language itself has changed, and he does not know "what sticum tacks words and tongue" (573).

We shall need a brief digression to fix this curious slippage of word and tongue. It has been a fairly common assumption among non-skeptics since Kant that in order to know something you must at least be able to say it. This assumption is implicit in both Kant's and Hegel's use of categories to constitute knowledge. Following the canon of the positivists, Wittgenstein eschews metaphysics entirely and concentrates on what can be said, assuming that what can be known will then be taken care of (but then changing his mind).

It is Wittgenstein's argument against a private language[4] that will be of use in investigating the slippage towards the unsayable in Bellona. Wittgenstein first asks whether it would be possible for someone to have a name E for a specific sensation for which there is no word. It would of course be possible, but there is no sense in which E is part of a private language. E is understood in exactly the way other words are, by its connection with an entire associative network of words and ideas, beginning with the word "sensation." The problem of constructing such a private language would be where to begin. If we did in fact create a word without a matrix of words in which to sit, in what sense could we be said to know what it means? For Wittgenstein knowledge is a linguistic function bound up with meaning.

It is not clear from a reading of *Dhalgren* exactly what Samuel Delany understands by that curious verb "to know"; but it *is* clear that, in Bellona, he constructs a certain class of experiences which, known or unknown, is linguistically inaccessible, not because it lies beyond or between the words, but because it is directly beneath them. *Three times* in the course of the novel we read sentences launched with: "Speech is in excess . . ." each followed by a different concluding term, three examples where the words are simply too large for what they need to say:

> Silent on the circuit of the year, speech is in excess of what I want to say, or believe. (297)
> Speech . . . is always in excess of poetry as print . . . is in excess of words. (297, 99)
> Speech is always in excess of poetry as print is always inadequate for speech. (783)

The "circuit" of the first occurrence suggests that is what we are dealing with here, a conjecture supported by the novel's circularity and other loops we shall presently consider. Here, if we take "words" to suggest "speech," we complete the small rhetorical loop:

SPEECH > POETRY > PRINT > WORDS (SPEECH)

We see that the "excess" of words is not simply some quantitative measure of reference, some inadequacy of resolution. It is a property of the network itself, which positions its elements so as to achieve maximum interdependence, so that translation tends, in general, to decrease that interdependence to imply more (and bury the original) in a positive feedback loop.

In the shifting world of Bellona, referents may utterly transform and remain bound to, under enormous tension, the same word. A room is still a room even though two moons and a gigantic sun have shone through its window. How can these enormous translations be made? Here is something "known," in the peculiar Bellonean sense of the word, but unsayable. Indeed it is the very phenomenon that Wittgenstein has described which freezes the tongue and halts the stream of utterance. The shift of one word cannot be described except by what has now become the inadequacy of the others towards the singleton. And how are words to express their own inadequacy? The singleton, like the sensation E, has been displaced from the network.

But the problem is one implicit in language from the beginning and not simply native to the Bellonean cosmos. We have an instinctive and completely false confidence that language makes a seamless armor over all of reality, that each word clicks in perfectly with its partner words and its counterpart thing. But language is always in a process of slow translation; its referents are always in rapid transition, and there is no built-in symmetry, either in the world or in language, to prevent the inevitable distortion. We have already alluded to Kid's unanswered question, "What is the simplest way to say to someone like Kamp or Denny or Lanya that all their days have rendered ludicrous their judgement of the night?" (573). It is a question that makes special sense in Bellona, since it has been immediately preceded by the rising and setting of Bellona's giant sun. The classic judgement of night: night is the absence of day. But what is the presence of day? Day and night are asymmetric; night falls, but the sun rises. What if day rose huge and opaque, like a vast sun, into the sky? Or what if night shone from a single heavenly body, a second orb placed beside the moon? Such imposed symmetries proceed from the island of ideal thought which is madness, where word and thing fit so well together that nothing is visible round the edges. Sanity necessarily entails that much be left inaccessible behind the word, lost in the shadow of its excess.

Bellona is a city in a book. That much we have taken for granted; and we have gone on to see it function like one, its myths typical fictional reductions (the coupling of a black man and a white woman brings destruction), its apocalypse a composite anxiety projection. But it is also a city of words.

The flow of its names and its people models that of any language space in continuous translation. Bellona's maddening mixture of the arbitrary and the formal mirrors the arbitrariness and the formality of language, at once marvelous in the multiplicity of its determination and the absolute haphazardness of what is determined. *Brass Orchids*, Kid's book of poems, is a Bellonean case in point. The title is a pun on brass in the sense of nerve or *chutzpah*, and the etymology of orchid, the Greek for testicles or *balls*. "Brass Orchids" is also the legend on a rack of ornamental weapons in the city's strange warehouse of artifacts; and "orchid" is the name of the steel weapon, given him upon arrival, that Kid wears strapped to his wrist. When we gaze, with Kid, upon the rack, the title of his book becomes a perfect triple pun and the language of Bellona a fraction more ramified.

The arbitrariness and formality of the Bellonean order are further underlined by other artifacts in the warehouse. There also can be found the optical chains, the holographic projectors, and the red eyecaps of Bellona, the last presumably for achieving the effect of a stare of red glass which Kid occasionally notes among Bellona's denizens. But how these quarter-sized circles of Ping-Pong ball plastic could possibly *work* is left unexplained, as is the purpose of this warehouse in the Bellonean matrix. That it is the Mateland Systems Engineering Warehouse, the same firm which employs Arthur Richards (who, we remember, goes *somewhere* from nine to five) does raise certain chilling specters of a middle class conspiracy, but these specters are like the red eyecaps, gestures towards explanation empty of content. Like the central compartment, this is the place in the network where we expect an explanation; and just as the eyecaps fall far short of explaining the Bellonean stare, so the gigantic spools of optical chain, the cartons of orchids, the holographic projectors labeled by bestial aspect, fail to explain chain, weapon, or aspect, or the privileged social position any of these artifacts have taken. Here in the warehouse they are signs as enigmatic as the drug company trademark would be to a Martian archeologist. The warehouse is not a source, merely one of numerous crossover points in the matrix, as arbitrary as the arbitrary sign itself.

Yet those signs which give us our *realest* vision of Bellona, Kid's poems, remain inaccessible to us. Each time Kid opens to a page of *Brass Orchids*, there is a sudden perceptual shift, and it is as if that page of print turned mirror: we are reflected directly back onto Kid. We go so far as to see the poems' entry into the machinery of impression, but the poems themselves we are denied.

In our closest approach, we move from impression (the narrative), to first draft, to second, but stop short of the completed poem. First, impression:

> Charcoal, like the bodies of beetles, heaped below the glittering wall on the far corner. The sharpness of the incinerated upholstery cut the street's gritty stink. Through a cellar window, broken, a gray eel of smoke slithered the sidewalk to vaporize in the gutter. Through another, intact, flickerings. . . .
> (86)

Seven pages later, Kid sits down to write and we read:

> "Charcoal . . . like the bodies of burnt beetles, heaped below the glittering black wall of the house on the far corner." He bit at his lip and wrote on: "The wet sharpness of incinerated upholstery cut the general gritty stink of the street. From the rayed hole in the cellar window a grey eel of smoke wound across the sidewalk, dispersed before," at which point he crossed out the last two words and substituted, "vaporized at the gutter. Through another window," and crossed out *window*, "still intact, something flickered . . ." stopped and began to write all over again:
> "Charcoal, like the bodies of beetles. . . ." (93)

We are treated to another entire draft and the first line of a third, but then, abruptly, we pull away: "He folded the torn paper in four and put it back in the notebook when he had finished the next revision." That next revision we are never allowed to see. It is as if, in becoming a completed poem, the text had ceased being part of this city of words and, though made of words itself, moved out somewhere beyond it.

In the crudest possible terms: Bellona is not just a city of words. It is a city of prose.

Kid discussed the difference between his poems and his other verbal efforts (to wit the journal, to which we *are* given access) in a passage labeled "the falsification of this journal":

> . . . When something really involving, violent, or important happens, it occupies too much of my time, my physical energy, and my thought for me to be *able* to write about. I can think of four things that happened in the nest I would like to have described when they occurred, but they so completed themselves in the happening that even to refer to them seems superfluous.
> What is down, then, is a chronicle of incidents with a potential for wholeness they did not have when they occurred; a false picture, again,

because they show neither the general spread of my life's fabric, nor the most significant pattern points.

    To show the one is too boring and the other too difficult. That is probably why (as I use up more and more paper trying to return the feeling I had when I thought I was writing poems) I am not a poet . . . anymore? The poems perhaps hint it to someone else, but for me they are dry as the last leaves dropping from the burned trees on Brisbane. They are moments when I had the intensity to see, and the energy to build, some careful analog that completed the seeing. (809, 810)

The poems, then, are *part* of the experience they portray. We are instantly supplied with one reason for the poems' departure from the text: they are parts of completed experiences. As such they belong to that set of experiences that "so completed themselves in the happening that even to refer to them seems superfluous." They are verbal constructs closing off a portion of reality, real rather than true, divorced from the fiction at hand.

It is notable that Kid tells us several times in the course of the journal that it is a failure; if he is trying solely to recapture his poetry then the reason is obvious. But his most keenly felt failures seem always to occur in some effort to fix words themselves. He is obsessed with the problem of speech and the vast quantity which escapes the written word:

> George's speech can't even be written down for the common reader. Throck-morton (at the party) speaks only in inane combinations of serial phrases that become satires on themselves as soon as they are recorded but that, during utterance, make miracles of communication. I suppose I'm just getting frustrated by what written words can't do. (754)

Or to return to the translation that began our rhetorical loop above, simply in moving from thought to words, he notes: "This is not what I am thinking; this is merely (he thought) what thinking feels like" (573). It is in the attempt to bend words back on words, always a work of radical translation, in which Kid ultimately fails, particularly the attempt, in the journal, to fix his poetry. Those places in the network where words will most often yield paradoxes like our loop are places where they point to themselves. Among the paradoxes of modern logic are self-referent statements of the form:

> *This sentence is false.*

Kid's description of his poems as completing the experience they portray castes them as self-referent entities. They are also self-referent in that, as verbal objects of high energy, poems are always partially about words themselves. Prose, even in a self-referent context like *Dhalgren's*, can only be about its subject, even if that subject is fiction's relation to reality.

"This is not what I am thinking; this is merely (he thought) what thinking feels like." Specifically this sentence refers to those first person paragraphs of splintered diction which circle round the edge of madness. Yet the same could be said of *Dhalgren*, if it is truly to be read as a work about fiction's relation to reality. It is not so much about what that relation is—the truth or reality of this link between the true and the real—but what it feels like; and let us say that "what it feels like" signals a gap between the text and its subject that may never be completely closed, but that the text may suffuse the network around that gap sufficiently to capture its shape and "feeling." Prose is opaque verbiage and can never capture its relation to the real without, as Kid tells us, its own bulk changing that relation. Poetry, with its aural effects, its energy, is able to become transparent, attaching itself to experience without obscuring it, and as both itself and part of that experience, it is implicit in the relation between the two, a pure rhetorical stance revealed in all its crystalline beauty.

In the last chapter of *Dhalgren* we move from ordinary third-person narrative, what, by fictive convention, is reality, to a journal, what, by the same fictive convention of privilege, is truth. Because the novel is circular, we then ideally proceed back to the beginning, making the transition back from truth, the gesture itself, that of flipping all the pages, removing us momentarily to the world of experience, the world above the page, "reality." The text of that transition reads, "I have come to . . . to wound the autumnal city." We have already taken this as a signal of the coming to consciousness that the novel enacts, the finding of a true self. There is another reading, which is simply that the *to's* at beginning and end are the same, a repetition, a stutter, an overlap. This overlap is the image of the gap discussed above, the interior of the transition from fiction to reality, that fragment of "truth," of "resemblance," which must exist for anything to model anything else, that single impurity which resides in both the truth and the fiction. If we view *Dhalgren* as a Moebius Strip, one side of which we begin by labeling reality, the other fiction, until we discover that the two run indistinguishably together, then the *to's* make up the narrow tabs where the ends of the paper join, the flaw by which we know there *is* a transition, although its location is forever indeterminable.

In order to appreciate the indeterminacy of this transition we shall have to examine more closely that concluding journal chapter, on which the greatest formal weight of the novel rests, where the key to *Dhalgren's* ruling triad of city, mind, and language may be found.

The central problems of Chapter VII do not become apparent until we try and wrestle its many fragments into some chronological order. To begin with, there is simply not enough information to establish a unique chronological order for the chapter. Many strings of events—such as the comings and goings of various nest members, Fireball, Black Widow, California, and various vignettes of nest life—run on parallel tracks. For example, we know because of a glass of water that Kid considers in the fragments describing three conversations in which Lanya took part (beginning p. 795), that it comes before the concluding apocalyptic sequences, in which Kid *asks* Tak about the strange bubbles observed in the glass. We also know, from mentions made in the text, that it comes *after* both the mugging fragment (p. 770) and the visit to Calkins at his monastic retreat (p. 807). But there seems no way to date *these* fragments against one another.

Far more troubling difficulties, however, crop up in connection with the fragments we *can* arrange. We can follow the entry marginal to the last entry (p. 864) back to where it picks up on page 734, now as a major entry. These two fragments chronicle Kid's stay at Madame Brown's and his return to poetry. We may assume that the stay at Madame Brown's, being marginal to it, occurs after the last apocalyptic entry (the editorial intrusion on page 735 *instructs* us to make this assumption). But then, when it takes up as a major entry, the rubric marginal to *it* involves the children Kid saved in the fire at the end of Chapter VI. This means the apocalypse occurs some time *before* the end of Chapter VI. We have come to a smaller loop within the large loop of the novel.

Or again, the entry marginal to the penultimate entry describes the abandoned women's commune to which Denny's girl friend belonged, complete with an abandoned sculpture of a lion. Upon his arrival in Bellona Kid meets a group of women, one of whom is said to have completed a sculpture of a lion. This places the bulk of the novel between apocalypse and the insert on page 862, which, since it happens after apocalypse, being marginal to it, happens before the bulk of the novel, and so on.

Clearly, the notebook is a jigsaw which may be reconstructed in a number of ways, but with many pieces missing, and those present tending to fit with either side up.

It is interesting that Kid's memory, once one examines the notebook, is such as to be at all times in harmony with a linear chronology; this keeps his sensibility entirely readerly, the reader being unable to *experience* circularity. Shortly after his arrival in Bellona Kid begins to forget the surrounding circumstances, so that by the novel's close he is unable to perceive any paradox. We are thus spared any troubling debate, full of ambiguities of tense, subject, and voice (ambiguities signaled at in the novel's opening), on which event, arrival or departure, happened first.

There may be a glimpse of the actual mechanisms by which Kid joins diverging chronologies in the entry in which he remembers two of his three names and an initial. We have already shown how the matter of the children and their rescue is a chronological sore point. They may fall into the readerly blind spot between departure and arrival. When the children are brought up in this scene, Kid is at first unable to remember them, then: "Inside it felt like two disjoined surfaces had slipped flush; the relief was unbearable" (857). At the same moment, various commune members and Scorpions dance within a taut network of their own optical chain; the resonance here is with Kid's arrival, the moment he receives his own chain: " . . . what he apprehended was insubstantial as a disjunction of the soul" (5). The temporal loops of *Dhalgren* are not concentric or even tangent; those of the notebook may rejoin the narrative in any of a number of places. The final image, focused by the optical chains, is of an intricate network controlling illusion. It is immediately after these two disjoined surfaces slip flush that Kid begins to remember his name, setting him onto a new chronological track which buckles at apocalypse.

One might attempt a simple cyclical reading of *Dhalgren*. For some reason time is circular in Bellona; and many of the journal entries were written *before* Kid arrived in Bellona (we see them shortly after the notebook is found) because, before arriving, he naturally left. But this fails to explain the discrepancies between early versions of journal sentences Kid reads in passing in the notebook, and their later incorporations into Chapter VII. As an example:

> . . . *first off. It doesn't reflect my daily life. Most of what happens hour by hour is quiet and still. We sit most of the time* (94).
> . . . first off, it doesn't reflect my daily life. Most of what happens hour by hour here is quiet and dull. We sit most of the time . . . (809)

The alterations here of orthography, punctuation, words, and type are all undeniable, but so minor as to seem almost pointless. The fact that the first version is set in italics, of course, allows us to read it as a reading, or a misreading by Kid, in this case, and take the second, notebook version as definitive. This would be fine except that other deviations, like that between two of the *speech is in excess* lines already quoted, seem too large for this explanation. There are also other curious distortions, not simply between notebook and notebook, but between notebook and text, that would remain problematic. For example, Kid's arrival and departure on Bellona's bridge bear a striking symmetry to one another, a man meeting women, a woman meeting men, each group with an artist, each newcomer given a weapon, the very dialogue of each scene almost line for line mirroring the other. One is in the notebook, one in the text, and the relationship between the two seems that kind only found in the transition from reality to fiction; on our Moebius Strip, we have located two points directly across from one another, on "opposite" sides.

The question of which is real is here undecideable, but the occurrence of reference, of one incident being *about* the other, and the distortive nature of that occurrence seem undeniable. It is not only in the relation between *texts* that distortion occurs in Bellona. There is, in *Dhalgren*, a whole system of imagery about false doubles or "stuttering": the names Kid, kid, and Kidd, the *to's* beginning and ending the book (which are and are not the same), the names Tak, Mak, and Jack, the gesture of fist against chin transplanted from June to Rose to Stevie (the last stutter indicated by our "editor" on p. 735), and the altered texts and scenes discussed above. All of these have to do with some kind of "fictionalizing" of real experience, even if, occasionally, the direction of the fictionalizing is unclear—fictionalizing represented in its microscopic form by transplanted gesture, in its vast all-consuming form by the lives of the Richards family.

Every fiction distorts; and those distortions are unretrievable because all we have to refer to are other fictions. The circularity of *Dhalgren* is the circularity of the search for truth, which depends entirely on a network of interdependent descriptions for its sense, on the decision we must make, just as the Richards have, of which are expendable and which are not.

Delany, by reinserting text into text, by all his crossing loops, here makes self-conscious the fiction-making process. His objectives do not differ that greatly from those of Gertrude Stein in much of her fiction, and particularly in her essays. Stein, with her repetitive, syntax-fracturing prose, constructs a number of sentential micro-loops; her many-jointed sentences reach back, by endlessly rebeginning, to the verbal processes behind the writing itself. With the various parts of the sentence mapped, as it were, onto themselves, what may show through is the nature of the links between them, the mental twist at each syntactic pause. Ideally, unattainably, the act of sentence generation would be fully experienced.

In his admirable critical effort *The American Shore*, Delany elaborates on a distinction originated by Roland Barthes, that between readerly and writerly functions, which will be useful here.

Stein's loops are writerly loops. She is interested in the act of setting words to paper and its relation to speech. Delany's loops are readerly; he is interested in the act of reading and its relation to perception. Hence, his intensively foregrounded prose, on the microscopic level, is one absorbed with perception, with the constitution of sensations. The concerns of both Delany and Stein intersect where speech and perception do, on the level of thought.

By its many repetitions of texts in various states, including the simplest (for the reader) state of pure narrative, *Dhalgren* minutely maps the passage from reality to fiction. Within a framework of distortion we have three (again the trinity) Bellonas: the Bellona of experience (narrative or notebook, undecideable), of report (the Bellona *Times*), and of fiction (narrative or notebook). Since all three are mutually dependent there is no end to the proliferation of fiction within fiction that makes up *Dhalgren*.

In such a flux, with all the moorings of reference loosened, there is no place to draw the final line between the ordering of perception and the structuring of the narrative. At the limits of self-distortion, the aesthetic and the perceptual become hopelessly entangled; representation and thing become one. Report becomes perception, if it is no longer fiction, and perception report, if it is stripped of the status of truth. Yet in ordering a fiction as readers we perform tasks of figure-recognition and arrangement analogous to those in the simplest act of perception. *Dhalgren's* fictional illusions, its momentary resolutions that quickly slide out of focus like the Mateland Warehouse, are in this sense no different from its giant suns and double moons, or the optical tricks of an Escher (who crops up as one of the artifacts of Bellona, one of his volumes of drawings stored in Denny's miniature collection of artifacts).

Similarly, to make the obligatory mirroring reading, to constitute a sensation is to perpetrate a small fiction.

As a final illustration, let us take the name Dhalgren which, throughout the novel, is no more than a readerly expectation, but out of which, with the reader as accessory, Kid constructs a small fiction. The name William Dhalgren is, first, one among an arbitrary ranking of names, an unexplained list in the notebook. Later, Dhalgren is the one name in the list that Kid remembers after it has been lost (again, his perception completely readerly). Still later we are given the subtlest of nudges in the letter from Calkins which bears, at the bottom, the intriguing legend, *RC:wd*. We have by then met Bill who, as a reporter on the Bellona *Times*, seems to be Roger's right-hand man. Thus when Kid, in the same scene where he spontaneously remembers part of his name, jumps to the totally unfounded conclusion that Bill is William Dhalgren, we are more than ready to cheerfully conclude that all questions of names and titles have been resolved.

Need we insist on it? The identity of Bill and William Dhalgren is never established.

The title of *Dhalgren* extends over no fixed thing in the world of Bellona, and connects only with a readerly expectation in ours: expectation, the quantity most commonly transferred from reality to fiction, its most powerful ordering force.

As readers not otherwise informed we must assume that Kid lacks the most important ingredient of our expectation, the knowledge that this is a novel called *Dhalgren*, but what he has instead is the constitution of the word itself, the experience that prepares its later elevation to a fiction. After hearing the word *Grendal* at orgasm, Kid later reports:

> "Grendal grendalgrendalgrendalgrendalgren . . ." still ran through my head. Suddenly I realized I hadn't been listening carefully enough; I'd stuck the brake in at the wrong place. The actual word I'd heard at orgasm and that, for the last few minutes, had been repeating in my head was " . . . Dhalgren ..."
>
> I wiped myself with part of the second page of the Bellona *Times*, January 22, 1776. (753)

Epiphany is followed, as in Raymond Chandler, by some stagey bit of humdrum. Dhalgren. Grendal. The allusion is chthonic, a journey into the underworld, a descent past the conscious and pre-conscious to the dangers of desire—of expectation—that lie beneath. Dhalgren: a word heard at orgasm, one of the tiny experiments in linguistic alchemy conducted eternally in our heads, out of which all reality is made.

Notes

1. Samuel R. Delany, "Of Sex, Objects, Systems, Sales, SF, and Other Things," in *The Straits of Messina* (Seattle: Serconia Press. 1989), 54.

2. Willard Van Orman Quine, "Methodological Reflections on Current Linguistic Theory" in *On Noam Chomsky: Critical Essays*, Gilbert Harmon, ed. (Garden City, New Jersey: Anchor Books, 1974).

3. It is time here to confess to a long and profitable association with Mr. Delany. Throughout the course of a friendship conducted from distances as great as the width of the Atlantic and as small as the (admittedly) sprawling confines of his Upper West Side apartment (one flight up from one of *Dhalgren's* dedicatees, Judy Ratner), we have had a number of exchanges around and about the extensive subject of *Dhalgren*, none ever completely breaching that admirable store of reticence Mr. Delany has concerning his work, but enough so that there is hardly an idea in this essay not in some way colored by that association, so that whatever insights it may have to offer concerning this difficult and ambitious work are thanks to the unique perspective

Mr. Delany's association has given me. I have chosen to acknowledge this debt over a point—Kid's novelistic name—specifically motivated by one of many criticisms and suggestions Mr. Delany made concerning the first draft of this introduction, but it is simply impossible to separate out all the various influences, direct and indirect, over an association of such long standing; so this acknowledgement is meant to be general.

4. Ludwig Wittgenstein, *Philosophical Investigations* (Oxford: Blackwell, 1953), 88–104.

"This You-Shaped Hole of Insight and Fire"

Meditations on Delany's *Dhalgren*

ROBERT ELLIOT FOX

Dhalgren can best be characterized by the words that Kid, the novel's protagonist, uses to characterize his own book of poems: "a complicitous illusion in lingual catalysis, a crystalline and conscientious alkahest" (709). This is the sort of language one would expect to find in contemporary criticism, not in a work of fiction, except that, since the advent of the postmodern, the borders between these ostensibly different sorts of texts, the creative and the critical, have been jumbled, if not abolished. Moreover, the choice of terms is interesting: one drawn from alchemy (*alkahest*, the sought-after universal solvent), the other drawn from chemistry (*catalysis*, the action of a catalyst, a substance that modifies a chemical reaction). One suggests "magic," the other "science," but chemistry grew out of alchemy, so the two are not fully dichotomous. Moreover, alchemy should be understood as a spiritual process, wherein the alchemist himself is the subject of transformation, from that which is "base" to that which is "golden," refined. We might say that whatever its materiality, there still is something magical about language; that this also is true of art; that our language may change as we change, and that we may also be changed by language (art).

Again, "magic" is the province of fantasy, "science" that of (classic) SF. Delany has written both, and *Dhalgren* participates in both.

• • •

At the start of chapter 2 of Book I, we are told that the past of the narrator/protagonist "fragments on the terrible and vivid ephemera of now" (11). The first line of the novel contains the word "wound" (used, like "fragments," as a verb), while the adjectives "shattered," "dead," and "broken" are found in the first three lines of the third chapter. If this is not the wasteland, it is, surely, an Ozymandian realm in which the pride of late capitalist society has been (at least within this particular "circle") shaken, if not yet fully humbled.[1] "Civility, for Europeans, has always been a life lived in cities. Outside the *polis*, as Aristotle said, there were only beasts and heroes."[2] Delany has reversed this scenario: the city of Bellona, at least, has lost all civility, and it is precisely within this city that we find the "beasts and heroes," or, at any rate, their anemic/anomic contemporary reflections.

"Very few suspect the existence of this city," we are told (15). Yet Bellona is (or was) a major mid-western metropolis[3], with a population of nearly two million now reduced to about a thousand. It can't really be a secret, yet, curiously, despite whatever catastrophe has occurred, the only "explorers" (temporary immigrants, actually) seem to be countercultural recruits (with some exceptions like the astronaut, Captain Kamp) drawn to Bellona the way aspiring hippies were drawn to San Francisco during the Summer of Love in 1967[4] (which was just two years before Delany began writing *Dhalgren*, and which I take to be one of the novel's prime catalysts; indeed, the first draft of the novel was written in San Francisco. Significantly, Kid's companions are described as the "slightly demonic heirs" of the "flower-children" [830]). Why would the National Guard, the news media, the Red Cross abandon Bellona to its unaccountable fate?

Bellona is like a cyst in the American body politic, present but encapsulated. *Dhalgren* was written, after all, during a period when this country's general population (seemingly a blind, rather than a silent, majority) was being surprised by sudden eruptions of an unpleasant reality which, for the most part, it had not bothered to acknowledge. When the previously "invisible" ghettoes of America exploded in violence, for example, it might have been said of the urban areas in question that "few suspected their existence," because the country had bought the illusion that the cities were steel-and-glass monuments to success and was unwilling to explore what lay in the long, deep shadows.[5]

There are three quotations from Geoffrey O'Brien's *Dream Time: Chapters from the Sixties* that provide illuminating resonances with regard to *Dhalgren*: (1) "Tribes are emerging from the midst of a terminally mechanized

civilization; our parents have mysteriously given birth to their own ancestors." (2) "Democracy had evolved into the most sophisticated con game
in human history. . . . Freedom was permitted as long as it didn't change
anything." (3) " 'To improvise is to invent heaven'."[6]

According to G. S. Kirk, "*Chaos* in archaic Greek means 'gap' rather than
'disorder' . . ." The earth and the sky had to be forced asunder before the
world of man could come into being; chaos was the gap between the two
realms.[7] There is clearly a "gap" between Bellona and the "real" world,
and, to get from one to the other, you literally have to cross a bridge.

Bellona is the labyrinth in which you stalk your self.

In classical mythology, Bellona, sister of Mars, is the goddess of war.
(Bellona is mentioned at least once in James Joyce's *Finnegans Wake*
[78.31]. This book's circular structure, its last, incomplete sentence leading
back to its first, likewise incomplete one, provides the model for *Dhalgren's*
own tale-in-its-mouth structure.) Indeed, elsewhere in his work, Delany
speaks of a city on the planet Mars called Bellona (it is mentioned frequently
in *Triton*, for example). Delany has claimed that the Bellona portrayed in
Dhalgren is the "original" city after which the Martian city of Bellona
is named.[8]

The exhaustion yet inescapability of myth seems to be one of Delany's main
themes in *Dhalgren*. Sandra Miesel has written that Delany "treats myth
as 'metacommunication.' "[9] As Kid thinks to himself about his own work:
"These things I'm writing, they're not *descriptions* of anything, they're
complex names" (198). If one thinks of names, not in the sense of "Dhalgren" or "Kid" (although they themselves are complex), but rather as subject, semblance, or essence—"hermetic syllables" (244)—Kid's comment
is applicable to Delany's work and the nature of mythopoesis in general.
    Kid's pilgrimage reflects the depletion of the hero myth. (Think of the still-
apparent need for heroes in our own society, and the feet-of-clay character of
many of those whom we turn into heroes.) Kid crosses the threshold (here,
a bridge) into an/other realm and comes back across that same threshold
after many pages, having gained no new awareness that will help to redeem
the wasteland, having, indeed, not even discovered who he is. Moreover,
the other realm is itself a wasteland, where mystery offers no revelations,
and where confusion and mundanity appear to be the rule.[10]

Delany is concerned, not with the duplication, but rather the replication of myth: with echoes, repetition, things folding back upon themselves. In *The Einstein Intersection*, those beings who take the place of the human race appear doomed to act out parodies of human mythology; in *Dhalgren*, Kid, along with some of the other characters, might well ask (with Bob Dylan) "what price you have to pay to get out of going through all these things twice." Which is why, as the "plague journal" notes, "In this city, where nothing happens, it is worth your sanity to refuse anything new" (738).

Dhalgren needs to be contextualized by reference to Delany's pornographic novel *Tides of Lust* (1973) and his autobiographical works *Heavenly Breakfast* (1979) and *The Motion of Light in Water* (1988).[11] In the case of *Tides*, we are provided with a far more extreme portrayal of sexual themes, while *Breakfast* and *Motion* re/collect personal experiences that in part inspired/incited the fictive "circle" that *Dhalgren* inscribes.

One of the characters in Delany's "essay" *Heavenly Breakfast* is named Grendahl. And some of the section titles of *Tides* read like they could have been employed in *Dhalgren*: "Riders of the Scorpion," "Alchemica," "Labyrinths." Delany's preface to his second porno novel *Hogg* is entitled "The Scorpion Garden."[12]

Why "scorpions"? Is Delany thinking of Kenneth Anger's film *Scorpio Rising* (1961), a homoerotic motorpsycho nightmare?

Anyway, the scorpions already have their counterpart in the pteracycle gang in Delany's story "We, In Some Strange Power's Employ, Move On a Rigorous Line." (In the case of *Dhalgren*, it is more on the order of, "We, in some very strange circumstances, move in complex loops.")

The "end" of the novel is identical to the last words in the notebook Kid finds (291). The "beginning" of the novel is identical to the first words of the notebook (36). The first and last pages have been torn out, so the "story" begins *in medias res* and ends inconclusively. *Dhalgren*, to the extent that the notebook contains the same story/information, thereby contains itself, making the novel the literary equivalent of a Klein's bottle, the inside of which is also the outside. There is, then, literally nothing outside of the text(s).

Pages 879, 1: "Waiting here, away from the terrifying weaponry, out of the halls of vapor and light, beyond holland and into the hills, I have come to // to wound the autumnal city."

"Holland" is Middle English, from the Dutch *holtlant*, meaning "wood-land." There is a Holland Lake in Bellona, which is where the monastery is located. But since the lower case "h" in "holland" in this instance is not a typographer's error[13], the word is employed here in its etymological sense.

Note the use of alliteration:

*W*aiting/a*w*ay/*w*eaponry/*w*ound; *h*ere/*h*alls/*h*olland/*h*ills;
ha*ll*s/*l*ight/ho*ll*and/hi*ll*s/autumna*l*,

as well as this repetition:

and/holl*and*/*and*.

"I have come to // to" : The repetition is a kind of stutter, in keeping, perhaps, with the broken grammar of some of the book's last sentences (e.g., "Just in the like that, if you can't remember any more if" [878]). There is at least one earlier example of this, when Kid is trying to describe his book of poems: "I'm trying to—to . . ." (709).

The "end" of the novel is really a pause before the *recorso*, therefore functioning like a comma: I have come to, to . . .

Moreover, to "come to" is to "come around," (re)gain consciousness, get "started" again.

Remember that Kid is a former mental patient, a partial amnesiac. He has to (re)discover what has already happened, what already is. Literally, as an artist (poet), and figuratively, as a damaged individual, Kid cannot simply write himself, he has to *re*write himself, which is one reason why it all comes around again. (The emphasis on revision in *Dhalgren*, especially with regard to Kid's poems, reinforces this notion.)

"Autumnal" may refer to the season, but it is also freighted with various connotations of decline, decay, etc. It is seemingly the twilight of Bellona, but is Bellona itself not symptomatic of the twilight of the city in general?[14] "Wound" presents more of a problem. If the city is "autumnal," in its last days, is it not already wounded? And in what way can Kid wound Bellona? Indeed, the very idea of wounding the city is a reversal of the traditional pattern of the quest, which is salvational, in the sense of reinvigorating that which is ailing or dying. Wounding Bellona only makes sense if Bellona is a threat to the outside world from which Kid comes, but insofar as it is a threat, it is so only to those aspects of ordinary reality to which Kid would be unlikely to give allegiance—aspects which, in fact, may have had something to do with his own breakdown. Karen L. Shuldner supplies a very suggestive reading of the meaning of "wound" when she refers to it as "an emotional plateau from which the book is scarcely allowed to descend" and when she reminds us that "The wound was long *the* symbol of both art and sexual love for Delany[.]"[15] Art and sex, after all, have been at the core of Delany's concerns since his first novel, *The Jewels of Aptor* (1962).

Kid's left foot is bare; he writes with his left hand; the lefthand pages of the found notebook are blank. On the level of political symbolism, is Delany suggesting that the right is an already completed (overdetermined) category, while the left has not yet been fully scripted? Or does this have something to do with right brain and left brain? Or ambidexterity?[16]

But then Kid writes his poems on the lefthand pages, filling the book and creating a complex of juxtapositions.

There is a confusion of narrative voices, first and third person. The third person voice is apparently that of the novel, while the first person voice is that of the journal, which Kid finds, but which he has also apparently already written.

If Kid is both narrator ("I") and protagonist ("he"), at what point does the latter become the former (while still remaining "in" the story)? And if Kid is the narrator and he is still partially amnesiac, he cannot be an omniscient narrator, nor can he be a reliable one. Recycling/recircling, "plot"-wise, brings, perhaps, greater awareness of detail, but it does not seem to unveil more essential "facts." The histories of Kid and of Bellona remain, to some degree, a mystery.

Kid wears a boot on his right foot and keeps his left foot bare. Mouse, in Delany's novel *Nova* [1968], also wears a boot on one foot and keeps the other bare. (And like *Dhalgren*, *Nova* ends in mid-sentence.) A few of Kid's other precursors are Hawk, juvenile delinquent poet in Delany's story "Time Considered as a Helix of Semi-Precious Stones," and Vol Nonik, poet and member of a gang of malis (malcontents) in Delany's *Fall of the Towers* trilogy.

What about Kid's mythological analogues? One would be Jason, a famous itinerant who was to be recognized by the fact that he wore only one sandal. There is also Dionysus. As Sir James Frazer informs us, "Another animal whose form Dionysus assumed was the goat. One of his names was 'Kid'."[17] Reinforcing this is the possibility that Kid is a cousin of sorts to George, John Barth's goatboy/messiah. George has a gimp; Kid, who wears only one boot, appears to hobble. Furthermore, George's discovery of Lady Creamhair's timepiece, which he wears around his neck (*Giles Goatboy* 77), parallels Kid's discovery of the loops of chain bearing the prisms, mirrors and lenses (*Dhalgren* 7ff.).

It is perfectly in keeping with the allusive, multiplicitous nature of the narrative in *Dhalgren* that the actual identity of the main character remains unknown. In fact, Kid himself never does learn who he is, though this would seem to have been a major element in his quest.[18] Kid is a kind of palimpsest of mythic and mundane identities, a sort of composite hero/antihero with selective amnesia. It is also significant that he is a former (incompletely cured?) mental patient.

Is *Dhalgren* properly classified as "science fiction"? The holographic projectors which the scorpions use are the only example of technology that we can't immediately recognize in our own world. The catastrophe that has struck Bellona is never explained or even specifically identified, nor are any explanations ever given for the odd phenomena of the two moons, the gigantically swollen sun, etc. (These things are reminiscent of the weird happenings, dismissed or ignored by science, that Charles Fort [1874–1932] collected.) Even the presence in the novel of a man who has been to the moon and back is something that is no longer speculative, since Neil Armstrong first set foot on the moon in 1969 and *Dhalgren* was published in 1975. (The actual writing of the novel occupied Delany from January 1969 through September 1973.) One might argue that apart from some examples of the seemingly gratuitous unknown, *Dhalgren* is very close to being a mainstream novel, if that mainstream can be said to include books like John Barth's *Giles Goatboy* or Nabokov's *Ada*. In fact, Delany's undertaking in *Dhalgren* is partly informed by his reading of three novels, two of which could be classified as "literature": Nobel laureate Miguel Angel Asturias' *Mulata*, Elias Canetti's *Auto-de-fe*, and J. G. Ballard's *The Burning World*, books which he did not particularly like but whose employment of fantasy or "magical realism" nonetheless intrigued him.

On the other hand: Tak says, of the circumstances in which Bellona finds itself, " 'I suspect the whole thing is science fiction' " (414). He bases this judgement on what he terms the "Three Conventions of science fiction":

> "First: A single man can change the course of a whole world: Look at Calkins, look at George, look at you! Second: The only measure of intelligence or genius is its linear and practical application: In a landscape like this, what other kind do we even allow to visit? Three: The Universe is an essentially hospitable place . . . Here in Bellona— . . . you can have anything you want . . ." (415)

Delany, when asked, "Isn't *Dhalgren* a dream outside of historical time . . . ?," replied, "It's very much a dream."[19] Science fiction dream, "mundane"[20] dream—these specific categorizations are probably only of interest to those hung up on definitional niceties. For the writer, and perhaps also for the reader, in science fiction (and, I would argue, in that fictional tradition which includes works like *Don Quixote, Tristram Shandy*, and *One Hundred Years of Solitude*), you can have anything you want, you can have it any way you want it, so that dream and waking reality, science fact and science fiction, imagination and reportage become no longer distinct, become (even) (perhaps) interchangeable.

The novel is divided into seven parts, or books, the last of which is entitled "The Anathēmata: *a plague journal.*" There is a lengthy poem by British writer David Jones entitled *The Anathēmata*, which W. H. Auden, a poet Delany knew and admires,[21] considered "very probably the finest long poem written in English in this century."[22] David Blamires, author of a critical study of Jones, calls *The Anathēmata* "a poetic counterpart of *Finnegans Wake.*"[23] Like the *Wake*, like *Dhalgren*, the poem is circular and encompasses much. In his Preface to the work, Jones quotes Nennius, from *Historia Brittonum*: "I have made a heap of all that I could find." This, Jones claimed, is essentially his own method. He intended his title to mean "as much as it can be made to mean . . . : the blessed things that have taken on what is cursed and the profane things that are somehow redeemed . . ."[24]

Pages 78–81: Joaquin Faust[25] claims not to "mean anything" by his use of the word "nigger," an epithet which is bandied about frequently in the novel, by various characters, including Kid.[26] Faust's argument is that his use of "nigger" is generic and in keeping with the common practice where he comes from. (Which is the West: Faust represents the European mythologem par excellence. Delany deals with this subject more fully [and obsessively!] in *Tides of Lust*. Here, the Hispanic first name invokes the identity of the first wave of conquerors of the New World, whose descendants, however, are viewed in the United States as minorities. We are reminded that multiculturalism has always been a reality in the Americas, and that this reality also has always harbored a congeries of prejudices, which have not been the exclusive "privilege" of the "white" man.) But Faust's occasional use of the term "colored" reveals that "nigger," for him, is indeed contemptuous; it is a word used to characterize "dangerous" or "undeserving" blacks, whereas "colored people" are those blacks he views as "respectable," with the inevitable concomitant that they are expected to defer to white hegemony.

Race and racism are not tangential; they are near the novel's center, especially when they overlap with the psychosexual, with patterns of desire.

Think, for example, of the superstar status of George Harrison, celebrated rapist, posters of whom exploit the very mythos of black male potency which, under different circumstances, would have gotten him lynched. In Bellona, however, a literally phallocentric (phallofocal?) picture of Harrison becomes a different kind of "wanted" poster than one marking him as a target of vigilantes or bounty hunters: the poster itself is a prized item, a "bestseller," and Harrison is a kind of idol. It says something about the nature of Bellona's culture that walls display George Harrison, "soul on ice,"[27] rather than George Harrison, Beatle. The poster of Harrison is, in fact, a visual equivalent of the sexual braggadocio (phal*logo*centrism) found in a good deal of contemporary rap music.

Although it may not always strike the reader, a sizeable portion of Bellona's population is black. (Kid's own racial origin is "ambiguous" [829].) So it would appear that the "fright flight" that so drastically reduced the population of the city was also a "white flight" of the sort that has turned many of our urban areas into minority enclaves.

The orchid, the weapon Kid inherits when he enters Bellona and which he passes on as he departs: Was this the inspiration for the weapon Freddie Kreuger uses in the "Nightmare on Elm Street" films?

Whether or not Delany influenced Hollywood, it is clear that he has been influenced by Hollywood's corpus of sci-fi and horror films, and by the Gothic in general. Consider the periodic vision that Kid has of people (and in one instance, a dog) whose eyes are blood-red orbs. Like much else in the novel, this suggestion of terror (vampires? demons?) is undeveloped and unexplained. Such scattered images raise expectations in the reader that are thwarted as the book refuses to pursue "predictable" or familiar avenues. The unreal, in effect, is rendered incidental. It is not the purpose of the novel to give us explanations for everything; its actual thrust concerns the responses of (ordinary?) people to the odd, the unprecedented, indeed, the inexplicable.

The loops of chain with attached prisms, mirrors and lenses to which Kid is led at the "beginning" of the book and which he wears until the "end" provide an analogue for the structure of the novel itself. The book (the experience) is a "you-shaped [w]hole," in that it is, finally, what you make of it; the chains loop around a person's body, making a "you"-shape. The book itself is a loop, whose "end" is its "beginning."

Lenses make things bigger and can also reduce: compare the swollen sun on the one hand and, on the other, the almost microscopically-focused details imbedded in the narrative (characteristic of Delany's writing more generally). Prisms break down, refract; much of the text is likewise refracted. Mirrors reflect, and may also distort. It is not simply that the book begins again by having the last word lead back to the first word; in fact, the things that happen at the beginning happen again at the end in reverse order: Kid crosses the bridge one way, he crosses back the other way; he is handed a weapon coming in, he gives someone else this weapon going out, etc. Is the Oriental woman Kid meets going out [875] the same one he meets coming in [2]? Answering such a question with confidence is difficult because "the same," here, does not necessarily mean "precisely equal to." Amiri Baraka has a potently apt phrase to describe the dynamics of continuity/spontaneity in black music, "the changing same," that seems highly applicable to Delany's own practice in *Dhalgren*. Or to borrow a parallel formulation from Henry Louis Gates, Jr., another formidable commentator on the aesthetics of black culture, what we are confronted with in *Dhalgren* is, in many instances, "repetition with a difference."

Notes

1. Mrs. Richards' comment that "Management must be having all sorts of difficulty while we're going through this crisis" (251) takes on a whole different level of meaning if we read "management" as implying "the established order" and not just the operators of one largely abandoned apartment building. This is not Mrs. Richards' own implication, but to the extent that Bellona represents, not just some paranormal event(s), but a crisis at the core of our whole system, the implication is the text's.

2. Anthony Pagden, "The Translation of America," *Times Literary Supplement* (December 13, 1991), 11.

3. An assumption based on the statement in the novel that New York and San Francisco are " 'a ways to go, either direction' " (13).

4. *Heavenly Breakfast*, in fact, documents what Delany calls the "The Winter of Love" on New York's Lower East Side, in the winter and spring of 1967/68. A literal winter, yes, but also a "winter of discontent," suggesting not simply a contrast to the neo-Edenism of West Coast psychedelection, but also implying that the Summer of Love itself had a cold underside, which *Dhalgren* surely reflects more than it does any hoped-for state of bliss.

5. Delany has stated that "American readers—at least most urban American readers—recognize [descriptions in *Dhalgren*], through the allegorical skrim, as all too realistic portraits of vast areas of our great American cities: burned-out, under-populated, all but abandoned. The specificity of those descriptions weights

the reading [of the novel's significance] away from the universal and toward the local" (Interview with Samuel R. Delany, *Diacritics* [Fall 1986], 36).

6. New York: Viking, 1988, 96, 129, 36.

7. *The Nature of the Greek Myths* (Penguin, 1974), 46.

8. Conversation with the author, February 13, 1975.

9. "Samuel R. Delany's Use of Myth in *Nova*," *Extrapolation* (May, 1971), 86.

10. In Brian Aldiss' *Frankenstein Unbound* (1973), two moons appear without warning in the sky, but Aldiss not only has given a possible explanation of this phenomenon (the breakdown of space/time which is crucial to the plot), he has also given the apparition a symbolic meaning, since it comes at the moment when the monster and his "bride" appear together for the first time. Similar apparitions in *Dhalgren* allow of no such clear reading; they remain inscrutable.

Time is supposed to be "out of joint" in Bellona, too, but this seems truer in the Shakespearian than in the science-fictional sense, apart from Kid's occasional temporal disorientation and the possibility that time may be looping to allow what has happened already to happen again, as the circular structure of the novel suggests. On the other hand, Roger Calkins' freewheeling dating of his newspaper (which lends a punning resonance to the last word in the name, *The Bellona Times*) has to do with historical "play," with a postmodernish pastiche of allusions, freedom *from*, rather than freedom of, information, at least as far as chronology is concerned.

"Roger Calkins," by the way, was the name of a young man who apparently disappeared around 1950. Ads seeking his whereabouts were printed frequently in alternative newspapers like the *East Village Other* and the Berkeley *Barb* during the late sixties. While working on *Dhalgren*, Delany realized that the sought-after Calkins probably would be approaching forty. Fiction could "solve" his disappearance. Thus Calkins "turns up" in Bellona, not as a burnt-out case, but as an entrepreneur with his own newspaper—one with a monopoly on the news in the absence of media competition, but nonetheless "alternative" in its approach to what passes for reality in Bellona.

11. It is worth noting that Delany has called autobiography "only another kind of fiction" (*Diacritics* interview, 44).

12. This preface, dated 1973, was published in *The Straits of Messina* (Seattle: Serconia Press, 1989). When *Hogg* finally appeared two decades later (Boulder and Normal: Fiction Collective Two and Black Ice Books, 1994), the preface was omitted.

13. There indeed have been numerous typesetting errors in *Dhalgren*, and Delany has been endeavoring to track and correct these from printing to printing.

14. Delany has explicitly stated, "I had a lot of cities in mind while I was writing *Dhalgren*—in a sense the city there is Every City, Any City." *Alive and Writing: Interviews with American Authors of the 1980s*, ed. Larry McCaffery and Sinda Gregory (Urbana: University of Illinois, 1987), 104.

15. "On *Dhalgren* and *Triton*," *Riverside Quarterly* 7.1 (March 1980), 6.

16. Delany has stated that some of the things that Kid experiences are based

on a dyslexic's experience of the world. "Some things are also taken from my being somewhat ambidextrous—which often goes along with my particular sort of dyslexia." *Alive and Writing*, 98.

17. *The New Golden Bough*, ed. Theodore H. Gaster (New York, 1964), 421.

18. In *Finnegans Wake*, there is a character named Kurt Iuld van Dyke, whose identity has yet to be discovered, and whose initials, fortuitously, spell KID (*FW* 100.31).

19. *Diacritics* interview, 36.

20. "Mundane" fiction is Delany's term for what ordinarily would be characterized as mainstream fiction.

21. The epigraph to the trilogy *The Fall of the Towers* is taken from Auden's *Horae Canonicae*. Also, see Delany's account of Auden in *The Motion of Light in Water*.

22. Sister Bernetta Quinn, O.S.F., "David Jones," *Contemporary Literature* (Spring 1973), 267.

23. Quinn, 268.

24. *The Anathēmata* (New York: Chilmark Press, n.d.), 9, 28–29.

25. Joaquin Faust is based on a real person, known as Bo Maverick, who sold the Berkeley *Barb* in the Haight-Ashbury district of San Francisco during the period when Delany lived there.

26. See my remarks on racist discourse in *Tides of Lust* in "The Politics of Desire in Delany's *Triton* and *Tides of Lust*," *Black American Literature Forum* 18.2 (Summer 1984), 49–56.

27. See Eldridge Cleaver's disquisition on his rapist impulses in *Soul on Ice* (New York: Dell, 1968).

Necessary Constraints

Samuel R. Delany on Science Fiction

DAVID N. SAMUELSON

Devising rules for themselves as they go along, creative writers can provide trenchant criticism and theory in paraliterature, while academic scholars often struggle under a load of knowledge and techniques more appropriate to defending values of the literary canon. Whatever their differences, commercial writers, fan critics, and academics have hailed Samuel R. Delany as a major theorist of the contours and composition of science fiction (SF). Examining the basis for that praise, this essay is a highly abbreviated exploration of Delany's body of writing about SF, inquiring into the extent of his involvement, into his major sources and central concerns, and into the long-term value of his contribution.

Extent

Theorizing permeates Delany's fiction as well as his non-fiction. The plots of several early novels turn on interpreting literary texts, while his idiosyncratic "takes" on conventions also demonstrated a critical eye. For the 1963–65 trilogy, *The Fall of the Towers* (see "Afterword"), he promulgated an elaborate architecture and programmatic rules for involving characters of both sexes and various classes in "purposeful, habitual, and gratuitous" actions. His manipulation of myth in *The Jewels of Aptor* (1962), *The Ballad of Beta–2* (1965), and *The Einstein Intersection* (1967) reflects at least an embryonic sense of literary theory. From speculative linguistics in

Babel–17 and the narrative-journal interaction of *The Einstein Intersection* to the novelist-commentator and explicitly tripartite emphasis on "physics, politics, and psychology" of *Nova* (1968), theorizing played a progressively more overt role.

In two pornographic novels, Delany apparently immersed himself in the darker side of his psyche, overtly linking sexual and criminal behavior ("Scorpion"). *Equinox*, written in 1971, saw publication as *Tides of Lust* (1973); *Hogg*, from 1973, remained unpublished until 1995. Sandwiched between them, "Time Considered as a Helix of Semi-Precious Stones" also explored ambiguities in art and criminal behavior. Such formal experiments, fed by something akin to a self-directed Freudian analysis, led to a greatly altered notion of SF in *Dhalgren* (1975). This textually and conceptually difficult novel, clinically explicit about both hetero- and homosexual behavior, implicitly critiques SF motifs. Its protagonist of indeterminate memory and character and its setting of indeterminate time and space almost demand an emphasis on reading signs or "codes" ("Remarks"). Delany's interest in semiotics and structuralism led to the post-structuralism of *Triton* (1978), *Return to Nevèrÿon* (4 vols., 1979–87), and the unconventional space opera, *Stars in My Pocket Like Grains of Sand* (1986).

Since 1967, moreover ("Sketch"), Delany has been writing *about* SF, with five volumes of SF theory and criticism published so far (a sixth volume, *Wagner/Artaud*, does not mention SF, but the background of modernism it traces is certainly relevant). Of the four, *The American Shore* (1977) is the core document, linking microcosmic and macrocosmic levels of analysis. In this detailed discussion of a Thomas M. Disch short story, which a surface reading would find minimally science fictional, Delany examines how SF readings shape reader reactions differently than those of mundane and fantasy fiction, which Disch also writes. Dividing the story into 287 "lexias" for individual commentary, this book elaborates many insights simplified in other writings, but the style is often crabbed, the analysis highly contextual, and the transfer of insights to other texts not always evident.

More accessible in expression, if more haphazard in construction, are *The Jewel-Hinged Jaw* (1977), *Starboard Wine* (1984), and *The Straits of Messina* (1989), comprising introductions, essays, open letters, addresses, workshop contributions, and reviews. Included in *Jaw* is a journal-like memoir, "Shadows" (1974–75), incorporated by reference into the appendix of *Triton*. That novel and the Nevèrÿon cycle comprise a mix of fictions and essays titled "Some Informal Remarks Toward the Modular Calculus." The most recent volume (1994) is *Silent Interviews*, comprising "written interviews," in which questions provide springboards for detailed excurses.

Uncollected items could fill several volumes. Several recent essays and lectures about SF have appeared in the *New York Review of Science Fiction*, for which he has served as a "Contributing Editor" since its inception in 1988. Although "The Discourse on Desire" has not found a publisher, his writings on sexual matters and AIDS have found appreciative audiences as public lectures.

As in his memoirs—"Shadows," *Heavenly Breakfast* (1979), and *The Motion of Light in Water* (1988, 1990)—the subject matter in Delany's critical writing is always mixed, be the ostensible focus on personal history, specific authors and texts, or broader theoretical constructs. As in his fiction, the expression is often playful, though with serious intent and implications. If change and development are visible over time, so is considerable repetition. As he told the Science Fiction Research Association Conference in 1985 when it honored him with the Pilgrim Award for his critical work, his strategy is that of the proverbial hedgehog who does one thing well, rather than that of the fox, who does many things with varying degrees of expertise.

Sources

A collage of theory, invention, and memoir, Delany's critical writings are atypical for SF in the nature and range of material to which he has been exposed, including personal experience. *Motion* portrays an observant child of the "black bourgeoisie" growing up in Harlem in the Forties and Fifties. Attending schools for the gifted across town, he saw at first hand disparities of class and caste distinguished by economics, skin color, and subculture. Homosexual in a repressed era and married at age 20 to a precocious poet, he could hardly escape noticing arbitrary gender distinctions, from the opprobrium heaped on "perverts" to the heterosexual economy of scarcity, from male dominance in job rewards and assignments to the different cuts of men's and women's jeans.

Delany's written sources range from childhood readings to social and linguistic philosophers. Introduced to African-American writers at home, classics and Modernists at school, and SF at summer camp, he came early to a grasp of conventions and complexity. Requiring intense attention to each word and its contexts just to understand surface meaning, dyslexia predisposed him to close (i.e., critical) reading. Conflicts between his sexual drive and his society's demands for conformity made him an acute analyst of social roles and behaviors.

Ambitious from childhood to be a writer, he was attracted to SF largely by its potential for alternatives. He began writing it highly conscious of theoretical concerns and their practical applications to the written word, and very aware of writing and living on the margin of reputability. Given this background, Delany was a natural audience for the insights, once he was exposed to them, of linguistic-related theorists with Marxist and feminist leanings, such as Paul De Man, Shoshona Felman, Michel Foucault, Barbara Johnson, Jacques Lacan, and Claude Lévi-Strauss ("Ken James Interview," "Neither"). Jacques Derrida's concepts of "free play" and "decentering," for example, were well-suited to Delany's practice in fiction. These theorists of language and behavior showed him "exciting ways of reading," which he adapted to his own writing. Self-consciousness about the act of communication increasingly filtered all he wrote in both fiction and non-fiction, making the differences between them problematic.

As a theorist, Delany's first concern is to raise audience consciousness of the act of reading, initiating a dialogue between readers and writers (who are themselves first and foremost readers). Central to this act is the interplay between the text itself and readers' expectations about life and literature. Thus all reading becomes genre reading and genre concepts are inescapable. Specific expectations rather than content differentiate how one reads SF vis-a-vis other genres. To examine these differences, obscured by the academy's monolithic idea of the "literary," requires paying attention to the genrification of literature in this century. Illuminating these conceptions may be the job of an educator, but recognizing both the enabling and crippling functions of genre is no mere academic distinction to Delany. His ultimate goal as a writer seems to be to bring about a recognition of the power of language to decenter the role of conventions in life as well as in fiction.

Genre and Language

Delany's critical writing always emphasizes interplay between reader and text. He started with letters to fanzines and the *Forum* of the Science Fiction Writers Association, thinking aloud his positions on concepts like "story-telling" and "characters." In his first publication for an academic audience, "About 5,175 Words" (1969), his own experience suggested a phenomenology of reading like Stanley Fish's "affective stylistics," each word modifying the experience begun by those preceding it. He also used the concept of subjunctivity to locate SF (which has not happened) between fantasy (which can not happen) and "mundane" literature (which could have happened). Downplaying the science in SF, moreover, he pointed to mystical visionary experiences in classic SF texts, commonly rendered by the device of synesthesia.

Coming to prefer a context-sensitive subjectivity like Fish's later position on "interpretive communities" ("Reflections on SF Criticism"), Delany continued to emphasize style, but came to see texts as products and facilitators of "reading protocols." More accessibly termed "codes" and "conventions" today, these are elements of reader expectation immediately perceived by those attuned to a specific "discourse." Specific to the discourse of SF, he finds certain kinds of verbal formulas and conventional expectations in SF open up to the world—or universe—in a different way than in other genres.

In his popularizations, Delany regularly exhibits certain words and sentences assuming special meanings in SF. Any term with a technological edge may signal futurity or artificiality until it becomes familiar; even a relatively familiar term can generate this effect in unexpected usage, like Disch's comparing skin to "lucite" (cited in *The American Shore* 53–4). A neologism like "ornithopter" (which he attributes to Cordwainer Smith), etymologically an air vehicle with moving birdlike wings, may require amplification in a specific text. A more complicated phrase (attributed to Larry Niven) demands a theoretical scientific context: "monopole magnet mining operations in the outer asteroid belt of Cygnis VI." Perhaps not impossible, monopoles have never been detected on the atomic level; there certainly is no known way to mine them in one of two or more broad bands of planetoids circling an alien sun. Readers for whom science and SF are unknown languages may be unable to grasp any of these concepts, let alone recognize their overtly speculative nature.

Somewhat less convincingly, Delany argues that certain terms and phrases with accessible meaning in mundane fiction may denote something completely different in SF. Context changes meaning, of course, but he typically shows SF literalizing implicit, even dead metaphors, like "Her world [read *planet*] exploded" and "He turned on [read *activated*] his left side." Comparable features can be found in other genres, both literary and paraliterary, however, and for a feature worth serious attention, it is odd how few instances turn up in his detailed studies of specific texts. This argument is hardly needed to show that SF's wider verbal latitude, including and supplementing so-called "normal" meanings, offers more scope than mundane realism on the level of words and sentences.

Other rhetorical features distinguishing SF discourse in *Shore* include grammatical tense, continuous exposition, and contextual orientation. For a future narrative in past tense, the teller is more removed from the reader than the tale's events, reversing the tradition of mundane fiction (lexia 2). Delany points out that this situation complicates the fictional nature of other tenses as well, though he does not discuss their zenith of complication in the time travel story. Because SF needs to maintain an outward discourse with the world it is creating, he argues that exposition never really ceases (lexia 232): the reader and the author lend the fictional world reality only by continuously creating it.

Contextual orientation can be equally complicated. Literal in space, "free fall" is a culturally significant metaphor in a future setting, where the reader (and writer) may never be fully oriented (lexia 218). Without a gravitational pull, preferences for "high" over "low" (or vice-versa) are meaningless. SF's vast potential for creation feeds a desire for fuller orientation. A response to this desire, he claims, is the ubiquity of SF series like his own *Return to Nevèrÿon*, Asimov's *Foundation* "trilogy," and Disch's *334* (where "Angouleme" appears in book form).

Expansions of potential operate at broader conceptual levels, in conventions of science and the future. Science is relatively unimportant as a "reality base" to Delany, since SF is not *about* science, nor does it claim to take place *in any real future*. As time overtakes SF "predictions" or "projections," he sees their settings shifting to "parallel worlds" (79). Like those at the sentence level, these verbal formulas *distort the present*. Both future and off-world settings offer writer and reader potentials unavailable in a mundane setting. SF protocols even let us literalize myth and visionary experience. Without overt mystical explanations, they may permit us to suspend scientific limits, as well as social and political constrictions we take for granted because they are in effect here and now.

One convention distinguishing SF for Delany is the familiar assumption that something *unproved* in our world is possible in the imagined world of an SF text. Delany sees such a speculation, in no way "predictive," as merely "tested" in the fiction; verbal formulas tie it to what we know of science and society today. What limits science sets for SF are elastic and negative; in "The *Algol* Interview" and elsewhere ("Letter" in *Exploding Madonna*), he approves the Australian critic John Foyster's contention that speculation should not controvert "what is known to be known." At the conceptual level as at the sentence level, SF offers a wider selection of options.

While Delany does not always distinguish explicitly between texts and conventions, he continues to oppose SF to mundane and fantastic fiction, now often conjoined ("*Dichtung*," "Disch"). The mundane purports to mirror quotidian reality, while fantasy specifically violates it, replaying age-old conventions of myth and folklore. Both use this assumed reality as a ground, however, and share "subjective" concerns, distorting perceptions of a "subject" (character, narrator, and/or writer). By contrast, SF does not assume any given reality; it manipulates landscape, distorts technology, and revises the social order, foregrounding the text's world as an "object."

Easy to overlook, this dialectic is also easy to overstate. Separating SF from mundane and fantastic fiction downplays its similarities to both. Emphasizing the construction of SF's "objective" world may imply that it totally lacks the "subjective" distortions of mundane and fantasy fiction, although SF characters are certainly subject to error and aberration. Landscape, technology, and the social order are themselves symbols of subjectivity, perhaps nowhere so overtly so as in the SF of J. G. Ballard. Writers of mundane and fantastic fiction must also construct their fictional worlds (Nabokov is an obvious example), and Delany has argued elsewhere that reading by SF protocols can help us see how arbitrary Shakespeare and Jane Austen are ("SF and 'Literature' "). Overtly constructed from both speculative and received materials, however, SF can include both the mundane and the fantastic. In its continuing dialogue with the present (strictly speaking, with the past), SF again has more options.

Hypothetical in the extreme, SF is more abstract than either mundane or fantastic literature, even more abstract than the trap of utopian/dystopian moralizing Delany seeks to avoid. Unlike utopia, SF features an almost limitless number of alternatives, in tension with continuing pressure to conform to the real world. In the "*Algol* Interview" and elsewhere, Delany went so far as to compare SF to serial music and abstract expressionism. While he has not pressed that issue, its relevance to discussions of postmodern fiction is marked. If every narration, every play, every poem is partial, its truth inevitably limited, SF may be unusual only in that it makes this selectivity one of its guiding principles. Indeed, Larry McCaffery goes so far as to argue that SF is paradigmatic for postmodern fiction.

Claiming no foundation for SF in scientific truth or any other *rhetorical* feature, Delany describes the discourse of SF (in *Shore* 58) as "trivalent":

> The s-f text speaks inward, of course, as do the texts of mundane fiction, to create a subject (characters, plot, theme . . .). It also speaks outward to create a world, a world in dialogue with the real. And, of course, the real world speaks inward to construct its dialogue with both. But as there *are* three different discourses involved, there is really no way any two of the three *can* be congruent, or even complementary to the other. At best, the s-f writer harmonizes them.

Delany credits this trivalence with larger effects. Inevitable gaps between these discourses and the overdetermined universe in which they function give SF writing a characteristic richness and resonance. Reflecting this universe, he argues, the best SF writing integrates such imaginative activities as art, science, and theology. SF's trivalence also determines its optimism against difficult odds, its transcendence of the personal and momentary, and its core of mysticism (lexias 8, 200, 287). He admits almost parenthetically that few SF texts actually approach these global ideals, but analysis of the Disch story at least substantiates the claim that SF redeems and revalues elements of the present.

What a less sympathetic reader might call Disch's failure to project a future different from the present, Delany interprets as redeeming the past. Mentioning today's commonplaces in a fictive future establishes their longevity, investing them with historical significance. Information and attitudes shared when the story was published (1972) are inevitably revalued in its fictive setting (the third decade of the 21st century). Even what we today consider settled facts may be forgotten, misunderstood, or newly conceived in a more scientifically or aesthetically satisfying way in the fictional future time (lexias 13–16).

Given parallels with Symbolist poetry drawn elsewhere ("Critical Methods"), Delany's argument in *Shore* that SF is impoverished in "symbolism" and "symbolic space" is curious. The former, however, he identifies with the subjectivism of character typical of mundane and fantasy fiction read through specific symbolic systems," such as those of Jung and Freud (lexia 12). He ties symbolic space to SF's trivalence, like those of classical tragedy, fairy tale, and myth (lexia 51), which can be transposed but not interpreted. While he sees SF compensating for this subjective "poverty" with increased richness of irony, Delany may be selling SF's symbolism short. It may not be easy for words constructing a new world to symbolize long-standing conventional beliefs as well. Every SF world is symbolic, however, and the world-view of characters seems to be as interpretable by symbolic systems in SF as in other fiction. These lexias themselves provide counter-examples in Disch, and symbolic readings can be richly rewarding in the pantheon of others he has written about in depth: Ursula Le Guin, Joanna Russ, Theodore Sturgeon, and Roger Zelazny.

Genre and History

Extending this highly theoretical set of oppositions into genre history is problematic. Claiming merely to describe, not define genres, Delany traces like Terry Eagleton the emergence of "paraliterature" to a redefinition of "literature" from Matthew Arnold to F.R. Leavis ("*Dichtung*"). What once meant literacy or the profession of writing became a body of received texts, requiring in turn a body of excluded texts, i.e., paraliterature ("Disch"). Situated outside both the canon of good taste and received opinion about reality, paraliterature is prone to distort objective elements, like past or future fictional settings. Unlike his theory of reading, which sees SF as liberating the word, his view of SF history seems highly constrictive, severely limiting the freedom of genre writers.

Delany's "material history" of SF can not help but be conditioned by his experience with the economics of publication and education (see "Popular Culture," "Another Letter"). These have predisposed him to reduce 20th century genres to publisher's categories, rising and falling with audience niches. An afterthought in paraliterature, SF reached impressive economic stature after World War II, spawning other genres or subgenres as it grew. Watching twentieth century publishers branch out, Delany sees parallel world and sword-and-sorcery stories as subsets of SF, horror and fantasy fiction as offshoots of it ("Gestation").

For the last three, this "history" varies significantly from what many scholars trace from 18th century Gothic to 19th century fantasy to modern horror, and from classical epic through medieval romance to Romantic and Victorian revivals to S&S and then Tolkien. Calling such genealogies "hypostatized" (concrete existence claimed for theoretical constructs), Delany denies they constitute a "living tradition" for editors and writers in paraliterature. Representatives of the tradition less known today, however, were read by others whose works persist, or who influenced contemporary writers. Robert E. Howard, C.S. Lewis, and Stephen King are among those who have seen themselves not as creators, but as revivers and transmitters, of their traditions.

Delany's vision of SF history is more provincial than one might expect from his breadth of reading. A key unifying element of SF for many scholars is the visibility in texts of the intrusion of science on popular consciousness, though they may argue over both terms. Delany generally locates the genesis in the 1920s, though he has let SF origins drift back to as early as 1890. By 1926–29, he argues, the codes of reading and writing SF were enough in place ("Reflections on 'Reflections' ") that a publishing outlet specifically for SF could exist. However sound the reasoning and whatever allowances are made for Edgar Rice Burroughs and his ilk, the practical effect is to make the Gernsback magazines seem a radical break in continuity, especially in the light of Delany's disavowal of other ancestors.

Dismissing as "preposterous and historically insensitive genealogies" derivations of SF from pre-19th century utopias and satires is fair enough (*Silent Interviews* 26; cf. *Shore*, "Science and Literature"); they are proto-SF at best, neither their discourse nor their audience scientific. However, he also dismisses Brian Aldiss' Gothic line of Shelley, Poe, and Wells ("SF and 'Literature' "). Because their moral fables were written in other discursive traditions preceding the emergence of SF protocols, he finds them thematically but not discursively related to SF. Delany would strip them from SF's "living tradition," virtually discarding the reprints on which Gernsback founded SF as a self-conscious genre, as well as myriad later variations and pastiches on them. Denying that even Verne's "encyclopedic" novels or Gernsback's own didactic fables should be read by SF protocols would also seem to rule out utopias, satires, fables, and encyclopedic works *after* 1926, even if they received SF marketing, which should matter in a "material history." Dismissing by name Borges, Calvino, and Lem as literary fabulists, he also omits many British and Continental writers who may have thought they were writing SF.

In the post-1926 period, Delany decries what he sees as Peter Fitting's attempt to make genre history fit changes in popular attitudes toward technology of the American middle class ("Historical Models"). Yet he distorts history himself in hypostatizing an internal dynamic in the field's development according to which earlier stories set in the far future allow later-written stories set in the near future to be read as SF ("Some Reflections"). A kernel of truth in this generalization is attested in memoirs by Arthur C. Clarke and Donald Wollheim, among others. The fact that near-future stories appeared in the Thirties and far-future stories as late as the Eighties, moreover, may only prove the rule ("Reflections on 'Reflections'"). If the principle is valid, however, some credit is due to writers he has read out of the tradition. After his first stop in Wells' *The Time Machine* (1895), the Time Traveler journeys forward millions of years to the near death of the sun. A hundred million years of human history are chronicled in *Last and First Men* (1930) by Olaf Stapledon, the even greater scope of whose *Star Maker* (1937) no space opera of E.E. Smith or Edmond Hamilton can match.

In more recent SF history, Delany complains of errant discussions of the "New Wave" and rightly points out its origin with certain editors inviting literary experimentation into SF ("Historical Models"). Broadening the base, however, enabled writers and readers to test a wider range of alternatives than he wants to admit within the gates of SF, let alone into the New Wave. It is not a fatal error to use the latter term to stand for that wider latitude, nor is it rare for literary movements to be defined for posterity by later observers rather than by participants who deny they ever formed a movement. If a writer loses control over what readers make of his texts once published, what control can a rebellious faction of writers and editors have over a nebulous ill-defined reaction to publishing policies they regard as straitjackets?

While no New Wave enclave acknowledged Delany as its own, he also protests too much at being confused with them. The confusion was evident among readers in the Sixties, usually hostile to both, and his relations were strained with only one of the rebel editors, *New Worlds'* Michael Moorcock, who only reluctantly published his "Helix" ("Historical Models"). Flashy and imbued with self-conscious form and style, Delany's early fiction stood out from his predecessors, but it was unlike the New Wave in its adherence to adventure fiction story-telling conventions. In his later fiction, however, Delany consciously adopted a *New Worlds*-like denial of common SF assumptions that the universe is hospitable, that ordinary individuals make history, and that intelligence is well-rounded.

Delany rightly objects to critics who fail to do their homework and who confuse genre history with their own acquaintance with it. Similar objections, however, can be made to his own blinkered view of SF history. His own departures from and reversals of conventions seem to require American pulp adventure narratives as a backdrop. Other readers, however, need not dismiss historical antecedents (Wells) and borderline contemporaries (Lem), in order to recognize special circumstances for American magazine and paperback SF.

Genre and Teaching

Striving to convince others to share his concerns is an effort at education, and Delany has done his share of literal teaching, from SF conventions and writing workshops to visiting lectureships and his present tenured appointment at the University of Massachusetts, Amherst. Although some academics oppose it in contemporary practice, literary theory has always had a place, if unacknowledged, in the classroom; indeed, some of Delany's own essays he generated in or for the classroom. Other classroom teachers, however, when he sees them blindly following false gods of literary study, he tends to give less latitude to differ with him than writers of theory, criticism, or reviews. More commonly, he finds ways to maximize the potential of all four roles, without restricting the freedom of an individual to change roles.

Theorists, Delany maintains, should explore rules of communication, as he does in focussing on reading protocols and genre history. Critics should tell interesting stories about their readings of texts, with other readers as their audience. His own favorite SF critics have been writers addressing fans: James Blish, A. J. Budrys, Tom Disch, Damon Knight, Judith Merril, P. Schuyler Miller, Joanna Russ. He observes that academic critics are unclear about both audience and purpose. They advise neither writers nor fans and their primary audiences may not regard as worthwhile either literary criticism (students) or SF (colleagues). Delany's own critical practice is mixed. An able and penetrating reader of his pantheon of writers fully engaged with the potential of both the English language and the range and scope he assigns to SF, he seems more perfunctory or restricted where his sympathies are less involved, as with Asimov, Dick, and Heinlein.

Sometimes his primary audience is obviously the writer of a text under examination, as in his fanzine critique of a beginner's story in "Crazy Diamonds" and his in-depth study of a Le Guin novel, "To Read *The Dispossessed*." On the other hand, his introductions to books by Heinlein, Russ, and Sturgeon approach what he asks from a review. Since SF reviewers have no effect on sales, Delany argues, they should ideally address writers and readers, advancing the dialogue of the art ("Discourse on SF"). Reviewing books and films (and occasionally music), he typically adheres to these principles, giving vent to his own general delight or disappointment in the accomplishment at hand.

For teachers, whose audience is often critically naive and typically distant from creative writers, Delany is more prescriptive, asking them to treat SF "as science fiction" (i.e., *his* definition), stressing issues implicit in his sense of SF rhetoric and history ("*Dichtung*"). Taking SF seriously as both vision and writing includes comparing and contrasting its best writing with canonical literary values ("Zelazny/Varley/Gibson—and Quality" is the most recent example). SF's unique history relies heavily on mass publishing practice, with its heavy editorial hand and proliferation of series. The shape SF has taken also depends on a dialogue between writers and readers (or fans), which exerts considerable pressure in maintaining its identity. Finally, in a suggestion equally applicable to literary critics borrowing from other disciplines, he reminds us sensibly enough that imported critical terminology usually carries unexamined literary assumptions into SF.

Genre and Life

In Delany's fiction and non-fiction, memoirs and criticism overlap and critical theory is not restricted to literature as a privileged mode of writing apart from life. The average readers and writers of SF may be young white middle class males, but the marginality of this genre offering alternatives to the present seems intimately connected for him with the marginality of the deprived. In a marginal genre, ruled by commercial concerns, Delany himself occupies a marginal position, as a gay black man driven by feminist, linguistic, and Marxist aesthetic concerns.

Delany seeks an ideal (para-)literature in which considerations of race and sexual preference are inclusive rather than exclusive, and in which science and technology take unexpected turns. Racially unbiased futures drew him into SF, which typically sees past skin color and other physical variations, even species differences, to intelligence and character underneath. Slower to free itself from gender bias, SF is slower still to accept sexual procliv- ities seen as deviant in the larger society. In this connection, Delany has supplemented characters in his fiction who are female, gay, and/or people of color with essays championing female, male feminist, and homosexual writers. It is surely no coincidence that Disch, Russ, and Sturgeon are in his pantheon of SF writers. Stylists for whom verbal expression has been equal to and interwoven with ideas, they have also been outsiders confronted with arbitrary social organization and the prevailing ideology of their time.

Materially deprived only by choice, Delany has identified with the op- pressed in his life as well as his writing. Often living in rundown urban neighborhoods, he has argued that such settings expose one to changes facing the larger society (*Motion*, "Sex Objects," Platt interview). Superfi- cially rational, this explanation may be an after-the-fact rationalization, too cerebral to be real, which begs more than it explains. In fact, he seems to crave some degree of danger in his life. Based on his memoirs and some of his more overtly autobiographical fiction, he has risked both life and limb in promiscuous sexual behavior. He has also befriended many marginal people, among them petty criminals and unappreciated artists. Having voluntarily undergone therapy in a mental hospital in 1964 to deal with stress resulting from the sexual, racial, and professional anomalies in his life, he is sensitive to both the mentally ill and the socially deviant. Seeing these categories as socially (not medically) determined, virtually as a genrification of human beings, he accepts criminals as well as artists, sadists as well as homosexuals.

In life as in literature, Delany shows the necessity of understanding codes and conventions in order to transcend them (see especially "Shadows" and the "Modular Calculus"). With Lévi-Strauss and Derrida, we should know the fallibility of our intellectual tools without believing that we can do without them. The protocols of language mirror those of society and genre. The arbitrary nature of all is the source of their strength, their hold on our imaginations. We must see the world through arbitrary categories before viewing categories critically; indeed, without such frameworks, we see nothing critically.

If individuals and groups can learn to overcome categories, such tran- scendence requires building on misunderstandings or opposition. It also requires a constant awareness that the codes are present and that one is inevitably involved in acts of transgression, if not outright criminality. Recognizing Douglas Barbour's argument that the repeated artist/criminal image in Delany's fiction is partly an artifice for embodying creative and destructive change in society, I believe it also reflects something of his whole writing enterprise.

Delany transgresses social and literary codes in several related ways. A writer on the racial and sexual margins of a predominantly white, heterosexual society, he provides a role model for readers otherwise disenfranchised. His art provides examples of individuals and whole societies celebrating cultural (including "racial" and sexual) diversity. As writer and critic, he has helped expand the boundaries of literature to embrace the paraliterary, as well as to transform the boundaries of SF itself. That his prose has enriched the language is recognized, albeit sometimes grudgingly, by critics inside and outside the SF community. His practice has made the genre resonate with mythic parallels, supplemented by a self-conscious awareness that they are indeed mythic parallels. In his later novels, moreover, consciousness of codes and conventions affects more than ever the reader's sense of social organization and the rise of science and technology, while pushing against the envelope of genre, mixing past and present, narrative and commentary, writer and writing.

Preliminary Evaluation

Any evaluation of Delany's contribution to SF theory must be preliminary. Fifty years old on 1 April 1992, he should have many fiction and non-fiction projects ahead of him. His career has taken unexpected twists in the past, and may well in the future. Since his first novel, however, his essential conception of SF has changed little, though it has been elaborated here and intensified there. Therefore, it may not be too soon to outline an evaluation of his strengths and weaknesses.

1. Conrad was not alone in wanting "to make you see" and many innovative writers feel the need to train their readers. Writing about his own work (both process and products) and adapting the theoretical insights of scholars of language to his critique of SF, Delany is motivated at least in part by the desire to create a more knowing and appreciative audience for his narratives.

2. Although some of his thorny rhetoric makes concepts seem more complex then they are and his own idiosyncratic erudition intimidating to the uninitiated, Delany even at his most abstruse (*Shore*, "Neither") is much more accessible than many of his sources. The biggest risk is that, faced with all this internal and external commentary, readers may be seduced into thinking the author has done their work for them, when it has barely begun.

3. Viewed outside those personal contexts, Delany's most influential challenge to critics in both commercial SF and the academy is his insistence on reading the *language* of SF, including its system as well as its texts. Less rooted but promising are his emphases on SF's abstract constructedness, its distortion of the objective world, and its dialogue with the present.

4. More problematic are Delany's genre history and some of the claims he makes for expanding language in SF. In addition, his genre protocols are not widely tested. A convincing demonstration of his theories would demand applications for a wider mass of texts including some that do not meet his specifications, such as proto-SF, utopian/dystopian literature, and European writings with SF pretensions, emphasizing where they fail.

In sum, Delany has produced a sizable body of theoretical and critical writings. Some of its brilliance depends on the empty blackness of its backdrop; even faint puffs of gas may stand out in the theoretical vacuum of most SF criticism. In the long run, moreover, its greatest importance may be its reflection of the thought involved in the fiction. Yet the scope of his project compares well with that of other SF critics, and Delany has done what other critics have not, by indicating and underscoring fundamental ways SF requires a unique kind of reading. In his efforts both to explain and to demonstrate this point, his best critical essays clearly shine with their own light.

Non-Fiction Cited

[N.B. Since periodical essays accessible in Delany's books often appear there in modified form, original sources are also included. Direct citation of specific sources does not exclude the topic's being addressed in others.]

Barbour, Douglas. *Worlds Out Of Words: The SF Novels of Samuel R. Delany.* Frome, England: Bran's Head, 1979.

Clarke, Arthur C. *Astounding Days: A Science Fictional Autobiography.* London: Victor Gollancz, 1989.

De Camp, L. Sprague, Catherine Crook De Camp, and Jane Whittington Griffin. *Dark Valley Destiny: The Life of Robert E. Howard.* New York: Bluejay, 1983.

Delany, Samuel R. "About 5175 Words." *Extrapolation* 10 (5/69) 57–66 [expanded in *Jaw* as "About 5750 Words"].

———. "*Algol* Interview" conducted by Darrell Schweitzer. *Algol* 13 (Summer 1976), 16–20.

———. *The American Shore: Meditations on a Tale by Thomas M. Disch— "Angouleme."* Elizabethtown, NY: Dragon Press, 1978.

———. "Another Letter from New York." *Wine* 207–214.

———. "Author's Afterword," *City of a Thousand Suns*. New York: Ace, 1964. 155–56. Rptd. in *The Fall of the Towers*. New York: Bantam, 1986. 398–99. Expanded successively as "Some Architectural Sketches for 'The Towers.'" *Algol* 13 (1/68), 17–18; "Some Reflections on *The Fall of the Towers*." *New Moon* 1:3 (Spring 1983), 2–13; "Ruins/Foundations" in *Straits*; and the first half or more of *Motion*.

———. "Characters." *Jaw* 171–79 [originally a letter in *SFWA Forum*. 11 (6/69) 6–10].

———. "Crazy Diamonds." *Empire* (1980) 21–22. [pp. 16–21 hold comments by Pamela Sargent and Michael Bishop on Alan R. Bechtold's short story, "Sweet Virginia."]

———. "Critical Methods: Speculative Fiction." *Quark/I*. Samuel R. Delany and Marilyn Hacker, eds. New York: Popular Library, 1970. 182–96 [rptd. in *Jaw*].

———. "*Dichtung und* Science Fiction." *Wine* 165–196.

———. "Disch." *Wine* 138–164 [originated as "Introduction." *Fundamental Disch*. Samuel R. Delany, ed. New York: Bantam, 1980. vii–xiii].

———. "The Discourse of Science Fiction." *SFWA Bulletin #76* (Spring 1981) 22–35.

———. "The Discourse on Desire" (typescript).

———. "Faust and Archimedes" [Disch and Zelazny]. *Jaw* 191–210.

———. "The Gestation of Genres: Literature, Fiction, Romance, Science Fiction, Fantasy . . ." *Intersections: Science Fiction and Fantasy*. George Edgar Slusser and Eric S. Rabkin, eds. Carbondale and Edwardsville: Southern Illinois UP, 1987. 63–73.

———. *Heavenly Breakfast: An Essay on the Winter of Love*. New York: Bantam, 1979.

———. "Heinlein." *Wine* 37–45. [Originally "Introduction," *Glory Road*. New York: Gregg Press, 1979. v–xiii].

———. *The Jewel-Hinged Jaw: Notes on the Language of Science Fiction*. Elizabethtown, NY: Dragon Press, 1977. New York: Berkley, 1977 paperback [subtitle misprints "of" for "on"].

———. "The Ken James Interview." *Silent Interviews* 233–249.

———. "Letter." *Science Fiction Commentary* #19 (1–3/71) 40–49. [Originally in *Exploding Madonna* #5 (1/69) 1–10. Not seen.]

———. *The Motion of Light in Water: East Village Sex and Science Fiction Writing: 1960–1965, with "The Column at the Market's Edge."* London: Paladin, 1990. [The British paperback is fuller than the American hardbound edition, subtitled *Sex and Science Fiction Writing in the East Village, 1957–1965*. New York: Arbor House, 1988.]

———. "Neither the Beginning nor the End of Structuralism, Post-Structuralism, Semiotics, or Deconstruction for Science Fiction Readers: An Introduction." *New York Review of Science Fiction* #6 (2/89) 1, 8–12; #7 (3/89) 14–18; #8 (4/89) 9–11.

———. "1985 Pilgrim Award Acceptance Speech." *SFRA Newsletter* 133 (8/85) 7–15 [adapted from "*Dichtung und* SF" in *Wine*].

———. "Of Sex Objects, Signs, Systems, Sales, SF, and Other Things." *Australian Science Fiction Review* 2 (1987) 9–36 [rptd. in *Straits*].

———. "Popular Culture, SF Publishing, and Poetry: A Letter to a Critic," *The Little Magazine* 6:4 (Winter 1973) 29–43 [rptd. in *Jaw* as "Letter to a Critic"].

———. "Reflections on Historical Models in Modern English Language Science Fiction." *Science-Fiction Studies* 7:2 (7/80) 132–49 [rptd. in *Wine* as "Reflections on Historical Models"].

———. "Reflections on 'Reflections on Science Fiction Criticism.' " *Science-Fiction Studies* 9:1 (3/82) 106–7.

———. "Refractions of *Empire: The Comics Journal* Interview" conducted by Dennis O'Neil and Gary Groth. *Silent Interviews* 83–126 [expanded from *Comics Journal* #48 (Summer 1979), 37–43, 70–71].

———. "Russ." *Wine* 101–128 [originated in "The Order of 'Chaos.' " *Science-Fiction Studies* 6:3 (11/79), 333–6. Expanded as "Orders of Chaos: The Science Fiction of Joanna Russ." Jane B. Weedman, ed. *Women Worldwalkers: New Dimensions of Science Fiction and Fantasy*. Lubbock: Texas Tech UP, 1985].

———. "Science and Literature." *New York Review of Science Fiction* #23 (7/90) 1, 8–11.

———. "Science Fiction and 'Literature,' or The Conscience of the King." *Analog* 99 (5/79) 59–78 [rptd. in *Wine*].

———. "The Scorpion Garden." *Straits*, 1–15. [Originally "The Scorpion Garden: The Author's Preface [to the unpublished novel, *Hogg*]." *White Pelican* 4 (Autumn 1975) 20–30. Not seen.]

———. " 'The Scorpion Garden' Revisited" [as by K. Leslie Steiner]. *Straits* 17–31.

———. "Shadows." *Foundation* #6 (5/74) 31–60; #7 (3/75) 122–54 [rptd. in *Jaw*].

———. *Silent Interviews*. Hanover and London: Wesleyan UP, 1994.

———. "Sketch for a Two-Part Invention." *New Worlds* #172 (3/67), 2–5, 76. Expanded in *Algol* #15 (4/69) 41–43.

———. "Some Reflections on Science Fiction Criticism," *Science-Fiction Studies* 8 (7/81) 232–9 [rptd. in *Wine* as "A Letter from Rome"].

———. "Some Remarks toward a Reading of *Dhalgren*" [as by K. Leslie Steiner]. *Straits* 57–91.

———. *Starboard Wine: More Notes on the Language of Science Fiction*. Pleasantville, NY: Dragon Press, 1984.

———. "Story Telling," *SFWA Forum*. 11 (6/69) 15–26 [rptd. in *Jaw* as "On Pure Story-Telling"].

———. *The Straits of Messina*. Seattle: Serconia Press, 1989.

———. "Sturgeon." *Wine* 56–80 [originally published as "Introduction." *The Cosmic Rape and "To Marry Medusa."* New York: Gregg Press, 1977. v–xxxiv].

———. "To Read *The Dispossessed*." *Jaw* 239–308.

———. *Wagner/Artaud: A Play of 19th and 20th Century Critical Fictions*. New York: Ansatz Press, 1988.

———. "Zelazny/Varley/Gibson—and Quality." *New York Review of Science Fiction*, #48 (August 1992) 1, 10–13; #49 (September 1992), 1, 3–7.

Derrida, Jacques. "Structure, Sign, and Play in the Discourse of the Human Sciences," tr. Alan Bass. Richard Macksey and Eugenio Donato, eds. *The Languages of Criticism and the Sciences of Man*. Baltimore: Johns Hopkins UP, 1970. 247–265.

Eagleton, Terry. *Literary Theory*. London: U Minn P, 1983.

Fish, Stanley. *Is There a Text in This Class? The Authority of Interpretive Communities*. Cambridge: Harvard UP, 1980.

Fitting, Peter. "The Modern Anglo-American Science Fiction Novel: Utopian Longing and Capitalist Cooptation." *Science-Fiction Studies* 6:1 (3/79) 59–76.

King, Stephen. *Stephen King's Danse Macabre*. New York: Everest House, 1981.

Lewis, C. S. *Surprised by Joy: The Shape of My Early Life*. New York: Harcourt Brace, 1956.

McCaffery, Larry, ed. *Postmodern Fiction: A Bio-Bibliographical Guide*. New York: Greenwood, 1986.

Meyers, Walter E. "Pilgrim Award Presentation Speech." *SFRA Newsletter* 133 (8/85) 3–6.

Platt, Charles. *Dream Makers*. New York: Berkley, 1980. Delany interview on 69–75.

Wollheim, Donald A. *The Universe Makers: Science Fiction Today*. New York: Harper-Row, 1971.

Nevèrÿon Deconstructed

Samuel R. Delany's *Tales of Nevèrÿon* and the "Modular Calculus"

KATHLEEN L. SPENCER

Preface: Return to "Deconstructing Nevèrÿon"

> "So far [said Pryn], this story sounds more confusing than exciting."
> "To the proper hearer," Norema said, "precisely what seems confusing will *be* the exciting part."
>
> Samuel Delany, *Neveryóna*

I once heard Samuel Delany explain that for each reader, there are two different kinds of writers. The first is immediately accessible, speaking our (psychological) mother tongue, the voice of home, familiar and revered. The second speaks an alien language, words which mystify as much as they enlighten, creating an initial reading experience of gaps and silence as the night sky against which bolts of excitement and partial comprehension flare like lightning. The first kind of writer offers us comfort and harmony, the pleasure of hearing our own beliefs stated with that artistry and grace we achieve only in our dreams; the second offers the thornier and more intellectual pleasure of learning a new tongue, of contemplating and grappling with ideas that our own experiences could never conceive.

For me, Delany is the second kind of writer. In fact, I was one of those readers who wrote him off after the first sixty pages of *Dhalgren*, so alien to the sensibilities and experiences of a small-town midwestern straight white woman. That was why, several years later, *Tales of Nevèrÿon* came as such a revelation to me. When my science fiction study group in graduate school chose this volume to discuss, I read it, at first dutifully and then with increasing excitement as I encountered Old Venn, Norema, and Raven for the first time. In his analyses of gender systems, Delany at last was speaking to my concerns in a way none of his previous novels had. And Kermit's essay in the appendix further appealed to my amateur's passion for history, anthropology, and linguistics. But the moment, somewhere in the middle of Kermit's text, when I realized that *the essay also was fiction*—a recognition so ravishing, so delightful in its unexpectedness that I still remember the feeling fifteen years later, though I could no longer tell you what accumulation of detail or what too-convenient coincidence revealed the truth of its fictionality: *that* was the moment Delany hooked and landed me. I had only the fuzziest notion what he was up to in this fictional enterprise, but because of his topic—one of his topics, at least; gender—and because of that intriguing and apparently unnecessary appendix, I was prepared to invest the effort to figure it out.

That was half the genesis of the following essay (revised slightly from its original form, published ten years ago in *Essays in Arts and Sciences*). The other half: a seminar on Jacques Derrida and the American Deconstructionists. Lost in the wilderness of philosophical discourse, I remembered Kermit's discussions of Derrida at the end of *Tales of Nevèrÿon* and glimpsed salvation. Perhaps, perhaps, I could use Delany to understand Derrida—and Derrida to understand Delany.

The degree to which I succeeded in either of these endeavours, you may judge for yourself; but certainly I have never found reason to regret the attempt. Nor have I ever encountered writers who made me work harder, or so richly rewarded my efforts to understand.

I. Models, Allegories

How can one text, assuming its unity, give or present another to be read, without touching it, without saying anything about it, practically without referring to it?
Jacques Derrida, "Borderlines"

The problem of the modular calculus, again, is: How can one relational system model another? This breaks down into two questions: (One) What must pass from system-B to system-A for us (system-C) to be able to say that system-A now contains some model of system-B? (Two) Granted the proper passage, what must the internal structure of system-A be for us (or it) to say that it contains any model of system-B?
Samuel Delany, "Ashima Slade and the Harbin-Y Lectures: Some Informal Remarks Toward the Modular Calculus, Part Two" (*Triton*, Appendix B)

Allegory is the purveyor of demanding truths, and thus its burden is to articulate an epistemological order of truth and

deceit with a narrative or compositional order of
persuasion. . . . From a theoretical point of view, there ought to
be no difficulty in moving from epistemology to persuasion. The
very occurrence of allegory, however, indicates a possible
complication. Why is it that the furthest reaching truths about
ourselves and the world have to be stated in a lopsided,
referentially indirect mode?

Paul de Man, "Pascal's Allegory of Persuasion"

During the last twenty years, Samuel Delany has devoted increasing attention to certain philosophical questions about models. How do we construct them? Especially, how does language function in the modeling process? How do the models adopted by individuals or cultures shape their perceptions and responses? How can we determine the relative coherence, accuracy, or appropriateness of competing models? To what extent can a model actually succeed in mastering the thing it models?

As a writer of science fiction novels (SF, in the accepted shorthand), Delany has addressed the problem through a variation of these questions: how can fiction model the real world?

As a genre, SF is ideally suited to the exploration of such questions, primarily as a result of its paradoxical relationship with reality, what Darko Suvin calls its "realistic irreality."[1] SF texts are clearly enough modeled on our world—on the commonly-held, external, sociopolitical world—that we can readily relate the model to the thing modeled, yet different enough that we have no difficulty distinguishing the one from the other. As a result of these characteristics, SF has much to offer narratologists and other theorists of fiction, and to critics concerned with the reading process. When we read mimetic fiction, we bring so much information about the world to our reading that it is difficult to be sure how much of our knowledge comes from the text itself, and how much we are supplying from our own previous experience. In SF, where there is no information about the subject world outside the text for readers to supply, both the author's techniques and the reader's interpretive methods can be examined in a context relatively purified of the ambiguity.

Although SF has received little attention from traditional literary theorists, intriguing work has been done by critics like Paul de Man and Jacques Derrida, exploring the boundaries where literature, linguistics, and philosophy meet. Their work does not specifically address SF; however, their analysis has created powerful tools for analyzing non-mimetic genres of fiction, SF included. For instance, the relationship between non-mimetic text and empirical reality which we have been referring to as metaphorical

Nevèrÿon Deconstructed   129

or modular could also be called allegorical, in de Man's usage of the term. By allegory he does not mean the traditional, fairly limited conception of the figure as "a sign that refers to one specific meaning and thus exhausts its suggestive potentialities once it has been deciphered"—like *Pilgrim's Progress*, for instance.[2] Instead he interprets it as a relationship in which one coherent system—the allegorical sign—refers to another sign that precedes it. "The meaning constituted by the allegorical sign can then consist only in the repetition (in the Kierkegaardian sense of the term) of a previous sign with which it can never coincide, since it is of the essence of this previous sign to be pure anteriority" (190).

Consider, for instance, an example that Delany offers to elucidate the relationship between a model and what it models: a tree in a garden in a rainstorm, and a drawing he made through a window of that same tree. It is clear that the real tree must precede the drawing, and that the meaning of the drawing derives solely from its recognizable repetition of the pattern "tree." But it is equally clear, argues Delany, that in their modeling relationship, the real three-dimensional tree and the two-dimensional paper-and-chalk drawing share nothing at all: "only the perceptive context imposes commonality on them. . . . There are only identical processes some thing else can undergo in response to both—emblem of their relation. And, presumably, different processes as well—emblem that the two are distinct and, possibly, hierarchical."[3]

But what exactly are these processes? It is one kind of process to look at a tree and then at a visual representation of a tree and to identify the similarity, but when the medium of the model is verbal or narrative, the difficulties increase. What is it, for instance, that allows us to identify *West Side Story* and *Romeo and Juliet* as the same story? And when we move to properly allegorical readings, the matter gets even more complicated. As de Man observes in a recent study, "Allegory is sequential and narrative, yet the topic of its narration is not necessarily temporal at all."[4] Consider, for instance, the narrative of *The Faerie Queene* which elucidates the virtues, or Ursula Le Guin's *The Left Hand of Darkness* which could be read as allegorizing the nature of androgyny. The radical disparity in allegory between model and that which it models raises serious questions about the referentiality of such texts. How can a narrative—sequential and time-bound—be recognized as a model for a situation which is atemporal?

Clearly, in reading allegory the most important task is to connect the model with its original. However, as de Man (quoting Hegel) points out, this task is so complicated that the surface narrative of the allegory is normally made as transparent as possible. When one task of interpretation becomes unusually complex, other aspects should be correspondingly simplified. However, this simplicity of surface does not affect the real problem of allegory, that "this emphatic clarity of representation does not stand in the service of something that can be represented" ("Allegory," p. 1).[5] Thus all writers of allegory, including writers of SF, must somehow find a narrative that will be the representational equivalent—a model—of the non-narrative, atemporal thesis they wish to demonstrate.

II. Modeling Modeling

Finding such representational equivalents is complicated enough; but with each new work, Delany reveals increasing concern for the philosophical issues underlying the aesthetic ones. His early interests in language, semiotics, and mathematics, all disciplines concerned with constructing models, led him to philosophers and critics like Quine and Wittgenstein, Derrida and Barthes, and the effect on his fiction has been striking. As early as the mid-1960s, he began not only seeking the right narrative model for his thesis, but also raising serious questions within his narratives about the very process of modeling.

That is, the atemporal situation he attempts to model is the process of constructing and interpreting cultural models.

Babel–17, published when he was 24, explores the implications of the Sapir-Whorf hypothesis about the relationship between language and thought-processes as his hero, the poet and linguist Rydra Wong, attempts to translate the language of alien invaders in order to understand their nature, their vision of the universe. What she discovers is that Babel–17 is not a real language but a deliberately constructed sabotage tool, one which shapes the thoughts of anyone who tries to speak it into patterns destructive to the Alliance. The novel concerns the process of her discovery, and her attempts to modify the booby-traps of the language so that the Invaders' own weapon can be turned against them.[6]

A year later in *The Einstein Intersection*, Delany explores the function of myths as models, as instructions for behavior and sources of personal identity. An alien race inherits the Earth after the disappearance (emigration? extinction?) of its original inhabitants. Though like humans in some ways, the aliens are significantly unlike us in others: for example, they seem to have three sexes rather than two, and to have mental powers and malleability of form beyond anything humans can do. Despite these differences, the aliens struggle to conform to the human model, at considerable cost to individuals like Lobey, who simply can't adapt no matter how hard he tries. So Lobey goes on quest for the "right" myth, one that feels comfortable, one that matches his experience. After trying a number of human myths, Lobey at last realizes that the only solution is to discover a new myth for himself: none of the old ones fit him.[7]

In both novels, Delany has constructed narratives which allow him to represent these issues rather than merely writing essays about them. But since 1976, his novels have explored the problems of modeling ever more directly and explicitly, which is to say in ways less and less traditionally fictional.

Triton, for instance, is still for the most part fairly traditional in form, yet there are some peculiarities creeping in around the edges. In the first place, the novel has two separate subtitles, "Some Informal Remarks Toward the Modular Calculus, Part One" and "An Ambiguous Heterotopia." The latter signals knowledgeable readers that *Triton* was conceived in dialogue with Ursula Le Guin's 1974 novel *The Dispossessed*, subtitled "An Ambiguous Utopia." But the former title—"Toward the Modular Calculus"—must puzzle many of his readers. It sounds scientific, all right—in fact, it sounds like a scientific paper; but it does not sound very fictional, not even science-fictional. Even more unexpected in an SF novel, each of the chapters is headed by a formidably intellectual epigraph from writers like Mary Douglas, Willard van Orman Quine, Michel Foucault, Spencer Brown, Wittgenstein—*Wittgenstein*? In a pop culture novel, a paraliterary genre? Something very odd is happening here.

But that is not the worst of it. At the end of the novel Delany includes not one but two appendices: "From the Triton Journal: Work Notes and Omitted Pages," and "Ashima Slade and the Harbin-Y Lectures: Some Informal Remarks Toward the Modular Calculus, Part Two." The first is precisely what the title describes, omitted passages from early drafts of the novel; the second is an essay about the mathematician/philosopher Ashima Slade, the father of "metalogic," a prestigious and lucrative field in *Triton*'s economy, though Slade never appears in the novel proper. The essay, whose "author" is an unnamed scholar living in the world of the novel, includes both a brief history of the life and death of Slade and some of Slade's observations on the subject of models in his final lecture.

But what is it that links this appendix, in form a traditional academic essay despite its fictiveness, with the novel? It tells us nothing about Bron Helstrom, the central character in *Triton*. Although Bron is a metalogician by profession, he admits that he is not really familiar with the work of Slade, the discipline's founder. It tells us a bit about The Spike, the playwright Bron becomes fascinated with, but nothing that seems relevant to her relationship with Bron—only that she once inhabited a short-lived commune with Slade.

What we learn here may be interesting, it may add depth to the background of *Triton*, but it has nothing to do with the novel—at least, it has nothing to do with the *story*.

So what is it doing here, it and the first appendix? They are commenting, first, on one of the major themes of the novel—the importance of models. Bron Helstrom, one of fiction's sincerely unlikable protagonists, is a classic (though unconscious) male chauvinist inhabiting a society which is not only totally egalitarian but no longer restricts itself to only two sexes. Indeed, we're told that Triton has "forty to fifty different sexes."[8] Bron's model, built on the hierarchical binary of male and female, cannot adequately map the world he lives in, so he finds himself continually at odds with his environment without understanding why.

What the novel does is to demonstrate Bron's problem, to represent in narrative form the importance of an accurate model for effective or satisfactory social behavior. However, *Triton* merely represents the problem; it does not explicate it. The explication is offered, after a fashion, in the second appendix, in Slade's theorizing about models. The appendix allows Delany to maintain a fictional stance and still discuss directly (non-representationally) the philosophical problems whose relevance the novel has just demonstrated. The second appendix, then, is both a guide to criticism of the novel and an additional text itself needing interpretation, its function in the artistic whole a question which must be answered to understand the point of the novel.

But how does the first appendix fit into the pattern? Why include rejected passages from earlier drafts of the novel? Primarily to emphasize the fact that this work is fiction, a construct, not a segment of real history whose form is dictated by external events but something entirely controlled by the author. The inclusion of these extra passages serves to undermine the convention of verisimilitude which reigns within the body of *Triton*. That is, both appendices challenge fictional conventions, challenge readers' expectations about the form or nature of fiction. Who ever heard of a novel that needed an appendix to be complete, especially an appendix in the guise of an academic essay?[9]

III. Sword-and-Sorcery

But if *Triton* breaks the rules of fiction in its subtitles, epigraphs, and appendices, at least it maintains them in the central body of the text. In Delany's next work, *Tales of Nevèrÿon*, even that bastion has fallen. The experience of reading this work (which is not quite a novel, though it is more than the collection of tales it appears to be) is distinctly vertiginous.

The vertigo results from Delany's use of two fundamental techniques. First, he knows his readers will approach the text with a series of expectations, based on their understanding of the various categories into which the work falls. The largest and most inclusive of these is fiction, of course, followed by a genre identification: not SF, but that genre known as sword-and-sorcery, the most formulaic of SF's many paraliterary cousins and offspring. Thus, the knowledgeable reader is likely to come to this work with an unusually specific set of expectations—and Delany systematically undermines every one of them.

Let us begin with the most explicit expectations, the generic conventions of sword-and-sorcery. The setting of a good sword-and-sorcery story is a land "on the brink of civilization"—a land in transition, then, a once-stable society gone suddenly fluid. The result is a loss of certainty, an increase both in conflict and in freedom as the established patterns lose their sway while new ones have not yet acquired wide acceptance. In traditional sword-and-sorcery, one key element in this instability is that the society is in transition from a barter to a money economy, a shift which, Delany argues, tends to reverse the values of the previous power system.

Unlike most fantasy, which is usually set in a world both rural and feudal, sword-and-sorcery deals with the transition from the rural and feudal to the urban and democratic. This makes perfect sense, considering that the primary readership for the genre is adolescent males: metaphorically we are dealing with the transition from childhood to adulthood, which both excites and frightens the adolescent. Hence the generic tendency to celebrate the liminal transition period itself, to emphasize the hero's competence and freedom. Within these texts, the limits of childhood have been transcended, but adult responsibilities not yet assumed.

This psychological substratum in turn leads to the typical sword-and-sorcery social geography. In the middle (in the background) is the feudal estate, the original source of cultural stability whose control is now weakening. The estate is represented by its two complementary classes, aristocrats and slaves. Flanking the estate on one side stands the city. Though in fantasy fiction the city is generally negative, a sign of expulsion from the garden, in sword-and-sorcery it is a place of opportunity and freedom for the adventurous—dangerous and confusing but also exciting. It is the center of the cultural flux, where all nations, races, and social classes may meet and mingle, where anything is possible.

On the other side of the feudal estate is the wilderness, the border lands roamed by wild animals and wilder men, where the only law is what one can make for oneself with a good right arm. This is a mirror image of the city, for both represent freedom from the constraints of the old order.

The importance of this fluidity and openness is mirrored in two other characteristics Delany notes: first, the land of sword-and-sorcery must have no connections, however faint, with real history, for that would be to limit its essential malleability; and second, a corollary of the first, the characters should have no identifiable nationality. True, the archetype of the hero is roughly Viking, but he has been denatured, denationalized, his hair half the time dyed black and his name indicative of no particular language group, but merely of strength and aggressive masculinity—like Conan the Barbarian, or Fritz Leiber's Fafhrd, or even Tarzan, who is generically a close cousin.

This hero is not the worthy prince of fantasy, nor the poor miller's clever youngest son of fairy tales: instead he is "the barbarian, an outlander, a stranger. . . . He is Caliban made human—indeed, he is Caliban rendered a little more than human thanks to the ultimately fragmented nature of the current organized society in transition" (*Jaw* 200). The sword-and-sorcery hero, that is, is not civilized: he is physically strong, skilled with weapons, dangerous, violent, but above all, he is independent, a loner (or he may travel with a single trusted companion). He is a man who flourishes in this society only because the flux creates gaps, open places uncontrolled by law or custom where he may move freely, according to his own code. Even the city of a later period will become too constraining, too civilized for him; but for the moment he is as at home in the wide open districts of the transitional city as he is in the wilderness.

So, with such a hero, what kinds of stories does sword-and-sorcery tell? What does this barbarian hero do? Mostly, he fights—villains, sorcerers, assorted monstrous livestock. His relationships with women are minimal; most often, what he does is rescue them. Since such damsels in distress are always young and lovely, he may sleep with them once or twice, so they can express their gratitude and he reap his proper reward, but then he is on to the next adventure. No permanent alliances, no binding ties to place or person (aside from the one faithful companion): that is the rule. The sword-and-sorcery hero is, in short, a teenage boy's fantasy: lots of adventure and excitement, sex whenever you want, but no awkward demands afterward, no responsibilities, no commitments; no worries about money, no wife or children or boring daily job.

These are, in outline, what readers expect of sword-and-sorcery.[10] And, at first glance, *Tales of Nevèrÿon* seems to measure up quite well. Certainly the landscape is right, and the social geography: we get the requisite teeming and wonderful city, the port of Kolhari; assorted wild lands on all the borders, and in between the great Court of the Eagles ruled by the Child Empress Ynelgo. The society, as required by the template, is "on the brink of civilization," and uneasily undergoing the transition from barter to money as the economic base.

Our hero, too, appears to fit the bill. Gorgik (whose name clearly belongs to the sword-and-sorcery tradition[11]) is huge and heavily muscled, skilled with weapons, horses, and men. Having grown up in Kolhari, he knows the city and the port; he has been a mine slave, a Vizerine's pet at court, a soldier, a smuggler, and assorted other odd occupations. He is obviously what we would call a barbarian (though not the characters in the tales: in Nevèrÿon, "barbarian" means "a member of the blond, grey-eyed uncivilized people of the south"): but for us, Gorgik bears all the conventional signs. His face is scarred from a knife fight; he wears heavy furs in the winter and goes naked in hot weather; he has brass rings on one ankle and a brass bracelet on his upper arm "chased with strange designs" which fits so tightly that it bites into the muscle, while around his neck he always wears a bronze astrolabe, a long-ago gift of the Vizerine. He speaks several languages passably, knows the land from one end to the other, and is "at home with slaves, thieves, soldiers, prostitutes, merchants, counts, and princesses."[12] Gorgik is a man with a hundred unexpected competencies who is at home everywhere in the society—and consequently homeless. He seems the ideal evocation of the sword-and-sorcery hero.

Yet if we look more closely at Gorgik, he does not fit the pattern so closely after all. In the first place, he is really too old—thirty-six instead of eighteen or twenty-three. That would not be a problem, perhaps, except that Delany chooses to emphasize both his age and his maturity: his hair is rough and thinning and dusty, while his face adds a full six years to his age. *That makes him middle-aged.* A middle-aged sword-and-sorcery hero is an absurdity. Further, the narrator remarks that "for the civilization in which he lived, this dark giant, soldier, and adventurer . . . was a civilized man" (78). This is not what readers of sword-and-sorcery expect, or desire, from their heroes, for civilization implies a recognition and acceptance of certain social constraints on behavior. But the point of having a barbarian for hero is precisely that he is not constrained in that kind of external, "artificial" way. His codes of behavior must be all personal, individual, "natural," rather than social, group-imposed standards.

Worse, the sword-and-sorcery hero is normally a great sexual athlete whom women find irresistible; but Gorgik, so far as we know, sleeps with only one woman in his life—the middle-aged, rather depraved Vizerine Myrgot who frees him from slavery in the mines; and even then, in effecting his rescue Myrgot is motivated less by awe at his sexual prowess than by her awareness of his many social talents going to waste in the mines, primarily his gift as a storyteller. When Gorgik has his free choice of sexual partners, he chooses not a woman but the barbarian boy, Small Sarg, whom he in turn has rescued from slavery.

Nor does "The Tale of Gorgik" fulfill any of the other expectations of the normal sword-and-sorcery tale. Promising situations abound—Gorgik's days in the mines, his sojourn at court with the Vizerine, certainly his years in the army—yet nothing conventional comes of any of them. There are no villains to murder, no ladies to rescue, no dramatic slave rebellions, not even a daring escape; Gorgik never kills anybody or rescues anybody or has any great adventures that we are told about. "The Tale of Gorgik" is a kind of peculiar bildungsroman, the story of Gorgik's education from youth to maturity, told in the least dramatic way possible. Like Gertrude Stein's remark about Oakland: there's no *there* there.[13] What looks like a sword-and-sorcery tale finally says nothing about either swords or sorcery.

Nor do the rest of the tales in the collection come any closer to fulfilling the genre pattern—with two exceptions, the last two stories in the collection; but even they are more than a little peculiar as sword-and-sorcery. Something keeps happening to the template.

In the penultimate story, "The Tale of Potters and Dragons," we finally get a true sword-and-sorcery hero—tough, barbaric, violent, capable, confident—all the normal characteristics at last. The only problem is, this hero is a woman named Raven. Not that classic sword-and-sorcery has no room for women: in addition to the willowy and willing ladies needing rescue, the genre includes a tradition of the fighting swordswoman, able to take care of herself and even of the hero in a pinch. She is the strong reliable companion for whom the hero need not be responsible, but to whom he can still feel, automatically, just a little superior. He can rely on her for help when he needs it, knowing that she will not need much taking care of in turn, will not make demands on him, emotional or sexual (a sexual encounter with a woman "nearly" his equal being far too unsettling an idea for the average adolescent male). She will not make sexual demands on him because she does not, herself, have much use for sex, nor for men either. Most of these women are, in fact, "virgin huntresses," the type who would surely lose their prowess if they were ever to fall for a man—which of course never happens (*Jaw* 202).

In fact, it is quite clear that these women are not real women at all, merely another adolescent male fantasy, the complement to the weak and willing lady who will sleep with the hero and then let him leave gracefully with no fuss. Both give him what he wants from them without making any demands on him. This is why (Delany observes), despite her competence and strength, the traditional sword-and-sorcery fighting woman is an archetype of very little use to the women's movement, for if she has no genuine relationships with men, she has none with women either. She "never appears on stage with another woman (unless to slaughter a villainess); much less is she concerned with how women—whether men consider them heroes, villainesses or just ignorable—are treated in such an overmasculinized society" (*Jaw* 201).[14]

But Raven, hero of "Potters and Dragons," the masked woman from the Western Crevasse with the double-bladed sword, does not match this image any more than Gorgik matches his stereotype. She is, quite simply, the exact image of the usual male sword-and-sorcery hero, independent, confident, always ready with the proper response to any situation, knowledgeable, suspicious at the right times, and coolly capable of murder when necessary. These are also the characteristics of the traditional swordswoman, but Raven's expansive, rather crude good humor is not: it belongs instead to the hero, the male.

Nor do her relations with either sex match the ordinary pattern. No virgin huntress, Raven, but the confident and randy sexual aggressor. When the sailors carrying her and Norema and Bayle to the south try to draw her curious double sword, she grabs it away and grins at them: "Watch out, men! You are not so pretty that you can handle a woman's blade!" (176). Or again, to young Bayle, the potter's apprentice: "Do you want my cabin for the night, pretty man? . . . Oh, don't worry, I shall not set on you in the night and besmirch your honor" (185). This is a blatant parody—or rather, an exact quote which, thus reversed, becomes parodic—of the way ordinary sword-and-sorcery heroes talk to pretty young women. Also unlike the archetypal swordswoman, Raven is very much concerned with the way other women are treated—which is also to say that, unlike ordinary sword-and-sorcery, there is at least one other woman in the tale (neither a villainess nor a clinging vine) who must be taken seriously as a character. So, though Raven zestfully performs the regulation kinds of swashbuckling, "The Tale of Potters and Dragons" is not quite regulation sword-and-sorcery.

Nor is the volume's final story, "The Tale of Dragons and Dreamers," despite its political schemings and violent deaths, depraved aristocrats, busy torture chambers and slave revolts. At first this may seem like the sword-and-sorcery we have been waiting for, but on consideration it too appears a little odd. For one thing, though there is a lot of running and hiding and fighting and slashing, it isn't our hero who does it: Small Sarg, too young and small for the archetypal role, accomplishes it while Gorgik hangs in the dungeon reluctantly providing amusement for the torturer. More importantly, this exciting action does not form the climax of the tale, as it properly ought to do, but instead is restricted to the first half. The rest of the tale is given over, anticlimactically, to quiet conversation between Gorgik and Small Sarg on one side, and Raven and Norema on the other.

What their conversation does is to tie together the dangling threads of the fictional tapestry, illuminating them, solving little mysteries left over from the preceding tales, and demonstrating just how tightly woven the apparently loose web of the tales actually is (much too tight for anything but fiction). However, none of this mystery-solving has anything to do with the plot, such plot as there is; the revelations all have to do with the way the characters— and readers—have perceived or interpreted earlier events, new information which leads to a shift in perspective or a growth in comprehension.[15]

And then the tale ends with an improbable, mysterious, hopeful image— of an absurdly fragile and awkward dragon managing to sustain a flight which should end in catastrophe but, for the moment, does not. It is a tiny touch of magic, the only mystery which is not eventually explained. Perhaps, since it is, after all, a dragon, which even in Nevèrÿon is a legendary beast, this small episode is the "sorcery" to complement the "swords" in the first part of the story, a final unexpected satisfaction of the readers' long-frustrated expectations—if we have the perceptiveness to recognize it for what it is.

But to say that it requires unusual alertness to interpret the significance of this event is precisely to reinforce the anticlimactic nature of the tale's conclusion, and in this respect "Dragons and Dreamers" is not alone: every tale in the collection is exactly like this. The narrator simply refuses to include the normal dramatic events, or rather he refuses to treat events in the normal dramatic fashion, with details chosen to emphasize their significance or emotional intensity. Instead of placing them at the center of his tales he observes them, so to speak, out of the corner of his eye, his voice detached and matter-of-fact. What ought to be the climax never quite seems climactic. The result is a peculiarly unfinished feeling for readers at the end of each tale, the impression that nothing much has happened.

IV. Reading Fictions

We are no longer talking about the conventions of sword-and-sorcery here: now it is the very notion of fiction itself that is being undermined, our collective sense of what to expect from a story. We expect a story to talk about important events, dramatic events, in the lives of its characters; we also expect that the most important and dramatic of those events will form the climax. Delany has here created five tales which refuse to satisfy either of those expectations. "The Tale of Old Venn," for instance, which mainly details the philosophical lectures of the island's teacher to her pupils, also includes an episode in which the islanders stage a sneak attack against the strange red ship which has sailed into their port. Without warning they set fire to it in the middle of the night, burning it to the water line and its crew (all women but one) along with it.

This has all the earmarks of an ideal sword-and-sorcery incident—drama, tension, violence, horror, primitive expressions of primitive emotions. But we perceive the event through the eyes of teenaged Norema, whose reactions are curiously distanced. As she sits on the dark beach waiting for the flames, she is thinking about the technique for firing a free-anchored ship which, like the men at their awful work in the harbor, she has learned from one of Old Venn's stories. When the flames suddenly spurt up, all she can think of is the story, how exciting its "burning and battles, its brave feats and betrayals" seem in the telling. Watching it in real life, she knows the tale's effect has been reversed, as in a mirror, its meaning changed, but cannot specify the effect of the reversal—only that it is, surprisingly,

> not something horrible. The reason she held the branch so tightly, pressed herself back against the tree, was not from any active fear, but rather from a sort of terrible expectation of emotion, waiting for the sound (amidst the faint crackling she could just make out) of screams, waiting to see figures leaping or falling into the ring of flaming waters. All she actually felt (she loosed her hand from the branch beside her) was numb anticipation.
>
> *There are people in there*, she thought, almost to see the result of such thought, *dying*. Nothing. *There are women dying in there*, she tried again . . . still it was just a curious phrase. Suddenly she raised her chin a little, closed her eyes, and this time tried moving her lips to the words: "There are women in there dying and our men are killing them . . ." and felt a tickling of terror. (134; second ellipsis Delany's).

She is moving toward a hint of the meaning of this incident, but it is only a hint (the true nature of this ship, its crew and cargo, is one of those little mysteries which will be cleared up at the end of "Dragons and Dreamers"); and meanwhile this great dramatic scene is occurring in a disconcertingly undramatic—virtually an *anti*dramatic way. If Norema ever hears the screams, we do not, nor do we see the flames or experience the terror of the scene. It remains doubly distanced from us, presented to us through the perceptions of a numbed observer and the climactic moments left unvisualized. The closest we get is the (parenthetical) observation that "in the bay's center, fire fell back to the water's surface, with things floating in it aflame." *Things*: a neutral colorless word, one which does not allow us to picture anything specific, though with effort we might remember that some of those floating, flaming "things" could be bodies. This sentence is followed by the observation that "several largish pieces of flotsam were drifting inland." That is all we ever see of the disaster. The ship must, by this point, be completely destroyed, along with its unfortunate crew; yet the story persistently refuses us the drama. It is blank, its meaning unspecified and unspecifiable. Though this episode provides the most striking example, Delany repeats this effect, using a variety of techniques, in each of the tales.

In addition to this "undramatizing," Delany finds ways to undermine our other expectations of fiction as well. One fairly simple technique is the epigraphs, which are drawn from the same kinds of sources as *Triton*'s, only even longer and more intellectually intimidating; and of course the appendix, "Some Informal Remarks toward the Modular Calculus, Part Three" (of which more later). Such apparatus is just not a necessary part of the usual fictional work, certainly not in an unabashedly low-brow genre like sword-and-sorcery. Then there is the fact that the narrator, and occasionally a character like Old Venn, always seems to be interrupting the story to deliver a lecture on civilization or writing or the nature of money.

Most important of all, there is the matter of verisimilitude. *Tales of Nevèrÿon* is a disconcerting mix of gritty realism and the most blatant improbabilities and anachronisms, manifested by narrator and characters alike. On one hand, Delany does not indulge any of the formula's normal romanticizing (or more accurately, sentimentalizing) of its subjects. Quite the opposite, in fact: many of the narrator's observations are designed explicitly to undercut romantic notions. For instance, "The Tale of Small Sarg" begins:

> In that brutal and barbaric time he was a real barbarian prince—which meant that his mother's brother wore women's jewelry and was consulted about animals and sickness. It meant at fourteen his feet were rough from scurrying up rough-barked palms, and his palms were hard from pulling off the little nodules of sap from the places where new shoots had broken away. . . . It meant his hair was matted and that hunger was a permanent condition relieved every two or three days when someone brought in a piece of arduously tracked and killed game, or a new fruit tree was (so rarely) found; for his tribe did not have even the most primitive of agricultural knowledge. (141)

This is a far cry from the normal sword-and-sorcery celebration of the noble savage living a life of simple splendor in the forest. Slavery and the aristocracy are likewise viewed with the same clear debunking eye, described not with the simplified outlines and colors of the formula, sweepingly idealized or sweepingly vilified, but as complex institutions in which the powerful experience profound limitations and the weak sometimes acquire significant powers. Even the dragons—the one suggestion of magic in the tales—are thoroughly deromanticized, perfectly natural and surprisingly awkward beasts who do not truly fly but can only glide, who cannot take off from level ground at all, and whose wings are fragile and very likely to tear. A poor pale shadow of the mythical creature—though precisely the kind of seed from which the myth might have sprung in the first place.

However, running counter to this naturalizing strain is the marked tendency of the characters to be self-conscious in an entirely unnaturalistic way, to perceive themselves not from within their own historical framework, but from ours. This anachronistic quality of the text is reinforced by the chatty and confiding tone of the narrator, who clearly shares our point of view rather than that of the characters: "The mark of the truly civilized is their (truly baffling to the likes of you and me) patience with what truly baffles," he remarks (151). From this perspective he makes frequent observations like "these were basic and brutal times" (74), or "in that brutal and barbaric time" (141). In "Potters and Dragons," young Bayle says to himself of Norema, his financial rival, " 'She probably lusts after me and feels guilty at the same time that she must fight with me over money,' for these [the narrator observes] were barbaric times and certain distinctions between self and other had not yet become common" (187; it was, of course, Bayle who was lusting and feeling guilty, not Norema). Again, "because these were primitive times when certain conversational formalities had not yet grown up to contour discourse among strangers, certain subjects that more civilized times might have banished from the evening were brought quickly to the fore" (238).

Though the narrator draws attention to himself with such observations, he does not completely shatter the illusion of verisimilitude with them. It is permissible to have a narrator contemporary with the audience rather than the historical period he discourses about. However, when the characters manifest the same kinds of awareness the effect is quite different. For instance, Old Venn tells her students, who have just invented a system for writing names, "Civilized people are very careful about who they let write down their names, and who they do not. Since we, here, do not aspire to civilization, it is perhaps best we halt the entire process" (85). The potter, sending Bayle on his journey south, tells his apprentice to be sure to reach the ship an hour early "since we have yet to invent an accurate timetable for shipping traffic in and out of Kolhari harbor" (164). Madame Keyne, sending Norema on the same trip, reminds herself "we civilized peoples are always romanticizing the barbaric" (171). A final example of many: Small Sarg observes that freeing slaves from their iron collars is easy because, although they are locked, all locks have the same pattern, so "in these strange and barbaric times, any key will do" (239).

All these remarks demonstrate, not the consciousness of people in the midst of change who do not know what the end of such changes will be, but rather of those who understand the whole pattern, as if it were a story with a familiar (*formulaic*) plot, against which they can measure the progress of their own movement. Far from being convincing inhabitants of their own time and place, with a realistically local point of view, these characters see their own world from our perspective in time. The effect is to undermine the verisimilitude of the text, our ability to respond to it as a self-contained and consistent universe whose fictionality we can, while we are reading, forget.

And, just in case we have missed the point, Delany offers us an unmistakable sign that he wants us to be conscious, even as we read, that this is fiction. In "Old Venn," just after Norema has learned of the plot to burn the red ship, the narrator remarks:

> Certain storytelling conventions would have us here, to point and personalize Norema's response to Enin's news, go back and insert some fictive encounter between the girl and one or more of the sailor women: a sunny afternoon on the docks, Norema sharing a watermelon and inner secrets with a coarse-haired, wide-eyed twenty-year-old; Norema and a fourteen-year-old whose dirty blond hair was bound with beaded thongs, sitting knee to knee on a weathered log, talking of journeys taken and journeys desired; or a dawn encounter at a beached dinghy between Norema and some heavy-armed redhead falling to silent communion at some task of mending, bailing, or caulking. Certainly the addition of such a scene, somewhere previous to this in our text, would make what happens next conform more closely to the general run of tales. The only trouble with such fictive encounters is, first, they frequently do not occur, and second, frequently when they do, rather than leading to the action fiction uses them to impel, they make us feel that, somehow, we have already acted, already done our part to deploy a few good feelings—especially when the action required goes against the general will. (131)

He will not include the usual scene, that is, because it is characteristic of fiction rather than real life! Because it is part of the formula, the way we expect things to happen in fiction rather than an accurate model of life. It is a surprisingly direct statement of the point behind all these other devices:

to call into question our model of fiction (and of certain genres of fiction), occasionally—as here—by explicit identification of our expectations and his refusal to satisfy them, but more often implicitly, by the discomfort we experience when the model simply is not fulfilled. He forces us to notice simultaneously both the model's existence and its conventionality, its inadequacy as a map of life.

V. Self-Deconstructing Texts

But even an inadequate model has its uses, a point which Delany's second major technique is designed to demonstrate. If his first technique—the frustration of expectations—can be suspected of owing something to his reading among the literary philosophers, there is no question about the second: it explicitly derives from the work of Jacques Derrida. Within the text Delany establishes a series of binary oppositions—civilization/barbarism, freedom/slavery, master/slave, man/woman, text/appendix (which could alternatively be identified as literature/criticism), and then proceeds to reverse the values within each pair. This process of reversal is one of the central elements of deconstruction. As Derrida argues, "in a classical philosophical opposition we are not dealing with the peaceful coexistence of a *vis-à-vis*, but rather with a violent hierarchy. One of the two terms governs the other (axiologically, logically, etc.) or has the upper hand." Faced with such a binary opposition, Derrida's strategy is to privilege the devalued term, to reverse the polarity of positive and negative, strong and weak, authentic and inauthentic, within the pair.

> We must traverse a phase of *overturning*. . . . To deconstruct the opposition, first of all, is to overturn the hierarchy at a given moment. To overlook this phase of overturning is to forget the conflictual and subordinating structure of opposition. Therefore one might proceed too quickly to a neutralization that in practice would leave the previous field untouched, leaving one no hold on the previous opposition, thereby preventing any means of intervening in the field effectively.[16]

But this overturning phase, however crucial (as the politics of the last twenty years readily demonstrates), is not sufficient. "To remain in this phase is still to operate on the terrain of and from within the deconstructed system" (*Positions* 42). To argue that black is better than white, female than male, is to be trapped in the same opposition, the same construction of the world as meaningfully divided into those two categories, one of which must still be superior to the other, since "the hierarchy of dual oppositions always reestablishes itself." Reversing the polarity does not change the structure of the system. What is required is "the irruptive emergence of a new 'concept,' a concept that can no longer be, and never could be, included in the previous regime" (42). This new concept, however, is not to be the Hegelian synthesis of the original binary pair, nor is it the structuralist mediating term: it is instead the permanent destabilization of the binary pair, the undermining of faith in their binarity. The "new concept" suggests that the terms are neither so completely opposed nor so discrete as the traditional formulation implies: there may be more than two categories, or these two categories may in fact interpenetrate, or the difference between the terms may be less meaningful than certain similarities which the habitual opposition has obscured from us.

What Delany has done in *Tales of Nevèrÿon* with all of the binary pairs he evokes is to overturn the opposition, to suggest the inability of such pairs to model the world adequately. If we study the pairs he devotes most attention to—man/woman and literature/criticism—we can see both how he challenges these traditional oppositions and how it is his choice of genre which makes his challenge possible.

The key to the challenge is reversal, symbolized by the mirror. Mirrors abound in these tales. With their use, Old Venn demonstrates to her students that a message written on paper means one thing; if you read the message in a mirror, the symbols run backwards and the meaning is reversed. But if you then reverse the mirror image with another mirror, you do not get the original message restored, but an entirely different message—the one written on the back of the original piece of paper. A reversal of a reversal does not reproduce the original meaning, but produces something altogether new.

To illustrate, Venn tells the children about an experience from her youth. Alone on a sailing ship, she was attacked by a great sea monster which, after a terrifying and uncertain battle, she succeeded in fighting off. But for the rest of her long trip home, she did not know whether the monster was following her, did not know whether she would survive the experience. When she returned to port, exhausted and still suffering the aftereffects of fright, she told her friends about the battle and the monster, stuttering, partially incoherent, going back to put in details as she remembered them.

> But as I told them, as I watched them, I realized: While for me, the value of the experience I had lived through was that, for its duration, I had not known from moment to moment if I would live or die, for them, the value of the telling was that, indeed, I *had* lived through it, that I *had* survived it . . . the more evidence they had, by my onrush of living talk, that I *had* lived through it, the more certain they were that I had survived *some*thing, though the "what" of it, just because of that certainty, was quite beyond them. (89–90)

Reflecting on what she had said about her experience and on her friends' reactions, Venn begins to reorganize her story, selecting details that her audience had seemed to recognize as true or accurate and putting them in order "so that these reactions would build as my reactions to the remembered experience had built." The next morning she tells her story again, smoothly this time; and the reactions of her audience are much more satisfying, much closer to the form of her original experience. But despite the fact that she uses the same words to describe the beast in both accounts, Venn observes that, "ordered and recalled in calmness, she is an entirely different monster" (91). As the children draw the parallel, the original experience is like the message on the paper, the first telling is "like what we saw in the first mirror, with its meaning all backward," and the revised story like the second mirror image, "something else entirely, with its own meaning" (91).

A few days later, a thoughtful Norema asks Venn if men and women might be another example of the same idea. Suppose, the girl said, somewhere there was a plan or model of the ideal human being (note, please, the word *model*). Then, if men were created first, in the image of the original, they would reverse all the values (thus explaining their greed, violence, and so on); and women, being made after men and thus an image of an image, would take on an entirely new pattern of values. Or, of course, if women were created first, then it would work the other way around. But Venn reacts with alarm to her pupil's speculation:

> That is the most horrendous notion I've ever heard. . . . What I've observed—
> the pattern behind what I've observed—explains why what happens happens
> the way it does. It makes the whole process easier to see. Your idea is a
> possible explanation not of observations but of a set of speculations, which,
> if you accepted them along with the explanation, would then only make you
> start seeing things and half-things where no things are. (105)

For instance, Venn says, if one took green-eyed people as the image and grey-eyed people as the image of the image; or fat people and thin people, or people who like to fish and those who like to hunt (or, as Venn does not say but we can readily supply, light-skinned people and dark-skinned people)— one would create a system with great power but no basis in observation, no truth. As Venn says, that is the trouble with all really powerful ideas: "What it produces is illuminated by it. But applied where it does not pertain, it produces distortions as terrifying as the idea was powerful" (105).

However, having (through Venn) denied that this pattern of images and reversals applies to women and men, Delany proceeds to demonstrate that our culture has in fact so applied it, that we perceive male and female as a fundamental opposition. To challenge this opposition, he merely reverses its polarity, not once but twice, first among the Rulvyn, the hill tribes of the Ulvayn Islands, and second in the culture of the Western Crevasse, Raven's people. Both these societies are, each in a different way, mirror images of the relations between men and women in our own culture.

Among the Rulvyn, as Venn tells Norema, the women really control the tribe, because they are active, strong, and clever, because their gardens provide most of the food and their labor produces most of the other necessities of daily life. But, being rare, meat is culturally important, so "the hunting men are looked upon as rather prestigious creatures" (92). The prestige is not the sign of social power, however, but rather a compensation for its lack. The hunter normally lives as the single valued male in a women's work commune, so that the sign of the family is "a fine, proud hunter content to be made much of by the women who constitute the family itself" (94). The male thus has prestige and ceremonial power, but little practical control of either family or tribe.

So far this merely sounds like a fairly idyllic version of tribal culture. But when Venn describes the way the Rulvyn treat their children, suddenly the hierarchical nature of the opposition stands out unmistakably. The hill tribe, she says, values daughters much more than sons, though to the casual observer, just the opposite seems true,

> that they make much more fuss over sons. They pamper them, show them off, dress them up in ridiculous and unwearable little hunting costumes and scold them unmercifully should any of it get broken or soiled—all of which seems eminently unfair to the child . . . [while] they let the little girls run around and do more or less as they want. But while all this showing off and pampering is going on, the demands made on the male children—to be good and independent at the same time, to be well-behaved and brave at once, all a dozen times an hour, is all so contradictory that you finally begin to understand why the men turn out the way they do: high on emotions, defenses, pride; low on logic, domestic—sometimes called "common"—and aesthetic sense. No one pays anything other than expectational attention to the boys until they're at least six or seven; and nobody teaches them a thing. Girl children, on the other hand, get taught, talked to, treated more or less like real people from the time they start to act like real people—which, [says Venn] as I recall, is at about six weeks, when babies smile for the first time. Sometimes they're dealt with more harshly, true; but they're loved the more deeply for it. (99)

Surely no one, male or female, who has grown up in our culture needs help identifying this description as a mirror image of the ways we have traditionally treated girls and boys. What the reversal points out is the arbitrariness of the pattern, and the way the system itself produces those characteristics considered "natural" to each sex, a self-fulfilling prophecy on a cultural level. More than this, it reveals the inherent unfairness in the system, the way the system is designed to maintain the hierarchical ranking of the two terms, male and female. This is the value of the reversal, that it helps us to see such things. When Norema first looks at the message in the mirror, it reminds her of her father's shipyard: "when they painted the prow designs . . . , frequently for the more delicate work that could not be done with the cut-out stencils, the painters checked their outlines in mirrors. The reversal of the image made irregularities more apparent" (87–88). As this episode demonstrates, a metaphorical mirror has precisely the same effect.

But if relations between men and women among the Rulvyn reflect a clear hierarchy, at least those relations are friendly and mutually supportive, the women proud of their hunter's prowess and he gaining status from the fruitfulness of their gardens and the beauty of their pottery, their strength at work and their skill at barter. But then money gets introduced into the hill tribe in their trading with the coastal people—Venn and Norema's people—and, as Old Venn explains to her pupils, money, like a mirror, reverses all the values of Rulvyn society. "For both in time and space, where money is, food, work, and craft are not: where money is, food, work, and craft either will shortly be, or in the recent past were. But the actual place where the coin sits, fills a place where wealth may just have passed from, or may soon pass into, but where it cannot be now—by the whole purpose of money as an exchange object" (93).

In the days of barter, women held the power in the tribe because they were the ones who did the work, and they traded that work, or its products, for what their families needed. The strongest woman, the hardest worker, the one with the most skill, thus had the greatest power. But when money came to the Rulvyn, the woman with strength and skill had first to go to someone with money—usually a man, since handling money was held to belong to men as hunting did—and sell her goods or services to him, and then take his money and buy what she needed from someone else. If she could not get the money, then the skill and strength which formerly had supplied all her needs were worth nothing.

The shift from a barter to a money economy thus works a profound change on the relationships between women and men among the Rulvyn: it reverses the polarity of the hierarchical terms. Where once women held power as the producers of wealth, now men hold it as the guardians and arbiters of wealth. Where once several wives cooperated to support one hunter, sharing the results of their labor freely with each other, now one man carries the responsibility for feeding several wives. In order to do this he must have money; in order to get money, he must urge his wives to work ever harder at those tasks which can be exchanged for money. The tone of the family changes: new tensions, suspicions and resentments accompany the change in the balance of power. What emerges in money's wake is nothing less familiar than the classic pattern of patriarchy.

But one reversed image of our own sexual hierarchy (with its subsequent further reversal) is not sufficient to make Delany's point: he offers us a second, even more telling, example. Among the people of the Western Crevasse, the hierarchical nature of the relationship between men and women has been exaggerated into an overt pattern of dominance and submission, with all the emphasis on power which those terms suggest, exactly like the long-established pattern of our own society—except that, again, the polarity has been reversed. Women dominate, while men submit. If even the comparatively benign pattern of the barter-stage Rulvyn reveals a basic unfairness, what term could be strong enough to characterize this grosser version of the same pattern?

In a passage cited earlier, we heard Raven talking to men—condescending, familiar, suggestive, flaunting her superiority over them with good-natured arrogance. Then later, at the urging of the sailors, she tells Norema the story of how god made women and men. In the Western Crevasse, god created the world out of her own body (in the beginning was not the word, but the *act*). Once the world is finished, out of her flesh she makes a woman of her own shape to praise and adore her, to hear her words, and to marvel at the wonder of the act. God loves Jevim, while Jevim praises the act whose nature is diversity and difference. However, in order to praise diversity better, Jevim asks for a companion, so god makes Eif'h. But Eif'h is of a different mind than her companion; what she longs to worship is not diversity but unity, "the pure and unpolluted essence of the act" (180). She finally persuades Jevim to join her in this heretical worship, though Jevim does stop to eat an apple to praise god in the diversity of various fruits.

When god learns of her creatures' disobedience, she comes to punish them. She pulls two trees from the ground and beats Eif'h with them. Eif'h screams and pleads for mercy, but

> god beat her bloody about the face and breasts and loins. And where god beat her on the face, coarse hairs sprouted; and where god beat her on the throat, her voice roughened and went deep; and where god beat her about the breasts, the very flesh and organs were torn away so that she could no longer suckle her daughters; and where god beat her about the groin, her womb was broken and collapsed on itself, and rags of flesh fell, dangling, from her loins, so that

when they healed, her womb was forever sealed and useless, and the rags of flesh hanging between her legs were forever sore and sensitive, so that Eif'h was forever touching and ministering to them, whereupon they would leak their infectious pus. (181–82)

God has beaten Eif'h until she is no longer a woman; now she is called "'man, which means broken woman. And she was no longer called she but 'he, as a mark of her pretention, ignorance and shame." God also punishes Jevim, striking her with the tree across the groin so that she bleeds every month, as do all her daughters; but because Jevim ate the apple in praise of diversity, god's anger against her is abated. Then god sends her two creatures, Jevim and Eif'h, woman and 'man, out of paradise to roam the earth, suffer and cherish one another, and praise the act in diversity and difference.

Already, of course, the reversal is shockingly obvious, and disturbing as well; but Norema makes the point even clearer. She asks Raven what such a story does to the men of her country, making them into broken women, diminishing and demeaning them. Raven objects,

> But there *are* no men in the story. . . . Except Eif'h. And besides it is *only* a story. I like it—it is a good story for me. As for 'men—well, it explains to 'men why they are weak and ignorant, instead of setting up for them—as so many of the tales do in this strange and terrible land—impossible goals that no man could rise to and which must make all your 'men feel guilty when they fail. Believe me, our 'men are much happier with our stories than your 'men are with yours. But then, our way is the natural way ordained by god herself, whereas I have no idea whose set of social accidents and economic anomalies have contoured the ways of your odd and awkward land. (184–85)

And she adds, "The story of Eif'h is very healing and healthful and reassuring for men. It teaches them their place in society and why they have it."

Their place in society? The same, obviously, as women's in ours, inferior, weak, decorative, domestic, devalued, living in harems headed by a single strong woman. Automatically, by the terms of the opposition, they are inferior, yet Raven calls it "natural" and blithely believes them to be happy. The point is reinforced later in the tale when young Juni asks Raven to tell her how she can avoid having babies, something her mother taught her to believe inevitable, of course. Simple, says Raven: for the five days in the middle of her monthly cycle, she must merely "refrain from tackling little boys in the fields and bringing them down in the furrows. Besides, despite what we are always saying in the women's barracks, little boys actually appreciate being left alone from time to time" (204). In this society, women are the sexual aggressors, and treat men with the same lack of concern, the same cheerful contempt—like some kind of charming, useful, but insignificant lower species—as men have traditionally done to women in the world we know. What seems "natural" or at least inevitable in our familiar polarity is suddenly revealed, with the polarity reversed, as shocking, obscene—not that *men* are suffering such degradation unnaturally, but that *people* are, that it is not natural for either sex. "Reversing the image makes the irregularities more apparent," indeed.

But, as Derrida said, though the phase of reversal is absolutely necessary, it is not sufficient. One cannot stop there and solve the problem. Raven's cosmology, the pattern of relations between the sexes, has all the flaws of our own system. Though it has established women as the dominant sex rather than men, the pattern of dominance and submission remains. But this reversed image, because it makes the pattern clearer, also makes possible a more accurate critique of the pattern. Neither the original nor the reversed image will work: we must create an image of the image, a whole new set of values; we must rethink the binary terms. It is not that the differences between male and female do not exist, but that they are neither as categorical nor as stable as we have assumed. Looked at properly, the similarities may turn out to be more significant than the differences. (It is surely no coincidence, no mere decorative detail, that the language of the Rulvyn does not, like our own, use different words for male genitals and female, but one word—*gorgi*—for both: not two conceptually different things, but two different forms of a single thing. As *woman* and *man* are not two different species but different forms of a single species.)

This particular opposition and the effect of its reversal should also make clear one of the reasons Delany chooses to work in a despised field like science fiction. In what other genre would either of the two reversals he has created in *Tales of Nevèrÿon* have been possible, or any other kind of reversal of the terms which would have had equal power? Because science fiction is not limited by the real (only by the realistic), its writers have the freedom to construct such imaginative and telling critiques of what we accept unthinkingly as "natural." Delany's work demonstrates the power of this technique to make readers revise—*re-see*—their own unexamined attitudes.

VI. Literature vs. Criticism: Versus Reversed

Where the other oppositions that shape *Tales of Nevèrÿon*—man/woman, barbarism/civilization, freedom/slavery—are stated explicitly, this final opposition is never mentioned by name; its operation is merely implied. It is the opposition between the tales and the appendix, "Some Informal Remarks

Toward the Modular Calculus, Part Three," by S. L. Kermit. The title takes us back to the theoretical problems of modeling raised in parts one and two of the modular calculus, *Triton* and its appendix; then the body of the essay plunges us neck-deep into the briar patch of Deconstruction.

We can easily read the tales themselves without reference to Deconstruction, despite their rather thorny epigraphs (which can always be ignored). Derrida's presence there can be traced only in the pattern of reversals which derives from Deconstruction; but we don't need the theory to understand Delany's point. The appendix is a different matter. In the first place, the Derridean theme is announced explicitly: we find citations of *Of Grammatology*, Derridean terms like "dissemination," and a discussion which centers on some of Derrida's primary concerns—the search for origins, and the habit of privileging speech over writing. All these ideas interlock in Derrida's work in dauntingly convoluted ways, but a (necessarily over-)simplified— and therefore fundamentally antiDerridean—account of the major threads should serve to demonstrate their relevance to Delany's appendix.

In their search for truth, origins, essences, Being, the ground of meaning, and so forth, western philosophers since Plato have privileged speech over writing. Speech in this view is immediate, primal, spontaneous, a mark of presence, a guide to the true nature of the speaker and his thoughts: "In the beginning was the Word," after all. Writing, on the other hand, is secondary—a model, an imitation of speech, distanced from presence, and therefore a mark of the absence of presence. However, as Saussure pointed out, the spoken word is no less arbitrary and conventional a sign than the written one. The phonic sign is still a sign, still not the thing itself, not the origin for which the philosophers seek. Thus, as Derrida observes, there is always something before the beginning, something which has left a *trace* of itself in the word but is not the word. However,

> the trace is not only the disappearance of origin . . . it means that the origin did not even disappear, that it was never constituted except reciprocally by a non-origin, the trace, which thus becomes the origin of the origin. From then on, to wrench the concept of the trace from the classical scheme which would derive it from a presence or from an originary non-trace and which would make of it an empirical mark, one must indeed speak of an originary trace or an arche-trace.[17]

It is a typical Derridean paradox: the trace is not an origin, and hence has none of the weight of authority which philosophers attach to the origin, but it is as close to the origin as we can get, and so in some sense it can serve as a substitute or a mark of origin—as an "originary trace," an "arche-trace"—

as long as we never lose sight of the fact that it is only a substitute and not the thing itself.

Dissemination is a more difficult term. In the first place, when asked about its meaning, Derrida replies, "In the last analysis *dissemination* means nothing, and cannot be reassembled into a definition" (*Positions* 44)! However, having said this, he observes that dissemination is "seminal *différance*" (45). *Différance* is another of Derrida's key concepts, which can be most clearly explained by a linguistic analogy. Any sound pronounced by two different people, even pronounced twice by the same person, will produce repetitions which are not exactly identical, but which can be perceived as the same by virtue of their difference from other clusters of sounds. An analogous kind of identity can be found, Derrida argues, in readings of a text done by different readers, or successive readings by the same reader: the readings will be obviously related, but not quite identical. The fact that these readings all derive from the same text can only be determined in contrast with other texts. This nonidentical identity Derrida marks with the term *différance*.[18]

Dissemination, then, or "seminal *différance*," refers to the multiplicity of meanings—or better, the indeterminacy of meanings—of any given text, which Deconstruction foregrounds. However, this multiplicity or indeterminacy is not the same, he observes, as polysemia, which, though a step in the right direction, is still based on the assumption that at some level, the text's multi-valenced language can be unpacked to discover a finite, decidable meaning or meanings. That is, polysemia is based

> on a teleological and totalizing dialectics that at a given moment, however far off, must permit the reassemblage of the totality of a text into the truth of its meaning, constituting the text as expression, as illustration, and annulling the open and productive displacement of the textual chain [that is, closing off the play of meanings]. Dissemination, on the contrary, although producing a nonfinite number of semantic effects, can be led back neither to a present of simple origin . . . nor to an eschatalogical presence. It marks an irreducible and *generative* multiplicity. (*Positions* 45)

With these terms and concepts in mind, let us now turn to Delany's appendix. The essay which makes up the appendix is a discussion by S. L. Kermit of "the fragment known as the Culhar' (or sometimes Kolhare) Text . . . a narrative fragment of approximately nine hundred words" dating from neolithic times and known in many different languages. Kermit tells us the "strangely disseminated history" of this text and its recovery in modern times through the translative genius of a young mathematical theoretician named K. Leslie Steiner (247); he also tells us Steiner's history, and describes in detail the mathematical theory underlying her new translation of the Culhar' Text. Both the history of the Culhar' Fragment and the history of its young translator are fascinating, intricately circumstantial, and interwoven with real events (the discovery of the Dead Sea Scrolls), real archaeologists and linguists (Schliemann and Ventris), and real mathematical theory. They are also both entirely fictive.

The whole exercise, full of elaborate private jokes,[19] may seem merely an attempt, as Pooh Bah would say, to lend verisimilitude to an otherwise bald and unconvincing narrative, but actually the essay serves a number of quite serious functions. In the first place, all that inmixing with real history and archaeology tends to validate the text of the tales, to place what we thought merely a rather peculiar and unsettling piece of fiction in a larger, more serious context. In addition, Kermit's citations of Steiner's revolutionary new translations, in comparison both with earlier translations of the sentences and with the stories we have just read (which obviously derive from Steiner's version), also validate the text in another sense. Details that we might have found puzzling or even ineffective have been put beyond the reach of our criticism: Delany did not invent those details himself, but found them in the text of which *his* text is merely a kind of translation, a model. The model cannot be independent of the original, but must conform enough to its structure to establish the modeling relationship. Hence he cannot be held responsible for what may seem to be illogical or implausible or incomprehensible incidents which derive from Steiner's translations of their "original" text, the Culhar' fragment.

On the other hand, we learn that all of Steiner's translations are guesses, the *highest* probability for which is fifty percent. Where the earlier factors incline us to grant the text a higher degree of authority than usual for fiction, this bit of information undercuts that authority. What we had assumed was an authoritative text, the "true story"—the accurate model—turns out to be instead only one version of the story, a version whose accuracy is, in approved Derridean form, completely indeterminable.

In another and more explicitly Derridean echo, the Linear B fragment at the bottom of one very old version of the Culhar' Text declares, "Above these words are written the oldest writing known to wise men by a human hand." From this, Kermit deduces the reason why the Culhar' narrative was so widespread in the ancient world: it "was thought to be the origin of writing, or the archetrace" (252). Yet no one has yet been able to determine its language of origin. The beginning is not the beginning, but already a beginning again, one step removed from the original text. Even the archetrace has already been translated once.[20]

A little later, Kermit observes that while the classic text in western society normally derives from an oral tradition in which it is repeatedly told, passing from teller to teller and only after a long time written down, "the Culhar' clearly and almost inarguably begins as a written text—or at least the product of a mind clearly familiar with the reality of writing" (256). Since the Culhar' text "predates" every other known narrative, even in their oral stages, Derrida's challenge of the precedence of speech over writing is here being evoked and (tongue in cheek, perhaps?) supported. Finally, again citing *Of Grammatology*, Kermit observes, "Let us consider Derrida's reminder that the basic structure of written signification is not, as it is in speech, the signifier of the signified, but rather the signifier of the signifier, a model of a model, an image of an image, the trace of an endlessly deferred signification" (260). This is perfect description of the Culhar' text itself, which "seems to play through the spectrum of Eastern and Western languages as translations of translations, some older, some newer, but finally with no locable origin" (260).

Thus we can see that the appendix is overtly playing with several of Derrida's most important concepts by creating a text whose meaning is undecidable, whose occurrence is widely disseminated (in both the ordinary and Derridean senses of the word), and whose origin is unknown and unknowable. There is, however, one more Derridean theme playing through the appendix, one which is not announced but which, nevertheless, turns out to be the most important of all, once we know to look for it: the problem of the supplement.

The presence of a supplement to a text—a preface, an appendix, notes, and so on—creates a philosophical dilemma. On the one hand, we have traditionally assumed that the text itself is primary, and thus is complete and sufficient. However, supplements add something to the text, presumably something important and necessary: that means that the text is not complete after all, since it lacks something which the supplement is required to provide. Thus the supplement is both more and less than the text it supplements.[21]

In this work of Delany's, the paradoxical relationship between text and appendix is exemplified in peculiarly convoluted form. We have already seen that the essay seems designed both to validate and to call into question the text's authority, its determinability. But if the essay undermines the text, the text also undermines the essay. In his concluding paragraph, Kermit speculates about some possible new version of the Culhar' text, one based on Steiner's exciting new translations:

> If some writer were to actually put down these stories, just what sort of reflection might they constitute, either of the modern world or of our own past history? Could one perhaps consider such an imaginative expansion simply another translation, another reading of the text, another layer of the palimpsest? . . . Exactly what sort of imaginative act would constitute, as it were, the mirror of Steiner's own? (259–260)

However, Kermit adds, the answer to this question must be deferred since "such a tale, or set of tales, written in reflection of the extant versions of the Culhar' Text, has not been written." But the text whose non-existence Kermit laments is obviously the text we have just finished reading. Therefore, his essay, though it comes at the end of the book in an appendix, must have been written *before* the text. It does not completely master the text, as it first appeared to: rather, the text is a response to—in some sense a supplement to—the appendix, not the other way around.

On the other hand, the text is not complete without the appendix. Here is where the issue of the supplement takes its final, crucial form. The opposition between text and appendix, work and supplement, in this case also represents the opposition of literature and criticism, since the function of the essay is to tell us how to read *Tales of Nevèrÿon*. We traditionally assume that literature precedes criticism, that literature is superior to and independent of any commentaries made upon it. With Delany's text, however, it is only the criticism that makes possible the full interpretation of the literature, that completes the literature. Worse, in this case the criticism does not follow the literary work but precedes it, thus reversing the polarities of the opposing terms.

But Delany makes one more reversal: here the critical essay *is itself a fiction*. Despite its form, it is fully as literary as the tales it comments on, while on the other hand, those tales are as much philosophical and critical as they are fictional or narrative. The two terms, literature and criticism, can no longer be identified as a binary opposition, for in this work they have interpenetrated; they are inseparable, indeterminable. If Derrida has inserted literature into philosophy, Delany has inserted philosophy into literature, writing not fiction but metafiction, fiction about the nature of fiction, a model of the process of making and interpreting models. He has written, that is, "some informal notes toward the modular calculus."

In the process, he has also written an allegory, a narrative representation, of Derrida's ideas about language and literature and the relationship between them. Such a text requires a different mode of reading than the usual novel, even the usual SF novel; and offers careful readers a different kind of reward, not necessarily greater than, but other than, the rewards of good fiction.

Envoy

In the ten years since this essay was originally published, Delany has released three additional volumes in the Nevèrÿon series: *Neveryóna, or: The Tale of Signs and Cities: Some Informal Remarks Toward the Modular Calculus, Part Four* (1983), including the appendix mentioned in note 19, "The Culhar' Correspondence"; *Flight from Nevèrÿon* (1985), which consists of three novellas: "The Tale of Fog and Granite," "The Mummer's Tale," and "The Tale of Plagues and Carnivals, or: Some Informal Remarks toward the Modular Calculus, Part Five"; and *Return to Nevèrÿon* (originally published in 1987 as *The Bridge of Lost Desire*), consisting also of three novellas: "The Game of Time and Pain," "The Tale of Rumor and Desire," and "The Tale of Gorgik"—the opening tale of the series, now expanded and repeated to close the series.

The first three volumes were originally published by Bantam; *The Bridge of Lost Desire* was published by Arbor House, accompanied by an essay by K. Leslie Steiner, "Return . . . a preface." In 1989, Grafton Books published all four volumes as a uniform set, restoring Delany's original title to volume four, *Return to Nevèrÿon*, and adding two appendices: "Closures and Openings," Delany's meditation on the origins and sources of these tales, and "Buffon's Needle," more "Culhar' Correspondence" from another real academic, this time a mathematical critique of Venn's method for approximating *pi* as described in *Neveryóna*.

In 1993 Wesleyan University Press published another (and very elegant) edition of the complete series, placing the Steiner essay at the beginning of *Tales of Nevèrÿon* as an introduction.

On the level of plot, volumes two through four extend the stories of Gorgik, Sarg, Norema, and Raven into the future, while adding new characters, new relationships, and new problems. True to Delany's dictum that in SF everything must be mentioned at least twice, characters and events continue to reappear, though at oblique angles to our original experience of them, woven into a fictional web of extraordinary tightness. More importantly, however, these subsequent stories develop and modify the themes first introduced in *Tales of Nevèrÿon*, revealing new complexities behind the assertions in those first five tales and raising new questions about their conclusions—that is, engaging in the self-critique which Delany long ago identified as the hallmark of the SF series.

The Nevèrÿon series cries out for a full-length study, even though Delany himself has already told us (twice) what it's about, once in Steiner's preface and again in his own appendix. Steiner, who in this preface confesses to being a fictional character, explains that this "mega-fantasy" is "a fascinating fiction of ideas, a narrative hall of mirrors, an intricate argument about power, sexuality, and narration itself" (*Tales*, 14). It is also, she reiterates, not a text about some distant historical epoch, but "a document of its times—our times, today" (19). "What it presents us, even as it seems to lure us away to another age and clime, is our own home reviewed through the distorting (or, better, organizing) lens of a set of paraliterary conventions" (20).

In "Closures and Openings," Delany in his own voice tells us that the series which began as "A Child's Garden of Semiotics" developed, as he worked on it, into a discourse on semiology itself, on the process by which meaning is made out of the excesses of meaning. He also describes some of the other sources and influences which fed his vision of Nevèrÿon as a locus and as a series of texts, from his childhood readings of Robert Howard to the lost fragments of the first Nevèrÿon stories, to his readings in feminist theory and his understanding of the way narratives work, after an adult lifetime as a creator and consumer of narratives. He even defines for us, in detail, the Modular Calculus, and the "Informal Remarks" toward same. So what is left for the mere critic to do?

Yet there are, perhaps, still gaps and silences in the Master's voice where other voices might insert their commentaries, their readings. I intended to sketch out here the directions and emphases of the full-length study I have been meditating almost since completing this initial essay; but after some initial forays, I have concluded that trying to compact so rich a banquet as the Nevèrÿon series into a sampling of hors d'oeuvres—even for the pleasure of creating an appendix to my own essay—is a self-defeating project. I do not have the time to be so brief. So it appears I will have to write the book instead.

Notes

1. *Metamorphoses of Science Fiction: On the Poetics and History of a Literary Genre* (New Haven and London: Yale University Press, 1979), viii.

2. Paul de Man, "The Rhetoric of Temporality," in *Interpretation: Theory and Practice*, ed. Charles Singleton (Baltimore: Johns Hopkins University Press, 1969), 174.

3. *The Jewel-Hinged Jaw: Notes on the Language of Science Fiction* (New York: Berkley Books, 1977). This material is from "Shadows," section 25. For more on models, see also sections 26, 28, 32, 35, 51–53.

4. Paul de Man, "Pascal's Allegory of Persuasion," in *Allegory and Representation: Selected Papers from the English Institute, 1979–80* (New Series #5), ed. with preface by Stephen J. Greenblatt (Baltimore: Johns Hopkins University Press, 1981), 1.

5. This observation has considerable significance for the development of the poetics of SF. The genre has often been faulted by traditionally-trained literary critics for the flatness of its narrative surface, a lack of interest in style or characterization, certainly in comparison with modern experimental writers. Delany argues in *The American Shore: Meditations on a Tale of Science Fiction by Thomas M. Disch—"Angouleme"* (Elizabethtown, New York: Dragon Press, 1978), 60–61, that one reason for this is that the central task of SF writers—the creation of a believable imaginary world—is so complicated when done thoroughly and well that there is little time, energy, or need for "symbolism" of the usual high-literary kind (though the argument is at least partly ingenuous, certainly in regard to his own work, as the present discussion should make clear).

However, if (as I believe) we can consider the entire genre of SF as allegory by de Man's definition, then we have identified an additional aesthetic reason for the surface simplicity of most SF texts, a reason inherent in the nature of allegory itself: to allow readers to expend their interpretive efforts identifying the source of the model, the previous sign to which the allegorical text refers, rather than on decoding the surface.

6. *Babel–17* (New York: Ace Books, 1966) is also a very complex play on the formulaic pulp-style SF subgenre, "space opera." Delany's use of the formula in his novel is explored by William H. Hardesty, III in "Space Opera, Semiotics, and *Babel–17*," *Mosaic 13* (1980), 63–69. Prof. Hardesty has also presented an unpublished paper, "Theory as Narrative, Narrative as Theory: Delany's Tales of Never Yon," which touches on some of the issues raised in this paper, notably the idea of *Tales* as a text which "deconstructs itself," though without following up the Derridean influences on the text beyond that observation.

7. *The Einstein Intersection* (New York: Ace Books, 1967). In this novel we can see Delany grappling with the fact that, like Lobey, he was a man without a myth. America in the 1960s offered no stories to validate the existence of a black man in a white world, let alone a gay man in a straight world.

8. *Triton* (New York: Bantam, 1976), 117. My remarks on the novel draw significantly from the unpublished work of Dennis McGucken, "To Read *Triton*."

9. Except Tolkien's *Lord of the Rings*, of course, which seems to be an exception to many rules. There is also the case of Norman Spinrad's *The Iron Dream* (New York: Avon Books, 1972), which purports to be "Hugo Award-winning sf novelist Adolf Hitler's great classic," *The Lord of the Swastika*. Spinrad's book is an artifact from an alternate world in which Hitler emigrates to New York in 1919, becomes an illustrator of comics and SF pulps, and then a writer of SF himself. *The Iron Dream* is published complete with traditional advertising blurbs, a biographical note about author Hitler, "a popular figure at SF conventions, widely known in science-fiction

fandom as a wit and non-stop raconteur," and an Afterword by "Homer Whipple of New York University." The essay by "Whipple" manages to be both a wicked parody of academic writing and a devastating attack on the fascistic enthusiasms of SF fandom. The real payoff in *The Iron Dream* is thus in "Whipple's" essay, not in "Hitler's" novel.

10. My discussion derives in part from Delany's observations on the genre in *The Jewel-Hinged Jaw*, 191–209.

11. Gorgik's name is also a kind of internal pun. In the novel, among the Rulvyn the word for genitals (both male and female) is *gorgi*. The resemblance of the words can hardly be a coincidence.

12. *Tales of Nevèrÿon* (Hanover, NH: University Press of New England, 1993), 77–78, 144.

13. I am indebted to my friend and colleague, Prof. Carol Stevens, both for the Stein quotation and for its illuminating application to "The Tale of Gorgik," which gave me "a local habitation and a name" for my own puzzled dissatisfaction at the end of the tale.

14. If the traditional archetype is of no use to feminists, however, her potential is clearly there, given some important modifications. As Delany points out (*Jaw* 191–209), at least one woman writer, Joanna Russ, has turned the swordswoman to feminist ends in her Alyx stories, published together as *The Adventures of Alyx* (New York: Baen Books, 1986). In Raven, Delany himself has modified the archetype even further.

15. At issue here is more than just the usual thematic weaving, which in these tales includes the children's rhyme, "I went out to Babára's pit," the ubiquitous little rubber balls that go with the rhyme, mirrors, and money, along with the central oppositions of the text. The weaving reaches down to the level of detail, a network of coincidences that tie the characters and tales together. The greatest coincidence of all, of course, is the meeting of Gorgik and Small Sarg with Norema and Raven, the four most important characters in the tales; but there are many others. Gorgik's mother comes from the Ulvayn Islands, like Norema; the red ship that sails into Norema's village comes from Raven's country, and trades in the little rubber balls that come from the South, where Small Sarg's tribe collects the sap to make the toys. Raven in turn, though nameless, figures briefly in "The Tale of Small Sarg" as the masked woman who trains the young dragonriders.

16. Jacques Derrida, *Positions*, trans. and annotated by Alan Bass (Chicago: University of Chicago Press, 1981), 41.

17. *Of Grammatology*, trans. Gayatri Chakravorty Spivak (Baltimore and London: Johns Hopkins University Press, 1974, 1976), 61. For the discussion of speech and writing, see especially "Plato's Pharmacy," in *Dissemination*, trans. Barbara Johnson (Chicago: University of Chicago Press, 1981), 61–171.

18. *"Différance,"* in *Speech and Phenomena, and Other Essays on Husserl's Theory of Signs*, trans. and with introduction by David B. Allison (Evanston: Northwestern University Press, 1973), 129–160. The word is a deliberate misspelling of the French *différence*, to differ. In spoken French, the substitution of "a" for "e" in

this context cannot be detected; in some senses, therefore, it is still the same word, yet—Derrida observes—the change has significance.

19. Note some of the elaborate games Delany is playing in the margins of the serious issues raised by the appendix. For instance, Kermit's note (321) that "Steiner has written numerous personable and insightful reviews of science fiction novels that have appeared in several Midwestern 'fanzines,' many of whose readers are probably unaware of her scholarly accomplishment." Delany himself did indeed write SF reviews for fanzines, especially of his own novels, under the name K. Leslie Steiner. This fact gives extra kick to the observation that Steiner and Kermit have the same initials, while it must be considered yet another (and typically Delanyean) layer to the joke that he has turned his alter ego into a half-black, half-Jewish woman from the Caribbean.

The joke gets increasingly complex in the appendix to *Neveryóna*, which is called "The Culhar' Correspondence." A real academic named Charles Hoequist got so much into the spirit of the thing that he wrote to "Kermit," criticizing several points in the essay in the previous book. From a dig in the desert Kermit replies, through Delany, to the criticism (meanwhile wondering why they are corresponding through this unknown Delany person, and whether Leslie had in fact published the Culhar' manuscript in some trashy SF format as she had threatened). The letter also gives some background on Kermit's long friendship with Steiner (who does indeed, as one couldn't help speculating, call him "Kermie"). The appendix concludes with Hoequist's reply.

The whole production is charming, energetic, and funny—and yet a further blurring of the lines between literature and criticism, fiction and fact. Delany must have been delighted at elicting such a response to his work.

20. This difficulty with origins and beginnings explains Derrida's habitual coyness about "beginning" his essays. Take, for example, *"Différance."* There is nothing which could be identified as an introduction; Derrida merely leaps in with a remark about the verb "to differ," the root of *"différance."* Seven pages later, in the middle of the third section of the essay, he observes, "I do not know where to begin" with his topic of discussion, the significance of this term, *différance*. Four pages after that, he says, "Let us begin with the problem of signs and writing," and five pages later still, "Let us begin again"! For a slightly different version of the problem, see *Positions* (3–5), in which Derrida, asked to put his works into some kind of sequence, observes that on the one hand, *Of Grammatology* is a two-part essay into the middle of which one could staple *Writing and Difference*, while on the other hand, one could also insert the former into the middle of the latter. And as for *Speech and Phenomena*, it could be considered as a long note to either of the other two. No wonder the bemused interviewer exclaims, "I asked you where to begin, and you have led me into a labyrinth" (5).

21. When the supplement is a preface, the problem gets even more complicated. For discussions of prefaces see "Hors Livre: Outwork Hor d'Oeuvre/Extratext/Foreplay/Bookend/Facing/Prefacing" in *Dissemination*, 3–59; and *Of Grammatology*.

Delany's Dirt

RAY DAVIS

I. We Want to Take You, Cholly, When We Go

But it's always intriguing to discover the ways in which desire
fuels the systems of the world.

—The Mad Man 257

I want to talk about Samuel R. Delany's pornography. I
want to talk about it much as I talk about his other fiction, but I know that this
desire won't be satisfied easily, since its consummation requires an unlikely
level of cooperation from interlocutor or reader. Even in fantasy, I can only
go so far before imagining your objections on the basis of genre—unless
fantasy becomes so divorced from experience that it goes unsatisfactorily
flat, or unless I imagine a very limited (but so beautifully tailored!) audience
of like minds.

Don't get me wrong; I *like* talking to an audience of like minds. But I also
want to make some attempt, however misguided or inadequate, to talk to
the rest of you. (Members of the choir may wish to turn to the next section
of the hymnal.[1])

Those who read science fiction: Imagine that I'm writing about Theodore
Sturgeon's work for a group of academics in the late 1950s. Whatever
virtues I point out will be undercut by the perfectly obvious fact that
it *is* science fiction, and that it is therefore adolescent wish-fulfillment:
"Telepathy, mutants; I just don't read that stuff." Indeed, the science-
fictional or fantastic content is so embarrassingly obvious that I might be
tempted to de-emphasize it in Sturgeon's defense, to, in effect, admit that
content to be a flaw in itself, and therefore admit that Sturgeon can only be
understood as a failed artist.

162

My point is that genre-specific content is not a sign of weakness. Only a sign of genre. And I don't think it's particularly difficult to assimilate—rather than judge—those signs which mark a work *as* genre. Genres may assume reading protocols which are not those of a particular ideal of literature. But a given piece of fiction can fit more than one set of protocols, and the set of "literary" protocols is notable for its flexibility. True, a fan of a genre, who responds positively to genre-specific content for its own sake, might appreciate work within the genre more quickly (and feel more betrayed when genre conventions are sabotaged). But fannishness is not required. Sufficient to begin with is a willingness to let down one's guard, to admit that a book devoted to telepathy and mutants can tell us things a mainstream book can't.

So can a book devoted to careful descriptions of sexual acts, although porn is especially subject to dismissal-by-genre-content. One rarely hears biographies turned away with, "I prefer having a life to reading about one." Few people rush to assure one that they're "not an elf" or "not a detective" or "not a serial killer" when the title of a fantasy or a mystery or a thriller arises in conversation. John Le Carré's target audience may be fellow spies, but readers who aren't spies seem willing to apply the experiences of a spy's life to their own. Why is it so difficult to play the same game of similarity-through-difference with sexual material?

That's a rhetorical question, since I'm not willing to take the time to answer it adequately. I can answer it rhetorically, however: We *do* play this game, but under carefully circumscribed rules. Perforce, we must pretend to find ourselves in the mainstream lies of bestselling novels, Hollywood films, and advertising, although even the most vanilla encounter has infinitely more in common with the porn of Pat Califia and Marco Vassi than with the *Sports Illustrated* swimsuit issue. Society expends a great deal of energy on not very convincing simulacra to keep us from thinking or talking about the reality of sex.

The only way to approach that reality is through sexually explicit material—emphasis on "explicit"; I'm not talking *Playboy* here. And masturbation is not the only possible approach to such material.

Delany hardly clarifies that point by his whimsical citation of Auden's "pornography is that which gives me an erection"[2]—which is about as useful as defining science fiction by sense of wonder. For all practical purposes, porn is defined by its focus on sex. Tumescence and lubrication may help the writer maintain that focus, but what the *reader* does with that focus is up to the reader.

True, an aphrodisiac effect is as worthy an artistic goal as any other physiological effect; true, porn's greatest benefits may be to confirm, comfort, and trouble those with matching proclivities. When porn *isn't* aphrodisiac? Then it can still offer the benefits of other forms of fiction: analysis of the workings of the world; disabusal of solipsism; laughter, horror, surprise; those excessive intrinsic pleasures which we call aesthetic. . . . . You probably have your own ideas of what fiction is good for, and, when the pornographer fetishizes literature as well as more traditionally sexual pursuits, chances are you'll find those virtues in porn.

Along with porn's own peculiar, problematic virtues: Desire, like art, is privileged to cut across (although not erase!) those wavering boundaries which define the power systems of the world. As such, it can, like art, be used to shore up those systems. Or, as such, its expression can be a courageous, humanizing reminder of the limits of those systems. Porn, as the art which most directly expresses desire, thus has a great deal of power at its disposal—which may be why it's so circumscribed.

By any reasonable standard, these are important (and courageous) books: three novels in three very different modes by Samuel R. Delany from three periods of his career.

- *Equinox*, an archly artificial fantasy, was Delany's last novel of the 1960s, finished in 1968, a year after *Nova*.
- *Hogg*, a violent *roman noir*, was finished in 1973, around the same time as *Dhalgren*.
- *The Mad Man*, a realistic novel about urban life and academia, with elements of romance and murder mystery, was finished in 1995.

In fact, the three are so different in style and mood that one might wonder why they should be treated together at all. Their most clearly shared elements—besides the "explicit sex" which establishes their genre—are abiding interests in racial epithets and the consumption of bodily products. Which, it turns out, is surprisingly little to have in common, though enough to have kept all three out of public sight, to put off the idly curious, and to distract most critics from other aspects.

What can I say? "After a while, you don't hardly notice the smell." For me, having read all three books, those abiding interests have faded from the primacy of "content" to almost the invisibility of "reading protocol." Which is probably far from the author's intent—especially for *The Mad Man*, which could truthfully be called a book *about* the consumption of bodily products—but, I think, permissible as a temporary reading strategy, as a step in appreciating those abiding interests rather than simply being struck by them. At any rate, it's the position from which I write the remainder of this essay.

I'm not asking that you change what you find sexually attractive; only that you experimentally discard the requirement for compatible fantasy when reading about sex. Remember, it's just a book. And if you *do* occasionally find yourself responding—well, that's educational, too.

> I started to say, *Tony, please! Spare me!* Then I thought: But who knows when I'll need to know stuff like that.
>
> —*The Mad Man* 386

II. Digression: Sex Without Porn

> "Oh, I lied and lied in that book!"
>
> —*Equinox* 76

> . . . Honesty is the best policy; a policy is, after all, a strategy
> for living in the polis—in the city . . .
> —*The Mad Man* 78 [ellipses in original]

Admittedly, there's a difference between treating sex "honestly" as just one (very important) part of life, and treating sex "fantastically" as the only matter worth one's focused attention, as porn does. But there are very few works which *do* treat sex honestly as a part of life. Delany has supplied a good portion of those few examples, and he supplied them only after beginning to work with pornography.

Despite its energy and charm, Delany's early work was weakened by sentimental clichés which may have been daring within science fiction, but which were pretty familiar outside it. Though sexual experience and desire seem to spur much of the early fiction, the young Delany's active imagination and close observation weren't enough to break the established forms by which art (and, more specifically, the commercially constricted science fiction of the early 1960s) tames the erotic. We find them in the hollow pairings-off of *The Fall of the Towers*, the wistfully vague romantic memories of *Babel-17* and *The Einstein Intersection*, the ubiquitous unfathomable bare feet and bitten nails, the soft-focus parade of artist-criminals. . . .

Most often considered "about sex" is Delany's award-winning story, "Aye, and Gomorrah." It remains his most reactionary treatment of the subject, a gravity-well of loneliness whose perverts are miserable by nature. Delany may have meant to satirize the mainstream media's redirection of lust towards untouchable unsexed icons, but instead I'm reminded of the old belief that lesbians, by definition, must be frustrated—since, after all, they can't *do* anything. As one of the story's "frelks" laments: "A pervert substitutes something unattainable for 'normal' love: the homosexual, a mirror, the fetishist, a shoe or a watch or a girdle."

Now really, what could be more satisfyingly attainable than a shoe?[3]

A year or so later, "Time Considered as a Helix of Semi-Precious Stones" takes a conventionally tragic attitude towards its prominently-featured masochist—" 'Boy,' I said, trying to keep despair out of my voice, 'why do you do it?' "—even though the narrator himself has soundly whipped the boy at least once! If that scar-raising scene had occurred on stage, the sentiment's hypocrisy would've been too obvious to maintain; contrast it with Kid's treatment of Denny in *Dhalgren*, for example, or with *Return to Nevèrÿon*'s meditations on S&M.

Between the early work and the mature work came two experiments in pornography, a form able to portray desire with all the resources of realistic fiction. I believe that porn showed Delany a way to transform his love of *poésie maudit* into something more original, more rigorously *fictional*, than the suffering and insufferable *fin-de-siècle* artist who's still part of pop culture's stock company.

Beginning with *Triton*, Delany's novels and autobiographical work, as well as many of his essays, center sexual issues to such an extent that one can easily imagine them, in some alternate universe (or just some different time), being writeable and publishable only as porn. Delany's role in keeping those issues visible, beyond porn's constrictions of form and distribution, is one of the supreme accomplishments of a supremely accomplished career.

But that accomplishment doesn't eliminate the genre's special attractions. The fantasy of porn requires no more (or less) justification than any other form of fantasy, and the rules of porn can be just as enticing as the rules of any other form of writing. There are still things which are most easily shown "in sleazy books or in . . . what do they call them—underground comics?" (*Equinox* 106).

III. Equinox

> It is a magic book. Words mean things. When you put them
> together they speak. Yes, sometimes they flatten out and
> nothing they say is real, and that is one kind of magic. But
> sometimes a vision will rip up from them and shriek and clank
> wings dear as the sweat smudge on the paper under your
> thumb. And that is another kind.
>
> —*Equinox* 163

"Underground comics" are an appropriate association. *Equinox*'s characters are cartoons, and explicitly described as such. It's the only time Delany approached the flat effect of pop-culture experiments like Zelazny's *Creatures of Light and Darkness*. There's a narrative of sorts, but the book seems at first, like early issues of *Zap*, a sequence of fascinating panels which form no greater pattern.

In *Equinox* I'm bothered by faults typical of Delany's '60s novels: the book's "absent presence," wicked Duchessa Catherine, is not built up enough to have the resonance required—I picture her callowly played by the young Jane Fonda in leather pants, which certainly is *not* the idea; chief orgy-instigator Jonathan Proctor is too pompous to gain any reader's trust; in the last chapter, our supposed protagonist, the Captain, writes that "there can't be any more magicians because I have learned how that works," but the pivotal lesson must've occurred off-stage, where he's spent most of the previous eighty pages. . . .

In my first readings fifteen years ago, the old-fashioned decadent atmosphere of the novel seemed meant to bear more weight than it could possibly handle. *Equinox*, like its immediate predecessor *Nova*, is self-consciously decadent to an outlandish extent—one chapter is rather cruelly titled after John Ruskin,[4] with an epigraph by Valéry! Decadence is a protective pose for both its actor and its audience; self-aware, self-dismissive, and certainly not passionate, its admission into society is an admission of failure. Thus it was possible for Robert Elliot Fox, in an otherwise insightful essay on *Triton* and *Equinox*,[5] to keep the latter at arm's length with gloves on.

Yet I kept returning to *Equinox* over the years, particularly to those protagonistless eighty pages which provide half the novel's bulk. Though nothing else might be clear about the book, its hold was clearly tenacious.

If *Equinox* is finally more interesting to me than *Nova*, it's because its decadence—in all its desperate confusion—finds fuller, more accurate expression. Even more than in *The Einstein Intersection*, in *Equinox* confusion is both a narrative theme and the most insistent stylistic effect: confusion of voice, of sexuality, of narrative form, of audience, and even of reading protocol, as the Captain broaches in his log, remembering his encounter with Joanna Russ's short story, "The View From This Window"[6]:

> . . . The first paragraph had all sorts of words and colors like science fiction, so I got my mind all ready with this attention.
> The story didn't mean anything to me!
> I didn't know what it was about. But everything was clear and mysterious, bright and mixed up. Three pages to the end, I realized it was a story about a woman teaching school who gets one of her students to bed with her. I read it again. The story was clear. Only the first paragraph was like science fiction, and it was for the feeling, I think. My attention, you see, turned everything different.

> I want to write about me so that it happens when you read it like the first
> way I read that story.
>
> —*Equinox* 27

And the first way you read *this* story?

Well, the book's "plot" is pure contrivance of a sort often found in commercial porn: Will the "healthy buck" who captains the Scorpion achieve a seventh orgasm in the twelve-hour period which commences in the first chapter? That goal, arbitrarily decided on by the Captain, is later arbitrarily declared the trigger for a new "age of moral chaos" by magician-artist-debauchee, Jonathan Proctor.

To this quest for the seventh coming, Proctor conjoins the offputtingly vague goal of teaching his long-time associate, Catherine, a sharp lesson by making her the centerpiece of a massive orgy—which, on the face of it, is unlikely to "destroy" her, since she's said to be even more steeped in debauchery than he is.

And indeed, once stated, this second ambition is returned to only to point out its absurdity, much as the first ambition is returned to only to point out its triviality. Instead of focusing on those stated goals, the book wanders from character to character, episode to episode, style to style, like a roué casting about idly for some fresh stimulation.

Desiring some more secure structural hold, the reader is likely to seize upon Faust, since each chapter is headed by a quote from a different recounting of the story, and two of the novel's characters (Proctor and the Captain's first mentor, Herr Bildungs) explicitly compare themselves to the earlier magician.

But on a closer look, Faust appears to supply rhymes rather than theme. The book's impact is not that of the legend; rather, details from previous versions of the legend reflect on details of the book which quotes them. *Camp Concentration*'s delivery of "irrevocable damnation and despair" as "nothing more than an epigram," for example, is one of the effects Delany's often stilted prose aims for, although there is no obvious dialogue between *Equinox* as a whole and *Camp Concentration* as a whole. The Icarus-variation of a 1565 Faust tale heads the chapter which describes a horrendous hallucinogenic trip—but that trip is not taken by a magician. And so forth.

Proctor insists on casting the Captain as the "black devil" to his own Faustus, but the essentially passive Captain is no more Mephistopheles than his dog (also called "black devil") is. The Captain has little interest in changing the course of Proctor's life, much less the course of the world;

he merely plays a part in Proctor's absurd plan to build a hell of pleasure in heaven's despite. In this version, Mephistopheles is only in Hell when Faustus bring him there:

> "We have done a tiny bit to free the darkies in this country. But the devil is still very much our slave."
>
> *—Equinox* 60

And, as in Blake, the sufferings of Hell are actively created by the perceivers:

> "It's their law, not ours."
>
> *—Equinox* 170

Given the book's wavering point-of-view and point-of-control, where can we find a central perceiver, a central magician? For me, the keys are Herr Bildungs's guiding principle—

> "Always remember the objects you are working with. When you make a bridge, remember you are putting steel on stone and dirt. [. . .] Some day you will write poems to a little girl: marks with ink on paper. [. . .] When you are making love, you are moving flesh against flesh. That is the basis of all magic."
>
> *—Equinox* 30

—and the following quote from *Doctor Faustus:*

> Now will I make all the maidens in our parish dance at my pleasure, stark naked before me; and so by that means I shall see more than e'er I felt or saw before.
>
> *—Equinox* 79

This quote heads "Homunculi," first in a sequence of three chapters which cover an orgy, an enthusiastically willing turn-out in an alleyway, several grossly comic and erotic tales of bisexual incest, a discourse on the limits of fantasy, a murder-by-rape, a discourse on the purposes of the book and of the characters within it, an assault, the most effective depiction of a hallucinogenic trip I've ever read, a discourse on the failures of the book and of the characters within it, an amusing joke about painters, and a murder-by-decree. (Yes, these are the "protagonistless eighty pages" I earlier referred to.) The shift in this sequence is well illustrated by the contrast between the pseudo-sadistic genre conventions of the first chapters—merely boorishly brusque transitions to The Good Parts ("Turn *over!*")—and the horrifically anti-erotic rape of the innocent in "The Stones of St. Mark" chapter, the most realistic treatment I've seen in pre-1970s fiction.

I'm tempted to say that Delany is showing the power of the "real" over the "imaginary," but that would be foolish sentimentality. Delany has power over his characters' fates, and makes clear his complicity: "(She cannot fight. Watch her beautiful fear. I will not let her fight." *Equinox* 135). What *is* being shown is a shifting of imaginative focus: an attempt to speak truthfully in a genre marked as both offputtingly honest and offputtingly artificial. In wet dreams begin responsibilities as well as responses.

Marlowe's *Doctor Faustus* is a tragedy of imagination's limits; at extremes of high and low comedy, the limits are those of lust. Porn, being the expression of desire, is always an early product of creative omnipotence. ("What would you do with unlimited power?" movie ads ask, answering with a photograph of a supermodel.) The central magician of *Equinox* is thus the pornographic writer, taking the devil's dare to write fantasies into material form. And, finished in the autumn of 1968, the book's "equinox" is its own unstable age, bound to topple into one chaos or another; authoring such a book is, willy-nilly, a nudge to that instability. The book's difficulties with publication demonstrate well enough just which flavor of chaos won out.

Jonathan Proctor, overseer and casting director, unconvincing though he might be as a stand-in for Faust, makes sense as a stand-in for the author— but only if he is one stand-in among many. Porn lusts to know, or to invent, the lust of others. Proctor alone, with his baroque disengagement, can no more fulfill *that* lust than the disarmingly straightforward Captain, alone, can. Lacking a fully satisfying point-of-view, the author is forced to address the reader directly: through the Captain's log, in narrative asides, and, most outrageously, within dialogue issuing from a variety of characters:

"Yeah, nigger, you better grin. Niggers can't smile in this book."

—*Equinox* 87

"There are more of us than most of you think. Correction: there are more of us than most people who will read this will think. That is a truth: and that this book contains one is what makes it dangerous."

—*Equinox* 120

"And perhaps they, in whose honor we perform, will (inspired by us, shadows though we are) move a step nearer the entrance of the labyrinth— which is so cunningly reduplicated about itself that, even with feet on both sides of the final doorsill, it is still impossible to be sure whether movement in either direction will take one out or in."

—*Equinox* 148

This contested narrative, with its crossweave of authorial puppets, conveys its own odd poignance. When the Captain writes that his may be "a bad book," but "it would be too much trouble to have to write this down then to tear it up," one senses the conflicting emotions involved in creating any art that "contains a truth." Proctor's disdain for narrative and for subjective identification gives him power but also blinds him; or at least the novel with which his paintings are sometimes conflated contains important information which he lacks. In the most disturbing display of his lack of omniscience, Proctor imparts mellow wisdom and sympathy to both the novel's non-initiates before expelling them from his haven—to their deaths, which follow almost immediately after.

Artistically ambitious porn—the sort of thing which is sold to the mainstream with blurbs like "Erotic!" and "Sizzling!"—suffers from a compulsion to turn any story of obsessive sensuality into a story of degradation and death. By punishing the two most innocent characters of the novel and leaving the novel's monsters of vice happily free, Delany obtains the formal satisfaction of this default storyline without its hypocrisy. Instead, in *Equinox*, as in many other works by Delany, the leading cause of death is social ignorance. Form and symmetry are "icily instructive" (as Delany writes in his dedication) because they distance the worker from the object; much is sacrificed in objectification, true, but objective mastery of material determines one's own survival when the "material" is human. Such analysis comes naturally to porn as the genre which most obviously objectifies while most obviously addressing the human need for contact.

Equinox is porn written by a sharp-eyed tourist; it is *about* porn, much more than it is about sex or such ephemera as character, story, and setting. The Captain and Catherine both mistakenly identify each other as paragons of "complete, unbridled lust" in their first encounter: pornographic desire idealizes the viewed, but on close inspection finds only a mirror, only a choice between figuratively-fatal self-consciousness and literally-fatal lack of awareness. As the artist looks into the givens of the genre, skeptically testing the limits of pornotopia (the imagined world in which sex is all), the characters arise from—

> "So Faust seeks to gather to him a greater public; one who, by definition, will participate. You have been consorting with them these past hours. They generate in the tensions of the diction that describes them.
> —*Equinox* 120

—and fall prey to the insupportable symmetry—fantasizing writer, fantasizing reader—which splits porn's core dream of all-devouring passion.

Having so acidly explored the limits of porn in his first attempt, why would Delany return to the form? There is a type of artist who masters a new tool or technique by composing an analytical virtuoso piece, and who, having taken that tool thoroughly apart, then feels free to use it as simply another tool. (Compare Antonioni's use of color in *Red Desert* with his use of color in *The Passenger*. . . .) In fact, *Equinox* ends with nervous jokes about the "new age" it's initiated, a retreat back to the sea, and a preview of Delany's next porn novel:

> "Where are we going now?" Gunner asked. "I liked the big one, with the gun."
>
> The captain laughed. [. . .] "The big one with the gun, hey? Stay around one like that for a week and you'll scare yourself to death."
>
> *—Equinox* 169

IV. *Hogg*

> To speak the unspeakable without the proper rhetorical flourish or introduction; to muff that flourish, either by accident, misjudgment, or simple ignorance; to choose the wrong flourish or not choose any (i.e., to choose the flourish called "the literal") is to perform the unspeakable.
> —Samuel R. Delany, "On the Unspeakable," *Avant-Pop* 150

> " 'Cause people don't even wanna see shit like that. I mean, they'd be happier pretending it didn't even happen. But you're gonna see enough of the kind of stuff I usually do."
> *—Hogg* 39

The old liberal line on "sexual liberation" was "There's too little love in the world. Why begrudge it?" Which doesn't quite ring true. Love is troubling, unreliable, and often corrupting.

Hogg is a love story. (Man meets boy. Man loses boy. Man finds boy.) It's also the most purely evil novel I've ever read.

In his introduction to Michael Perkins's *Evil Companions*, Delany writes that that book's "fundamental conceit" is to suppose "the new breed of pot-puffing, long-haired young people—beatniks or hippies—really were as perverted and sexually dangerous as a hypostatized American Middle Class and Working Class then claimed to fear." Similarly, one could say that *Hogg* is the (otherwise imaginary) porn which '80s anti-porn crusaders attacked: made up of violence against women and sexual abuse of children, with a dash of racism, all rolled in a thick coat of filth.

I doubt it needs pointing out that Delany hardly matches the crusaders' imagined pornographer, nor that *Hogg*'s publishing non-history hardly matches the crusaders' imagined porn industry. So I'll restrict myself to noting the equally unanticipated *effects* of the work:

Imagine Lautréamont as tight narrative, de Sade as gritty realism, Bataille without preciousness, and Genet without sentimentality. Then imagine the resulting work as constructed with brilliant meticulousness—a book whose only possible defense might be that it erupted in a fit of passion, but which instead wears its badge of shame polished to a high gloss.

And finally imagine this most sophisticated and depraved of books as written in a flat voice so quintessentially American that the first comparison to come to mind is Dashiell Hammett.[7]

In virtually all his work, Hammett subverted point-of-view assumptions with extremes of emotional distance. The cold reportage of his narrative voices gives an impression of complete control, of a man who's always a few steps ahead and likes it that way, even at the cost of becoming a "monster."[8] Some of the most powerful moments in Hammett's fiction come when it's made coldly, distantly, clear that such control is merely the most convenient side-effect of extreme emotional damage.

Hogg's first-person narrator is as suspicious of expression and as compulsive about accurate observation as any Hammett hero. He's as nameless as Hammett's Op, and, like the Op, shows no interest in reporting reactions beyond the physiological: "it felt good," "it stung." Devaluing or simply not recognizing what fiction defines as *psychology*, his all-purpose analysis of any more complex inner state is "It made me feel funny."

The foundation for all Delany's horrific effects is that, instead of placing a middle-aged authority figure into this strong silent role, *Hogg* is narrated by a sexually submissive eleven-year-old boy. This casting against type undermines easy application of labels like victim, or collaborator, or agent; despite his blatant powerlessness, the narrator never describes himself as forced to do anything against his will, and he's able to casually, silently, leave those who think themselves his owners. Admittedly, this impression of independence is achieved by reducing force of will almost past existence, since in the world of *Hogg*, as in our own, power is no illusion. But *control*, mercifully, is. It's a small mercy, but one worth clinging to, and the only one offered by *Hogg*'s painstaking portrayals of attempts to assert control.

Refusal to communicate is one rebellion of the powerless, and Delany does Hammett's reticence one better by keeping *Hogg*'s central character almost completely speechless as well as nameless. In this 212-page novel, the boy utters only one word. It's the last word of the book, worried out of him only because he cannot walk away from his insistent questioner. And that word is nothing but a borrowed lie, taken from the narrator's almost-invisible opposite number (every '70s Delany novel has one), a twelve-year-old girl enslaved by her father.

I got up but, as I stepped over the nigger, I looked back at her. She was staring at me . . . I felt my face trying to mimic hers, as though that would let me know what was going on inside her.

—*Hogg* 189 [ellipsis in original]

In some ways, *Hogg*'s closest American cousin is that other novel of constrained rebellion, *Huckleberry Finn*: in its use of dialect (particularly the omnipresent "nigger"; Twain might've had occasion to use "cocksucker" as well, if printing standards had been different), the childish exclamations ("Cheese tastes *awful* good!"), the handing-off of the narrator between rapacious scallywags on land and on water, the taken-for-granted gulf between male and female experience, and the narrator's concluding secret intention to light out for the territory. But this is a boy who's never been permitted the decision of whether to go to hell—nor is he out of it.

The book he writes is, as its first line claims, mostly about Hogg, the most imposing and articulate of its monsters, Shakespearean in his villainy. Hogg is the nightmarish Other who understands both the "systems of the world"—

"I think I ain't never met a normal, I mean *normal*, man who wasn't crazy! Loon crazy, take 'em off and put 'em away crazy, which is what they would do if there wasn't so many of them. Every normal man—I mean sexually normal, now—man I ever met figures the whole thing runs between two points: What he wants, and what he thinks should be. Every thought in his head is directed to fixing a rule-straight line between them, and he calls that line: What Is [. . .] On the other hand, every faggot or pantysucker, or whip jockey, or SM freak, or baby-fucker, or even a motherfucker like me, we *know*—" and his hands came down like he was pushing something away: "We *know* man, that there is what we want, there is what should be, and there is what is: and don't none of them got anything to do with each other unless—"

The bartender was shaking his head.

"—unless we make it," Hogg went on anyway.

—*Hogg* 121

—and also how those systems depend upon the surreptitious assistance of those "outside" the system. The status quo's assumption of control is unspoken; therefore, when endangered, it must be re-established via the unspeakable.

Oddly, though Hogg is a sadistic misogynist, he's not blindly *sexist*. Like some nightmarishly literal Hitchcock, he is, if anything, unusually perceptive and articulate about the operations of sexism in the world; he's obsessed with women's suffering because he enjoys seeing women suffer. Some of his monologues are downright consciousness-raising in their own fashion:

> "Men hate bitches the way white men hate niggers [. . .] Long as they do like we say they're suppose to do, everything always looks fine. But let one of them get even a little, teeny, weeny bit out of line, then you watch what happens—we wanna kill. We may *not* kill, but we *wanna* kill. Well, if I was a bitch and knew what I know 'cause I *ain't* one, I'd get out there and start killin' first."
>
> —*Hogg* 82

Around this pair of dark stars, one silent as death and the other an embodiment of destruction, orbit a host of lesser monsters and victims. After the introductory chapter (in which the narrator claims he'll "tell you some about me," only to give a clinical summary of his final day in an impromptu lemonade-stand of a whorehouse), the first half of the book introduces us to four rapists (gruff blond leader, black guy, Italian guy, awkward teenager—Hollywood war movie casting), then follows them to work on three rapes through three carefully constructed and varied chapters.

It's hard work, as they point out. Our band emerges victorious, but not wholly without injury, even if the most serious wound, a hideously incompetent attempt at a Prince Albert, was self-inflicted, and even if their one (very satisfying) fatality was merely a tag-along amateur.

The second half of the book contains a kidnapping, a car crash, incest, slavery, coprophagy, the surprising appearance of two straightforwardly affectionate biracial couples, cop-fucking, a not-especially-premeditated-or-violent rape of a child, a brutal fight, and mass murder. Which is to say the mood is more relaxed and expansive.

I don't much like criticism-by-plot-summary, but here a plot summary seems necessary if only as a warning. A book such as this simply can't be recommended to everyone; or maybe I've just grown mellower about the need to push through certain limits, more cognizant of the occasional healing benefits of keeping limits in place.

However, as the receptions of Thomas Harris's and Dennis Cooper's comparatively tepid novels (not to mention self-examination) illustrate, there *are* readers who welcome—or, if "welcome" is too strong a word, at least are willing to pay for—explorations of those limits, which are, after all, limits of expression rather than limits of imagination or of the world. That's pretty much what "evil" signals as a literary term: anything from flirtation with, to a direct assault on, the terms of the unspeakable.[9]

The unspeakable finds a perfect spokesperson in Delany's mute narrator. And the strangest, most unreal moments of his tale do not arise from the superhuman physical endurance of its characters, but from his impossibly accurate transcriptions of attempts to tell the unspeakable "with the proper rhetorical flourish":

> "Of course the only thing anybody is interested in, in tonight's news, is Dennis Harkner. Young Harkner, as of this broadcast still on the loose, has been on an afternoon—and evening-long—rampage—*allegedly* been on an afternoon and evening-long rampage of mayhem and slaughter. . . . And the latest tragedy?"
>
> —*Hogg* 144

"Young Harkner"—Denny, the gangly teenager among the rapists—is another of Hogg's protégés, older than the narrator but more naïve. Or at least more direct in his application of Hogg's teachings: Nothing is true; everything is "all right." Crucified by over-the-top adolescent horniness, Denny finds some temporary relief in the distraction of physical agony, only to have his stymied sexuality then work itself out through murder. Having created this monster, Hogg watches Denny's progress with the fond disbelief of a TV dad dealing with normal growing pains, even going to some effort to rescue him.

Hogg also goes out of his way to rescue the narrator; Hogg's world holds its own forms of kindness—which, of course, aren't rewarded. And it holds its own forms of humor and suspense, its own variety of character and incident. . . . What it lacks is the illusion of shelter. In *Hogg*, home is where the violence is. There's no respite. Nor is there the possibility of communication: language is useful only to incite, to command, or to pile up into unattended monologues. The elements of *Hogg*'s world are pleasure and pain; everything else must be sketched with those bare terms, and they're no more separable (and no more mistakable for each other) than the black-and-white terms which make up the world of an etching.

Of course, the viewer's perception of an etching is *not* a matter of black lines on white space; similarly, the reader's reaction to *Hogg* is not a matter of the reactions portrayed by the narrative: art brings about effects very different from what one defines as its *material*. What are those effects? Or, as the question's usually asked, "Why would you want to read such a book?"

This sort of treatment of "such a book" usually explains from high regretful moral ground that, even though (it goes without saying) the reading affords us no pleasure, "we"—the insinuatingly inclusive "we" of politicians and reviewers—cannot *afford* to ignore such dreadful goings-on; it speaks of the artist's painful obligation to diagnose societal ills, despite the protests of the patient that she feels fine, just fine. . . .

Such rhetoric is well-intentioned, but, given the book's own stringency, I think—to quote Hogg again—"that would just turn my stomach, somehow."

Yes, I may be able to say (with some smugness) that my pleasure in *Hogg* isn't overtly sexual; nevertheless, I take pleasure in the book. By virtually any definition, this must be a perverse pleasure. I can claim (and the claim somehow gives relief) that the pleasure is inextricably threaded with pain—but that hardly makes the pleasure less perverse.

On the contrary, I'd say, perversely, that both pain and relief are essential aspects of the readerly pleasure to be taken in *Hogg*. The book provides an unusually pure (because unusually "evil") example of a complex pleasure, peculiar to narrative art, which combines anxious passivity and complete control, a feeling of novelty and a feeling of recognition, innocent transgression and guilty confession all in one. Perhaps the mechanisms binding these feelings together have something in common with those which motivate Denny's self-mutilation and murder spree, or with those which lead Hogg and the narrator to their own peculiar habits; perhaps that's why I find *Hogg* so fascinating and so indefensibly satisfying.

And, as I begin to stray outside the bounds of criticism, perhaps it's safest for me to simply recommend *Hogg* as a perverse pleasure, with all the inconvenient intellectual and spiritual rewards attendant on such.

V. *The Mad Man*

> Lying there, I thought: people feel guilty about *wanting* to do stuff like this. But this is the reward for actually *doing* it, for finding someone who wants to do it with you: The fantasies of it may be drenched in shame, but the act culminates in the knowledge no one has been harmed, no one has been wounded, no one has been wronged.
>
> —*The Mad Man* 458

The history of sex in narrative art—particularly of gay and lesbian sex—is a history of double-cryptology, of codes which may be overlooked by the many, and which, when deciphered, still deliver a message reassuring to the status quo: the message of Dorian Gray's collapse, of Plato's fatal expulsion from *Rebel Without a Cause*'s family-valued utopia, of *Nightwood*'s helpless misery. At best, for the happiest of the happy few, that coded message itself is discarded as mere cover, and the hint of representation is enjoyed for its own sake.

But even at their most benign, the codes enable unthinking condescension like that with which *Masterpiece Theater*'s insufferable Russell Baker dismisses E. M. Forster's "rather sad" passion for working-class men. ("And how sad is *your* sex life?" we mutter to the screen.) In return, such liberal condescension ensures that the codes remain firmly in place.[10]

The codes have structured brilliant pieces of art, and we have to marvel at the courage and skill needed to master them. We have to be grateful for the messages smuggled out through their agency. And we also have to remember—as if we have a choice!—the costs they've exacted in human lives: despair, fear, violence, suicide. . . . In the 1980s and 1990s, not daring to speak of the love which dares not speak its name has led to untold numbers of deaths by AIDS, through processes which Delany has often described: culturally dictated denial at both individual and institutional levels, following close on the heels of lust's irrepressible bravado ("All right, then, I'll GO to hell!").

Yes, tragedy happens to perverts. But to introduce the "perverse" into a tragic situation is by default to imply that perversion itself is to blame. A serious story involving the perverse (that is, a story in which sexual activity plays a pivotal role, since all sexual activity, closely observed, partakes of the perverse) must ensure that "perversity" in itself cannot be mistaken as the cause of a tragedy which would've been averted by some universal (and unexamined) "normal" sexuality. Or at least it must do so if it's to have any hope of disturbing the status quo.

Written twenty years after Delany's first two porn novels, *The Mad Man* is a very different contract of marriage between heaven and hell, between desire and the world.

The jacket copy for its first edition[11] reads:

A TRIP THROUGH THE ELECTRIFYING, FRIGHTENING DARK SIDE OF HUMAN DESIRE. . . . shocking, depraved sexual entanglements . . .

"Well, yes, sort of, but . . . ," as one could also say of the hilariously misleading original jacket copy for *Triton* ("INTERPLANETARY WAR. CAPTURE AND ESCAPE. DIPLOMATIC INTRIGUES THAT TOPPLE WORLDS . . ."). In Delany's earlier porn, appalling acts are executed by dehumanized monsters. In *The Mad Man*, perversion, like other violations of taboo, is instead a profoundly humanizing act of courage.

Thinking about going over to help him, while the sun's warm fingers rubbed the back of my neck, I actually felt scared: that coldness at the throat's base when you're about to do something no one is doing, or wants to do, or would approve of if *you* did—the feeling before swiping something or starting to sing on a crowded sidewalk or going over to help some homeless guy tossed out on the street.

I *hate* that feeling more than anything.

I walked back to the corner, stepped off the curb over black water trickling in the gutter, and squatted: "You okay?"

—*The Mad Man* 292

A realistic novel about promiscuous gay sex in the age of Reagan, in the first decade of AIDS—what's shocking is not just that it's so clear-sighted, but that it's so *happy*. Although the book predictably quotes Yeats's "place of excrement" line, it could just as well be said to illustrate Blake's "lineaments of satisfied desire." "Am I reasonably happy or, happily, reasonable?" wonders Bron Helstrom (a fine specimen of Hogg's "normal man") in *Triton*. *The Mad Man*'s narrator, John Marr, is both, thanks to behavior that many (including himself, at times) would characterize as insanely dangerous.

Not only is *The Mad Man* the cheeriest of Delany's novels, it's also the most straightforward. John Marr has messages to deliver, and he doesn't deliver them with ambiguity, or even with concision. Far from sounding tormented or depraved, he writes his story in an easy-going, affably convincing style even chattier than Delany's autobiographical work, larded with nods, qualifiers, repetitions, and exclamations. My first impression was of a big old friendly dog of a book, with, like many big old friendly dogs, habits and appetites which might offend the finicky.

"Yeah . . . !" the big guy said; and took another swallow of beer. "Ain't nothin' like peein' on a white boy, is there?" Nodding to us, he turned—"It just makes *everybody* feel good, don't it?"

—*The Mad Man* 165–166

The scrupulous meanness of *Hogg*'s prose and the structural puzzles of Delany's other novels would be out of place here, in a book dedicated to the pleasure of shaping one's life—philosophical, economic, social, *and* sexual life—out of emotional and physical "messiness":

But what is inchoate in Hasler's work, from beginning to end—what he best represents—is the realization that large-scale, messy, informal systems are necessary in order to develop, on top of them, precise, hard-edged, tractable systems; more accurately, structures that are so informal it's questionable whether they can be called systematic at all are prerequisites for those structures that can, indeed, be recognized as systems in the first place. . . . For Hasler, the messy is what provides the energy which holds any system within it coherent and stable.

—*The Mad Man* 284–285

Delany's Dirt   **179**

The Hasler mentioned there, Timothy Hasler, is a (fictional) philosopher murdered in a gay hustling bar in 1973 at age 29. Seven years later, John Marr is a young scholar specializing in Hasler's work; he describes himself at the beginning of the book as:

> a young, bright, moderately middle-class black kid from Staten Island . . . naively certain my thesis would be a 600-page tome on psychology, history, reality, and metaphysics, putting them once and for all in their grandly ordered relation.
>
> —*The Mad Man* 8–9

By narrating his life in Hasler studies (which turn out, in the grand philosophical tradition, to insinuate themselves into a surprisingly broad range of experiences) from 1980 through 1994, that 600-page tome is pretty much what Marr delivers—except that it takes the form of pornographic fiction rather than academic philosophy. The result is a rare portrayal of the life-affirming pleasures of research and influence, as well as sex. Ecstatic John Marr, much more than cold-fish Jonathan Proctor, can believably say, "Metaphysics, thou hast ravished me!"

Of course, a relaxed appearance is not the same as bonelessness. This is Delany's novel as well as Marr's, so, as one would expect, it's thickly webbed with variations and reflections—on interracial attraction, on the association of physicality and death, on the place of the intellectual and on self-styled intellectual incapacity; most of all, as Reed Woodhouse writes in "Leaving No Button Unpushed" (*The Harvard Gay & Lesbian Review*, Fall 1994), on "the kindness of the sexually satisfied [and] the deliciousness of natural bodily secretions." And there are the expected lovely set pieces, including beyond-Al-Capp tales of life among the lowly, and two descriptions of a (very) wet bar which are so warmly enticing that I can't imagine a reader vanilla enough to resist them.

Beneath the surface attractions lies a typically audacious structure: The book's first half leapfrogs every few years from 1980 through 1990 on the backs of detailed sexual encounters, conveying on the side the history of AIDS, Marr's and his city's complex reactions to the disease, and the progress of Hasler studies. In contrast, most of the second half covers less than a month, with the final two parts (and 200 pages) of the book mostly devoted to a single week's worth of sex (with a few serious distractions along the way—a killing, a rape), capped by publication of a rather different version of *The Mad Man*.

The most blatant formal device is provided by the novel's murder mystery, solved at almost the same moment as it is hopelessly replayed. But, despite its Lambda Literary Award nomination for "Best Gay Mystery," *The Mad Man* doesn't *read* like a mystery. (Although one can easily imagine, in a better world, a popular series following on the success of *The Mad Man*, with amateur sleuth John Marr solving some new academic or urban crime in each new volume, ably assisted by his down-to-earth lover Leaky . . . followed by the TV show . . . ah, well.)

Equally misleadingly, Delany's "Disclaimer" calls *The Mad Man* "a pornotopic fantasy."[12] It's true that hundreds of pages are devoted to the sort of social activity whose description is usually called "graphic" (as opposed to "muddled"? to "verbal"?), and it's true that all the material of the novel has *some* connection with sex. But the connections are by no means always direct. Pulitzer-Prize-winning poet Almira Adler gets no fuck scenes, for example.

No, aside from the surprisingly large percentage of very nice people who character it, the world implied by the novel, and the genre it seems to inhabit, is unmistakably that of mainstream realism. Which is a considerably more startling way of presenting this material than porn fantasy would've been!

Admittedly, to some readers obtaining an apartment by careful application of blow jobs and Myers rum may seem like "fantasy." Or it may simply, as Marr says, be New York, for, among many other things, *The Mad Man* is a valentine to the city. Magic consists of remembering your materials; over and over, Marr is rescued (and endangered) by the special power of that magic in New York, where values are not so much proscriptive as descriptive. In Delany's novel of 1980s gay life, I don't find the dance clubs, faux-Western bars, and West Village brunches with which I was familiar, but such divergences of shared experience are precisely typical of New York, a hive made of interlaced hives, hidden to each other despite their blissful blatancy. In New York, focus—the active component of observation—is everything, as brought out in the book's frequent (and frequently undercut) division of the world into alert "cocksuckers" and oblivious "baseball players."

In the philosophy of language, the study of this sort of *contextual* truth, of meanings which are dependent on the context of speaker and listener, is called *pragmatics* (in contrast to semiotics and syntactics). In the 1960s, pragmatics was more-or-less initiated as a branch of mathematical linguistics by the nearest "real life" model for *The Mad Man*'s Tim Hasler: Richard Montague, a young (if not as young as Hasler) gay philosopher, murdered in 1971 by persons unknown. Under the banner of pragmatics, Hasler and his students treated such themes as ethical obligation, scientific explanation, and the practical consequences of belief, all in stringently logical terms.

Montague is not Hasler. But there are intriguing connections between Montague and Hasler, and between Montague's work and *The Mad Man*, as witness this 1986 treatment of "Montague grammar":

> We may safely state that sentences with "generic" terms *Man*, or *a man*, and *Woman*, or *a woman*, when they occur as subject terms in syntactically unambiguous purely juxtapositional sentences, [. . .] cannot, given the said syntactical conditions, be given a clear meaning-in-critical-use, i.e. they have no logic.
>
> —E. M. Barth & R. T. P. Wiche, *Problems, Functions and Semantic Roles* 64

As if to demonstrate practical applications of this insight, in the course of *The Mad Man*, Marr learns that child abuse, sexual harassment of students, and "putting things like that in your mouth" can only be considered evils in context, rather than categorically. However, these contextual specifics of life are the stuff of memoir and fiction rather than of categorical logic. One of the central notions of *The Mad Man* is that philosophy can aid rethinking of cultural values, even if that rethinking cannot be fully expressed in academically "philosophical" form.

The title of *The Mad Man* reflects on all of Delany's porn. Sex, though defined as unspeakable or even "unimaginable" madness, actually enables and expresses sanity. The sizable bulk of the book is stuffed with reflections on the relationship between madness and systematic thinking; a process of reflection which can be defined as "the philosophic life." No system is self-consistent; simply to live is to be in flux between what has been defined as sane and what has been abjured as unspeakable. And therefore, to follow desire outside culturally dictated boundaries—though never, of course, outside culturally *determined* boundaries—is to enable survival within the culture. *The Mad Man* is an instruction manual for the sane use of one's madness.

Which suggests considerably wider-reaching effects than the "self-help" book Marr self-mockingly imagines writing. *Equinox* is a fantasy with flatly cartoonish characters; *The Mad Man* is a realistic novel where sex involves fantasizing oneself into cartoonish roles. Yet *The Mad Man*'s reality is what *Equinox*'s characters long for: a life of directly expressed passion. With all its disarming assuredness, *The Mad Man* is Delany's most thoroughgoing push towards a "new age of moral chaos."

Delany's ambitions are hinted at by the titles and epigraphs of the novel's five sections. Drawn from *Tristan und Isolde*, Novalis's "Hymns to Night," Nietzsche, and Yeats, they're a garland of night-for-day, bad-for-good inversions. In "Atlantis Revisited: Some Notes on Hart Crane," Delany summarizes the central trope:

> to those of a certain sensibility (often those in deep grief, or those with a secret sorrow not to be named before the public) the day, sunlight, and tile images of air and light that usually sign pleasure are actually hateful and abhorrent. Night alone is the time such souls can breath freely, be their true selves, and come into their own. For them, night is the beautiful, wondrous, and magical time—not the day.

This double paradox of "expressed/secret treasure/sorrow" is one of the codes which traditionally indicate homosexual content. At first one might think its use here wholly ironic: Marr certainly can't be accused of an overdeveloped sense of privacy! There's no need to hide one's actions when society is so intent on repressing knowledge of them.

But Marr begins his story and his post-college life in New York in a state of secret mourning for a lover killed in a car accident, a lover who cannot be acknowledged. And if more secret treasures of sorrow are needed, plague can certainly provide them. Darkness spreads over the book not from the narrator's descent into "depravity" but from the slow spread of AIDS information and misinformation. For years at a time, Marr lives every day convinced that he will die, and that his death will be due to what's keeping him spiritually alive. This is tragic Romanticism with a vengeance.

The Mad Man doesn't make much direct use of the "wondrous realm of night" trope; many memorable sequences take place in broad daylight. Instead, the allusions point to a more general transfiguration of values, in which hell's lost pleasures are regained via the hostile terminology of the angels. "Nigger," "piece of shit," and "dummy" are endearments; the "top" wears the dog collar while the "bottom" has the power; what is "low" is what is desirable.

> "Goddamn, man—" with my arm around little Tony's broad shoulders—
> "That's great—man! That's really fuckin' low—it really looks fuckin' good."
> And, you know, my dick had gone from half hard to almost painful inside my jeans.
>
> —*The Mad Man* 382

And Marr is redeemed (at least twice) through his association with "the damned"—who are, of course, blessed. Both the penultimate cathartic tragedy and the ultimate comedic happiness of *The Mad Man* imply a vision of insular utopia familiar from science fiction of all political persuasions: a wise community, whether of scientists, telepaths, or aliens, which the outside world would wish to destroy. Cocksuckers Are Slans. (Come to think of it, the cognitive leap when one learns that the guy walking down the street with a beer can might be drinking literal-not-figurative piss is a very science-fictional effect. . . .)

Delany breaks past the miasma lingering around hoary "transgressive" clichés not only through his refreshing assumption of centrality, but also through his attention to racial and economic boundaries. When it came to reversing value systems, Novalis, Nietzsche, and Wagner all drew the line at class divisions. Only the Delphic Oracle's punning advice to Diogenes, "Change the currency," points towards a re-valuation so thoroughgoing. John Marr begins the novel as a very experienced young man, sexually. Inasmuch as he becomes more "degraded" in the course of his story, inasmuch as he's "corrupted" by Hasler's example, it's not by the addition of new acts to his repertoire, but by his growing involvement with homeless men. In a democracy, there is no ignoble rot.

In this realistic transformation of realism's traditional morals, sex and desire aren't linked with death; only disease and money are. Considering how thoroughly out John Marr is, and his proclivity for propositioning potentially-psychotic strangers, one would think him at constant risk of bashing. But all the violence in the book results from commercial interests: the two would-be bashers are livid because Marr doesn't pay for sex, and the two murders are triggered by the incursion of charitable horniness into a hustling zone.[13]

Money inevitably becomes eroticized in capitalism. Which brings us to the most truly fantasy-like character of the book, Mad Man Mike, the King of Riverside Park. Mike—"the Mad Man"—was Hasler's last lover and is the most blatant source of the book's (or books') title. He plays father-figure and articulate mentor, Priapus incarnate and representative of the pre-diluvian age. Scarringly familiar with the dangers of erotic economics, Mad Man Mike has rather brilliantly evolved an approach which privileges erotic play instead of privileging exchange value.

Yet, at the same time, Marr insists on the Mad Man's violence, frightening unpredictability, and inability to communicate. Like the absurd nightmarish chimera of the novel's Proem, he's an unvisualizable unfathomable creature who's invaded from another sort of book (*Hogg*, perhaps) to focus energy in this one. The unspeakable mirror image of the deeply articulate Marr (whom he assaults "in the mouth"), Mad Man Mike still manages to provide social guidance and healing fantasy to his flock. In other words, he fulfills the role of the novelist in a non-literate environment.

The existence of such a role is key to the contrast between *The Mad Man*'s and *Hogg*'s emotional effects: John Marr always assumes the possibility of communication. It may be heavily coded or playful communication, but it's usually effective enough for all that. Marr's narrative, *The Mad Man*, is one outcome of that assumption.

Why take the risk of communicating such (potentially) unwelcome messages? Delany demonstrates by results, most obviously in the 110-page letter which Marr sends to a straight-and-clueless friend from college. A novella of mystic awakening, the letter details Marr's urine-soaked sex life, reflects on its meaning in the time of AIDS, and also reflects on his need to describe it. True, his friend at first views the letter as evidence of insanity; but years later, after making a number of previously unimaginable changes in her own life, she finds it perfectly sensible.

Similarly, Tim Hasler's honesty about desire—his own and others—was the most important lesson given to his student, Pete Darmushklowksy, helping to transform Darmushklowksy from a frustrated boor to a contented sweetheart who, in turn, "everybody thinks [is] some kind of madman" because of his own honesty. Hasler's journal of "degrading" sexual encounters is an impetus for Marr's thoroughly fulfilling experiences with the homeless. Even "the Old Poet," Almira Adler, who through most of her life has repressed any interest in Hasler's sexual practices, hoping they would just go away, finishes by accepting (if not particularly enthusiastically) the value of "talking about things like that."

Or, more succinctly, if "SILENCE = DEATH," then "EXPRESSION = LIFE." John Marr has escaped death (not alone) to tell us, and to help us escape as well.

(Speaking of logically invalid generalizations. . . .)

VI. Postscript: What You Mean, "We"?

"What I look for in a friend is someone who's different from me. The more different the person is, the more I'll learn from him. The more he'll come up with surprising takes on ideas and things and situations."

—*The Mad Man* 239

One would almost think that they [straight white males] felt empowered to take anything the society produced, no matter how marginal, and utilize it for their own ends—dare we say "exploit it"?—certainly to take advantage of it as long as it's around. And could this possibly be an effect of discourse? Perhaps it might even be one we on the margins might reasonably appropriate to our profit . . . or perhaps some of us already have.

—Samuel R. Delany, "The Rhetoric of Sex, The Discourse of Desire"

An explicit motivation for this essay has been to draw attention to marginalized work.

Less pleasantly, and equally truthfully, one could say that this essay attempts to teach, by example, how to profitably distort areas of discourse which were not originally constructed for my (or perhaps your) benefit.

Let's look at the assumptions of the statement above: "to draw attention"—*whose* attention? The attention of a gay man who's into grime and golden showers? If so, I've done a piss-poor job.

The work is "marginalized" by whose standards? The standards of underground gay porn? The standards of science fiction? The standards of the *New York Times* bestseller list? For that matter, the standards of the housing projects down the street?

And what is "the reader" to make of the insistence throughout these pages that books which are clearly intended to be sexually stimulating can profitably be read without sexual stimulation? Well, clearly that would depend on just who "the reader" is. For that matter, my inattention to (for example) *The Mad Man*'s speculations on transmission methods of AIDS is unlikely to be typical of "the reader."

As *a* reader—as my particular type of class-crossing hetero white man, reading—I think highly of these books and often talk about them, in pretty much the same terms I've used here. I do so from a peculiarly privileged position, and that position is no more detached or trustworthy than it is when I take advantage of the other pleasures available to my particular type.

Nor, naturally, am I inclined to give any of these pleasures up.

I hope the one other reader who can be particularized—that is, you (*mon semblable, mon frère*, as I might write if you were a particular type of hetero white man)—will not be put off by this intrusion of the tediously taxonomical. Because if any one formula can explain how Delany's porn fits (and doesn't fit) into academe's and the press's particular systems of the world, why it's confiscated at borders and why you may not be allowed to read it at all, it's this: that in their painstaking and pleasureful assumption of centrality, the books resist easy appropriation.

Nevertheless, I recommend the attempt—which could be called, more pleasantly, and equally truthfully, communication.

Notes

1. Or even to the "Postscript."
2. "The Scorpion Garden," *The Straits of Messina*, p.1.

3. For a contrasting view, I recommend Earl Jackson Jr.'s recent *Strategies of Deviance: Studies in Gay Male Representation* (Indiana University Press, 1995, p. 108–111). Jackson imagines my own reading, but then discards it as "the most impoverished interpretation of the text and the most ungenerous evaluation of Delany's achievement." Rather than taking the frelk's speech at face value, Jackson uses it to explore the Lacanian ramifications of a desire for that which explicitly lacks desire and an orientation which explicitly lacks sex.

4. The chapter is "The Stones of St. Mark," probably referring to the low-lives swarming below St. Mark's church as described in *The Stones of Venice*. It's safe to say that Ruskin's aesthetic is not Delany's; witness his reaction to a painting by Murillo: "Do not call this the painting of nature: it is mere delight in foulness. [. . .] We all know that a beggar's bare foot cannot be clean; there is no need to thrust its degradation into the light, as if no human imagination were vigorous enough for its conception." (*The Stones of Venice*, v. II, p. 194)

5. "The Politics of Desire in Delany's *Triton* and *Tides of Lust*," *Black American Literature Forum*, Summer 1984, pp. 49–56.

6. Published in *Quark/1*, ed. Samuel R. Delany and Marilyn Hacker, 1970.

7. K. Leslie Steiner, in "'The Scorpion Garden' Revisited" (*The Straits of Messina*, pp. 17–31), also notes the classically American prose of *Hogg*, although she oddly bypasses Hammett in favor of the more traditionally expressive and sentimental Raymond Chandler.

8. Hammett's Continental Op is described as "a bit of a monster" in *The Dain Curse*. Readers of *Hogg*, starting with Delany himself, have consistently applied the same term to that novel's characters. Also note that Blacky, the narrator of "We, In Some Strange Power's Employ . . ." is called "monster" at the end of the story.

9. Henry James's witticism at the expense of Baudelaire's *Flowers of Evil*—that if *this* is the ultimate evil, then the ultimate good must be "plumcake and eau de Cologne"—depends on confusing this aesthetic definition of "evil" with *ethical* "evil."

10. Among many other contemporary critics, Delany himself has discussed such codes at length—in his essay "Atlantis Revisited: Some Notes on Hart Crane," for example.

11. However, all quotes and page references are from the heavily revised (and impressively improved) 1995 paperback edition of *The Mad Man*.

12. The reader who finds the "surely self-evident reasons" of *The Mad Man*'s "Disclaimer" a bit disingenuous may be confirmed in her suspicion by *Equinox*'s thoroughly over-the-top "Note of Moral Intent," which assures us that "the dictates of the present's greater sense of moral responsibility" have been taken into account by adding "an even hundred years" to every age under 18 mentioned in the novel.

13. In a book so dedicated to violation of taboos, *The Mad Man*'s treatment of the sex industry seems oddly puritanical. Compare Pat Califia's "Whoring in Utopia": "Especially in utopia, there would be no reason for someone to play the martyr and try to be sexually satisfied [as defined by orgasm] by an act of charity. Cash would

even the bargain and keep the fetishist from becoming an erotic welfare case."
(*Public Sex*, 245) This resonates uncomfortably with Marr's self-characterization
as one who believes it's better to give than to receive. But since *The Mad Man* is a
book about academics and the homeless, some antagonism towards working stiffs
is probably unavoidable.

Editor's Note: One of the essays quoted herein, "Atlantis Revisited: Some Notes
on Hart Crane," will appear as "Atlantis Rose . . ." in *Longer Views*. Another,
"The Rhetoric of Sex, The Discourse of Desire" (not to be confused with the
former), appeared in *Heterotopia: Postmodern Utopia and the Body Politic*, ed.
Tobin Siebers, Ann Arbor: University of Michigan Press, 1994.

Subverted Equations

G. Spencer Brown's *Laws of Form* and
Samuel R. Delany's Analytics of Attention

KEN JAMES

I.

Statements tolerable at the beginning of arguments are not
acceptable as ends.

K. Leslie Steiner, *Tales of Nevèrÿon*[1]

On page 2 of Samuel R. Delany's *Dhalgren*, we encounter
a sentence which, if we are familiar with modernist fiction, carries a curious
resonance. The sentence—"The moon flung gold coins at her breasts"—
recalls a similar sentence from the first chapter of *Ulysses*: "On his wise
shoulders through the checkerwork of leaves the sun flung spangles, dancing
coins."[2] Notice that the former sentence does not merely allude to the latter,
but, like a mirror, inverts the value of its images: heavenly and mortal bodies
traditionally taken as primary, central and luminous are replaced by bodies
traditionally taken as secondary, marginal, and reflective.

And on page 721 of *Dhalgren*, we see that the concluding line of the
penultimate chapter—the one-word question, "Where?"—matches the concluding line of the penultimate chapter of *Ulysses*. But whereas *Ulysses* answers with Molly Bloom's terminal, unmediated, stream-of-consciousness
monologue, *Dhalgren* answers with a fragmented dialogue of marginal
texts, running down each page in a double column, framed by the offstage
activities of a pair of editors of dubious authority. This revaluation seems
to mimic in its form what the first revaluation indicated in its content—a
shift away from luminous singularity towards reflective multiplicity.

If these two examples suggest that a basic hierarchy of values in modernist
literature is being inverted, their deprivileged position within the text enacts
that revaluation. In *Ulysses*, allusions refer "back" to an original text or set of

texts that ground the entire enterprise: the experience of the coherence of the text is open only to readers with privileged access to the intellectual/cultural armature lying "beneath" it. In *Dhalgren*, the experience of the coherence of the text is open to any reader attentive to the play of sign relations "across" the text—and since the concepts of reflection and revaluation are explicitly supplied by the text, the above two allusions merely offer supplemental resonances to readers with a certain kind of literary background.

Indeed, by beginning with a discussion of these allusions, I have constructed a fiction which exactly reverses my own experience—for I read Delany's novel *first*. Only later did I encounter the "original" passages in *Ulysses*—where they struck me as so many reflections of an earlier, more "primary" text. But this was a primary text that refused its own authority, always giving back an image of secondary reflection, even though for me it had provided the primary illumination. The subjective effect of this was that of a resonantial loop, fully present in neither text alone, but cycling endlessly between them.

In *Flight from Nevèrÿon*, the third book in his four-volume sword and sorcery series, Return to Nevèrÿon, Delany sets up the conditions of my own idiosyncratic experience by placing an account of a real-life event (Delany's early-morning stroll through the Port Authority bus terminal) *after* the fictive passage (in "The Tale of Fog and Granite") which it supposedly inspired. For the reader encountering these two passages in the order in which they are given, all the resonances are in the "wrong" direction. We experience what "should" be the primary content of the tale (Delany's original experience, or at least its image in his journal) as a secondary reflection, while we experience what should be a reflection (the tale) as the original content. This reversal throws the authority of both passages into doubt, since it is plain that only the order of their appearance in the text has determined whether they express a "proper" referential relation, or a "paradoxical" one.[3]

As in *Dhalgren*, our apprehension of the ambiguous relation between these two passages is enhanced by explicit discussion in the text itself of the notions of content, image, and reflection. But while in *Dhalgren* this discussion is relatively spare and oblique, in *Flight* (and indeed in the Return to Nevèrÿon series as a whole) it is overt, explicit, and pervasive. Just about every major character, at some point or another, discourses at length on the topic—and once we have sufficiently internalized the concepts themselves, we can see that they inform and pervade nearly every page of the series. And while it is not necessary to know the textual source of this trope to enjoy its intricate play across the texts, nevertheless the tantalizing promise of greater knowledge impels us to seek other texts—to search for origins.

As it turns out, we need not search for long. In his Introduction to *Alyx*—the Gregg Press collection of Joanna Russ's sword and sorcery series—Delany reveals that the source of the content/image/reflection trope is *Laws of Form*, a mathematical treatise by G. Spencer Brown. Delany appropriates this trope to clarify what he sees as an essential relation between the genres of sword and sorcery and science fiction; namely, that "sword and sorcery represents what can, most safely, still be imagined about the transition from a barter economy to a money economy," while "science fiction represents what can most safely be imagined about the transition from a money economy to a credit economy."[4] Delany argues that this relation can be better understood if we read barter, money and credit as a set of systems which relate to one another as, respectively, an original content, an image of that content, and a reflection of the image—and that a society shifting from one system to another will experience that transition as a reversal of social values associated with the earlier system. We find an image of this argument in the second tale of the Nevèrÿon series, "The Tale of Old Venn," where Delany expands the descriptive field of the content/image/reflection trope to include not just the relations between different modes of economic exchange, but also the relations between different orders of experience, representation, and narrative, and even between different metaphysical discourses.

But if we read the above passages from *Dhalgren* and *Flight from Nevèrÿon* as expressing something typical about Delany's whole approach to extratextual sources, then we might expect that the content/image/reflection trope itself—no matter how powerful a descriptive tool it might seem to be—has not simply been appropriated wholesale. We might expect that it too has in some way been revalued. And indeed, in those same passages such a revaluation does seem to be taking place, a revaluation specifically affecting the first term of the series—the notion of an original "content."

Now, it is probably safe to say that the sort of reader who would be familiar with *Ulysses* would not, in all likelihood, be familiar with *Laws of Form* (and the fact that it is safe to say this is not without significance). I shall therefore review some key ideas and structural points in Spencer Brown's text before discussing their reappearance and revaluation in Delany's series. In my conclusion I shall re-read *Laws of Form* in light of Delany's critique.

II.

> . . . the determination of the complexity of a form depends, above
> all, on the choice of the simplest ground form, and in this choice
> lies a problem almost untouched by present-day topology.
>
> René Thom, *Structural Stability and Morphogenesis*

First published in Great Britain in 1969, then in the United States in 1972,
G. Spencer Brown's *Laws of Form* purported to offer a new calculus—a
new mathematical system with unique notation, axioms, and operations.
According to Spencer Brown, one could interpret this calculus as operating
at a "deeper" or "more fundamental" realm of mathematics than that
of Boolean algebra, the formal abstraction of algebras of logic and set
theory.[5] With its appeal to metaphysical intuition, the book was immediately
(albeit somewhat confusedly) hailed by such counterculture personalities
as Alan Watts and John C. Lilly as a way of approaching mysticism through
mathematics. At the same time, its formally rigorous argument (Spencer
Brown had studied under Russell and Wittgenstein) received a good deal
of scholarly attention from mathematicians and computer scientists. And it
sparked a raging debate in the pages of the highly technical *International
Journal of General Systems* which carried on well into the '80s. This debate
will have a direct bearing on our reading of Delany's reading of Spencer
Brown, but to make any sense of it we need to know something of the
mathematical discourse in which Spencer Brown's text is embedded.

An algebra generalizes an arithmetic by using variables to stand for
distinct entities (such as numbers, sets and set elements, and logical propositions), and then manipulating these variables according to operations which
hold true for all the entities under consideration. A Boolean algebra, in
turn, generalizes the laws of both set-theoretical and logical algebras, by
reducing—or elevating, depending on your theoretical bias—the shared
properties of these algebras to a collection of purely formal laws which
themselves have no representational content. For example, while propositions can be either "true" or "false," and elements can be either "members"
or "not members" of a given set, Boolean expressions can be either "0"
or "1"—a pair of values devoid of any particular content other than their
binary relation.

What Spencer Brown wants to know is, what is the *arithmetic* of Boolean
algebra? What are the distinct entities (not numbers, not sets and set
elements, not propositions) that are subsumed under the Boolean variables?

Notice that by even positing the existence of an arithmetic for a purely formal algebra—and by asserting furthermore that the entities of that arithmetic are in some way more "fundamental" than entities of other arithmetics—Spencer Brown implicitly locates the legitimacy of Boolean algebra in its movement towards a kind of ideal abstraction, rather than in the fact that it is derived from more recognizably representational systems; in effect, he posits an ontological hierarchy in which the formal ideal is privileged over the informal real.

Spencer Brown begins his argument by declaring that the Boolean postulates "can be seen to represent two simple laws of indication which, whatever the nature of their self-evidence, at least recommend themselves to the findings of common sense" (LF xiv). To long-time Delany readers, this appeal to common sense should be ringing bells of alarm, but let us not get ahead of ourselves. Briefly, the two laws are based on the idea of drawing distinctions. One draws a distinction by "severing" or "cleaving" one space from another—as when one inscribes a circle on a plane, or blows a soap bubble in the air, or passes temporally from the state before one drew the circle or blew the bubble to the state after one drew or blew, and so on. Spencer Brown suggests that on a formal or ideal level, these three kinds of distinction are the same—and his two laws express that notion of sameness. Using the mark " $\rceil$ " to indicate the "marked state" or "cross," and the blank "   " to indicate the "unmarked state" or "void," Spencer Brown puts forth his two laws as follows:

1. The law of calling: The value of the call made again is the value of the call [in notation,

$$(1) \qquad \rceil\,\rceil = \rceil$$

the "form of condensation"]; and

2. The law of crossing: The value of a crossing made again is not the value of the crossing [in notation,

$$(2) \qquad \overline{\rceil} =$$

the "form of cancellation"](LF 1–5).

Now, equation (1) does not mean that two equals one, but rather that two equivalent distinctions are, in the realm of ideal forms, identical. To give a metaphorical example (and if it troubles the reader, all the better): From an ideal point of view it does not matter whether you have two apples or one apple—they are both, formally, the "same apple." Moreover, even if you have just one apple, if you indicate it with its name and then indicate it again, these two indications are formally indistinguishable. And equation (2) does not express the idea of the double negative, but rather the idea that distinguishing an already-distinguished space from itself places one back in the unmarked state. Or, metaphorically, if you walk into a house, or a city, or a text, and then turn around and walk back out again, your journey—formally—cancels itself out. With these two laws and their typographical forms, Spencer Brown is able to generate strings of equations like:

As this string suggests, and as Spencer Brown proves in "Theorem 1" of his arithmetic, any well-formed expression can (apparently) be reduced to either the marked state or the unmarked state, thus (apparently) preserving the binary relationship at the heart of Boolean algebra. Using variables to stand for collections of marks and blanks, Spencer Brown goes on to prove, step by mathematical step, that this "primary algebra" does indeed generate Boolean algebra. The proof is rigorous, powerful, and convincing. By the time one reaches its conclusion, one is convinced that not just the empty Boolean values "0" and "1," but all similar binary oppositions can be formally reduced to the "first distinction" between the mark and the void. But, as we shall see, it is precisely the apparent extensibility of the argument that Delany calls into question.

The notions of content, image, and reflection first appear in Chapter 8, in which Spencer Brown uses his notation to metaphorically illustrate the relation of an algebra to its arithmetic:

> Of any expression e call e the content, call $\overline{e}\,$ the image, and call $\overline{\overline{e}}\,$ the reflexion. Since $\overline{\overline{e}} = e$, the act of reflexion is a return from an image to its content or from a content to its image . . . In the form of any calculus, we find the consequences in its content and the theorems in its image. (LF 42–3)

Which is simply to say that proving a theorem using algebraic variables is equivalent to—in the image of—demonstrating an arithmetical fact using the specific entities subsumed under those variables. Later, in his "Note" to Chapter 8, Spencer Brown elaborates:

> A demonstration, we remember, occurs inside the calculus, a proof outside. The boundary between them is thus a shared boundary, and what is approached, in either direction, according to whether we are demonstrating a consequence or proving a theorem. (LF 94)

In other words, a proof approaches certainty and a demonstration approaches exhaustiveness as each approaches the space of the other. But this idea clearly recalls—is in the image of—a passage in the Introduction, where Spencer Brown discusses the tendency of twentieth-century science to get tangled up in the problem of the presence of the perceiver:

> It becomes apparent that if certain facts about our common experience of perception, or what we might call the inside world, can be revealed by an extended study of what we call, in contrast, the outside world, then an equally extended study of the inside world will reveal, in turn, the facts first met with in the world outside: for what we approach, in either case, is the common boundary between them. (LF xix)

And at proof's end, Spencer Brown draws these two cloven spaces—the space of mathematical argument and the space of the physical universe—together:

> We see now that the first distinction, the mark, and the observer are not only interchangeable, but, in the form, identical. (LF 76)

The power of these passages, taken together in this way, is undeniable—and, yes, mystical. That they appear to be supported by an impeccably linear mathematical argument only adds to their power. But it must be noted that the order of the passages as I've presented them here is *not* the order in which they appear in the book. And only two of the passages appear within the mathematical argument itself. Yet the book's very structure seems to compel us to read these passages as though they are all informed, or pervaded, by the same linear argument—as though they can be shuffled into an order which suggests proof.

Laws of Form is divided into many textual frames. One must get through one Author's Note, two Prefaces, and an Introduction before arriving at the text "proper," which after just seventy-six pages gives way to a collection of Chapter Notes (half as long as the main text itself), two Appendices, and two Indexes. And, as we've just seen, these multiply-marginal texts are heavily dependent on one another for their own internal coherence. Another instance: the rules of proof governing the "central" mathematical argument are not formally justified until Appendix 2—and the significance of that justification is discussed not in the Appendix itself but in the preceding Chapter Notes. The overall effect of this interdependency is to give individual sections a greater apparent weight than they actually have—and to suggest that a rigorous proof of the ultimate reducibility of every conceivable distinction down to an original, ideal distinction has indeed been given. But *that* proof is nowhere to be found in the book. It resides instead within the cascade of resonances made possible by the book's intricately repetitive intratextual structure and activated by the reader's own tendency to find order in that repetition. It is, finally, not a proof at all, but rather a demonstration of a process—a specifically aesthetic process which depends precisely on the fact that to recross a textual space is *not* to cancel out the first crossing, that the value of a call made again is *not* the value of the call. And it is Spencer Brown's image of this process, as well as his structural method of generating it, which Delany appropriates and revalues in his own rigorously formal collection of marginal texts, the Return to Nevèrÿon series.

III.

> Imagine Plato's cave not simply overthrown by some philosophical movement but transformed in its entirety into a circumscribed area contained within another—an absolutely other—structure, an incommensurably, unpredictably more complicated machine. Imagine that mirrors would not be *in* the world, simply, included in the totality of all *onta* and their images, but that things "present," on the contrary, would be in *them.* Imagine that mirrors (shadows, reflections, phantasms, etc.) would no longer be *comprehended* within the structure of the ontology and myth of the cave . . . but would rather envelop it in its entirety, producing here and there a particular, extremely determinate effect.
>
> Jacques Derrida, *Dissemination*

The first overt reference to *Laws of Form* in Delany's fiction can be found about two-thirds of the way through *Dhalgren*. In this passage, the character called Reverend Amy preaches to the denizens of Bellona, the mysteriously burned-out Midwestern city within which most of the action of the novel takes place. During her sermon—which the protagonist of the novel, Kid, only hears in snatches—we get our first glimmer of what Delany's position might be vis-a-vis Spencer Brown's. Reverend Amy begins: " 'Who lives in this city? . . . Logicians love it here! . . . Here you can cleave space with a distinction, mark, or token, and not have it bleed all over you.' "(D 527) Later, when Reverend Amy is in mid-oration, Kid catches this fragment:

> " . . . of the crossing taken again is not the value of the crossing? Oh, my poor, inaccurate hands and eyes! Don't you know that once you have transgressed that boundary, every atom, the interior of every point of reality, has shifted

its relation to every other you've left behind, shaken and jangled within the field of time, so that if you cross back, you return to a very different space than the one you left?" (D 536)

Like the allusions to *Ulysses* mentioned earlier, these references to *Laws of Form* are, again, merely supplemental: the efficacy and coherence of the passages do not depend on prior knowledge of Spencer Brown's work. And as I've already mentioned, this is equally true of Delany's use of the content/image/reflection trope in the Return to Nevèrÿon series. But there his elaboration of the critical position implied in the above passages is so rigorous and systematic that if we *are* familiar with *Laws of Form*, we find we can read the entire series as an extended critique of the metaphysical grounding of the mathematical discourse in which Spencer Brown's calculus is embedded.

Our first encounter with Spencer Brown in the Nevèrÿon series comes with the second tale of the series, "The Tale of Old Venn." This tale seems to serve the function that Delany elsewhere has suggested most "second tales" serve in science fiction and fantasy series—as an explanatory account of the images in the first.[6] Certainly one cannot re-cross the space of the preceding tale, "The Tale of Gorgik," without spontaneously applying lessons learned in "Venn"; but this is of course the fundamental experience of reading the series as a whole. At the same time, by providing the first explicit discussion of the theoretical possibilities of the content/image/reflection trope, the tale also gives us an interpretive tool "that *precedes*, that prepares *for*, a later, intense image" (AS 229)—and indeed a whole encyclopedia of images. Moreover, the formal structure of the tale reappears in revalued form in subsequent tales—as, once again, the notion of content/image/reflection prepares us to recognize.

"Venn"—the very name recalls the Venn diagram, a visual method of representing the relations between sets, set elements, and universes of discourse. A brilliant, aged woman living in what appears to be a primitive observatory out on the margins of a port town in the Ulvayn Islands, Venn introduces many new ideas and inventions into Nevèrÿon's primitive universe of discourse, including celestial navigation, various kinds of writing, tools and machines, and certain mathematical proofs. Venn introduces most of these innovations rather offhandedly—in the case of this tale, as educational tools for the Ulvayn village children sent to Venn for daily lessons. During one such lesson, Venn presents a new idea to the three children present (two boys, Enin and Dell, and one girl, Norema), cryptically suggesting that there is something "funny" about this particular idea:

"I know something. I know how to tell you *about* it, but I don't know how to tell you *what* it is. I can show you what it does, but I cannot show you the 'what' itself." (TN 86–7)

As her examples indicate, this epistemologically problematic something "is" the repeated appearance, in several very different realms, of the notion of content/image/reflection as an organizing descriptive principle. Venn first shows the children that writing, when viewed through the Rulvayn boys' "belly mirrors," reverses itself—and that when this mirror-image is viewed through a second "belly mirror," not only does the writing reverse itself again, but one can now discern writing on the reverse side of the paper, which had previously been hidden from view (TN 87–8). Next, Venn tells three short tales: the first, of her terrifying encounter with a sea monster; the second, of her first breathless recounting of this encounter on the following night; and the third, of her later retellings, revised after evaluating the responses of her first audience (TN 88–9). Obviously this example suggests a mise-en-abyme image of the writing of the whole Return to Nevèrÿon series—which Delany has explicitly described as a self-critical narrative enterprise (RN 271). But a dilemma emerges as soon as we cross over from the act of narrating to the act of reading: for how are we to read the relation of this, Venn's *fourth* retelling, to its antecedents, which it summarizes and presents as examples of what so far appears to be a tripartite process? More to the point, what does it mean to us if our own "original experience" *is* the hearing of this fourth tale? Where are we to locate the original "content" from which the other two terms in the model emerge?

After listening attentively to Venn's account, Enin and Dell leap to draw the connection between Venn's first example and her second, with the girl Norema reluctantly completing the interpretation:

"What happened to you," Dell said, "was like the signs on the paper."
"And what you told the first night," said Enin, "was like what we saw in the first mirror, with its meaning all backward."
"And what you told again the next morning," Norema said, feeling rather like it was expected of her and terribly uncomfortable with the expectation, "was like what we saw in the second mirror. Something else entirely, with its own meaning."
"As much as mirrors and monsters can be alike," mused Venn, whose sudden distraction seemed one with Norema's discomfort. (TN 91)

Venn's closing comment suggests that while one may readily see the similarities between two different things (as the boys did), one cannot reduce that similarity to identity—an implicit critique of Spencer Brown, who, we remember, claimed that one could formally reduce the human subject and the mark of distinction down to the same ideal first distinction. At the same time, in this passage the problem of reduction is rather ingeniously linked to problems of gender representation within the rhetoric of patriarchal discourse: for, as Norema uncomfortably realizes, a kind of strange rhetorical inevitability seems to have placed her as the third term in a series of individual speakers, and is now compelling her to "follow the boys" and complete the analogy. But if we carry this notion of a "series" of speakers further, then Venn, the last speaker in the above passage (and whose "distraction" Norema identifies—accurately? or reductively?—with her own "discomfort"), occupies both the *fourth* position in the series—which we've already identified as problematic—and the position preceding the first, since she told the original tale. And if we carry the idea to its logical conclusion, then we must include my own reading of the text, my presentation of that reading to you, and your reading of this reading as the fifth, sixth, and seventh position in the series respectively—with Delany and Spencer Brown occupying positions somewhere at the other end. But the point, of course, is that there *is* no "end"—there is no original "content" which provides the ontological ground for all the rest. The problem begins with the positing (both in the sense of postulating and in the sense of positioning) of a "first term." For once this (wholly arbitrary) *postulation* has been made, where one chooses to *position* that first term can have gigantic consequences for the ontological hierarchy that grows out of it—as well as for the individuals who find themselves subsumed within this hierarchy, as Norema dimly realizes.

We find a reflection of this argument in Venn and Norema's discussion of economic systems. Since in Nevèrÿon's primitive economy there is no such thing as credit, Norema and Venn must take the content/image/reflection concept, which up to this point has been used as an interpretive tool, and try to apply it speculatively or predictively to generate the third term in the economic series—thus inventing credit on the spot (TN 102–3). But despite this apparent confirmation of the power of her model, Venn swiftly realizes that to use the model in speculative fictions rather than descriptions is to change the model's status—to re-position it within the hierarchy of terms which it itself describes/generates. When Norema goes on to speculate that perhaps men and women are the image and reflection (or reflection and image) of a plan for an "ideal human being" (TN 104–5), Venn immediately and vehemently denies this possibility:

> "Look girl: where *is* your 'ideal' plan? Floating in the clouds somewhere? *I*
> start with the real thing, like barter, words written on reed paper, an experience

at sea, and discuss what happens to their value when series of reflections occur. *You* start with a value—an ideal human being—that is the result of so many real and imagined people's real and imagined actions, and then try to say the people are a result of this value . . ." (TN 105–6)

At this point Venn launches into a fascinating and minutely detailed account of her experiences in the neighboring Rulvyn tribe—a tale which we must here forego, as its complex interrogation of Freudian and Lacanian conceptions of sexual development and representation places it well outside the scope of this essay. When Venn is through, she challenges her listener to "think about my idea until you see what's wrong with yours—and indeed you may find out in the process things wrong with mine as well" (TN 117). Norema then begins a series of experiments, observations, and speculations to try to discern the real nature of Venn's inexpressible principle—an exploration ending with a sudden insight into the structure of human signs which, in its intensity, approaches the mystical. Norema suddenly realizes that while

> the world in which images occurred was opaque, complete, and closed . . . this was not true of the space of examples, samples, symbols, models, expressions, reasons, representations, and the rest . . . everything and anything could be an image of everything and anything. (TN 121)

What Norema has discerned here is the endlessness—and beginningless-ness—of the content/image/reflection principle. She has discerned the one property of the principle that Venn's very first example hints at, but which Delany does not explicitly reveal: namely, that when you gaze into a reflection of a reflection, what you get is not just a revelation of hidden perspectives, but an image of an endless hall of mirrors.

Although Norema at first considers her new conception "a glorious and useless thing to know" (TN 121), we may speculate over whether it is in fact so useless. After all, it dissolves the problem of ontological hierarchies suggested by the first model, rendering Venn's materialist interpretation and Norema's Platonic interpretation as simply two possibilities to be chosen at will by the interpreter—with neither model carrying any epistemological privilege over the other. More to the point, if we leap ahead to the opening chapter of *Neveryóna*, we find that later in life Norema has herself become a storyteller, whose narrative technique—involving leaving several choices of interpretation to the listener—rather resembles Delany's own. Clearly, Norema has appropriated something vital and powerful from this vision.

But appropriation cuts both ways, as we learn at the tale's conclusion, where, in a fit of xenophobia, a group of Ulvayn men put a visiting foreign ship to the torch. The significance of this event is not revealed until the end of the very last tale of the book, where we learn that the ship had been full of women from the Western Crevasse, a land where the gender hierarchy favors women. Carrying this image back to the story under consideration, we now perceive the ghastly irony in the fact that the men probably learned their torching method from one of Venn's other tales (TN 134). But despite this cautionary concluding note, we cannot help but notice that "The Tale of Old Venn" has been presented as a kind of proto-feminist, materialist "reflection" of a Platonic dialogue. We have already seen one passage in which boys are merely accessories to the insights of the women. There are many other examples throughout the book. But if Venn's critique of Norema's Platonic model starts precisely with a critique of her arbitrary hierarchizing of men and women, then how are we to interpret the gender hierarchy of *this tale*?

Let us jump ahead to "The Tale of Potters and Dragons." Armed with Venn's analytical model, we find complex patterns of images and reflections in both the content and form of the tale. It opens with a dialogue—or rather, with two parallel monologues, for the characters have not yet met—between two citizens of Kolhari, the bustling capital city of Nevèrÿon. The first character, a potter named Zwon, while preparing to send his young apprentice Bayle on a business trip to the southern Garth Peninsula, celebrates the power of money to bring people together and make "us all one" (TN 163)—reversing an earlier argument made by Venn that money, an image of the items for which it is exchanged, tends to "flatten" those items (which can include people) into empty commodities (TN 101–2). This dialectic mirrors the theoretical debate over the status of algebraic variables—which can, we remember, be read as either "reducing" distinct entities down to empty combinatory values, or "elevating" them to a higher, more ideal realm. The second citizen, a shrewd businesswoman tellingly named Madame Keyne, argues with her young secretary (the now grown-up Norema, also being sent on a business trip to the Garth Peninsula) that "money draws to money" (TN 166)—recalling, though not reversing, Venn's earlier point that in a transition from barter to money, power tends to reorganize itself around those who have money (TN 93–4). At the end of the tale, we find a continuation of this dialogue—a genuine dialogue now, for Zwon and Madame Keyne have finally met. Only this time, the two have reversed their positions: Zwon now believes that money *divides* people by emphasizing the distinction between incomes over any other relationship that people might have, while Madame Keyne appears to be rid of her few misgivings about money, which, she tells Zwon, is "the greatest invention in the history of mankind" (TN 213). We can see, then, that this tale is framed by reflections: at its opening by two parallel monologues in which each speaker takes a position that mirrors positions found in an earlier tale, and at its close by a dialogue in which both participants have reversed their own positions.

But to discern just *why* these two characters have reversed themselves we must cross into the space of the embedded tale. In it we find that Bayle and Norema have in fact been sent on the *same* mission—to petition Lord Aldamir, the mysteriously absentee southern governor, for an import franchise of a popular children's toy, the little rubber balls which bounce their sinister way all through the "Nevèrÿon" series. Having boarded the same southbound ship, Bayle and Norema meet a third passenger named Raven, who turns out to be from the matriarchal Western Crevasse. And while Raven is clearly something of a female chauvinist, she is not completely blind to the workings of oppression and appropriation. When, after much wrangling, she consents to tell Norema and the crew her country's creation legend, she warns Norema that the men "will try to take it away from us, as men take everything from women in this strange and terrible land" (TN 117). But her warning must be taken with a grain of salt, since it is rooted in her society's prior construction of a devalued maleness—as her story of genesis amply demonstrates.

Raven's doubly-embedded tale posits Paradise as a kind of radical separatist-feminist space where two women, Jevim and Eif'h, tend the garden—with no man in sight. When Eif'h transgresses against her goddess-creator, the goddess mutilates her until she is "castrated"—she becomes a "broken woman," or "'man" (another parallel: woman/'man, Raven/Venn) (TN 182). Like *Laws of Form*, this story valorizes the act of drawing distinctions (TN 179). But like "The Tale of Old Venn," it critiques the notion that real distinctions can be reduced to ideality—or rather, it morally forbids it: the transgression for which Eif'h is punished is precisely her attempt to conceive of an ideal distinction (TN 180–81)—an image of Norema's attempt in "The Tale of Old Venn." But in Raven's legend the transgression is explicitly identified *with maleness* (though, significantly, this "maleness" is bestowed after the fact; the story reverses the order of events of the Judeo-Christian myth in a way which highlights the constructed nature and retroactive logic of the cultural valuation of gender). Thus, this embedded tale does explicitly what we have seen "The Tale of Old Venn" do implicitly: it subverts its own critique of essentialism by gendering both sides of the debate in a way which presupposes an essentialist ontology. In other words, the tale deconstructs itself.

On the other hand, by the end of the frame-tale Raven's warning has come true. Once the franchise has been revealed as an elaborate sham, leaving Bayle most likely dead and Norema and Raven wandering the southern province, two messages are sent back to their employers which precisely reverse the true events. Zwon is told that Bayle, tempted by the lack of constraints on his actions in the south, has run off with the meager funds the potter had given him; while Madame Keyne is told that Norema had been immediately set upon by bandits—and that even though she'd been saved by the "good and loyal workmen on the dock," her injuries were fatal (TN 210–12). Significantly, these two stories actually confirm the "worst fears" of both employers, who "know" how common such stories are. Zwon muses:

> "Truly the south is a strange and terrible land, where every evil we here in civilized Kolhari can imagine of it comes reflected back to us with an accuracy as perfect as the image in the belly-mirrors that the young men of the Ulvayn from time to time wear on our docks." (TN 212–13)

Nevèrÿon's patriarchal discourse has appropriated the true story, reversed its value, and linked those new values to an implicit message about money: that men, in their autonomy, should be given more of it, and women, in their helplessness, should be kept away from it.

But this new message has not discouraged Madame Keyne, who, we learn, intends to make a killing by replacing Kolhari's ubiquitous three-legged cooking pots with new *four*-legged pots (TN 209). This can be read as an image of the transition from a three-termed interpretive model—which always rests on an original "ground"—to a four-termed (or many-termed) model—which always wobbles between at least two positions in an endless dialectical process. And just as Norema's appropriation of Venn's model and Raven's internalization of her society's metaphysics allow them both to resist—or at least recognize—Nevèrÿon's patriarchal discourse, so too does Madame Keyne's invention allow her to resist the implicitly patriarchal message she has just received—by making a lot of money.

Leaving the last narrative frame of "The Tale of Potters and Dragons," we may believe that we have reached the outermost discursive "space" of the text. But when we reach the text's final Appendix, we find that we were mistaken. Like its formal precursors, the two Appendices to *Triton* (a novel peppered with epigraphs from Spencer Brown's text), this Appendix provides information which partially explains, as well as disrupts, everything that has come before. We learn here that all of the tales we've just read had originally been "inspired" by the recent translation (actually a fourth, comparative translation of three earlier translations—another image of Venn's tales) of an ancient text called the "Culhar' fragment," by the young mathematician K. Leslie Steiner. Just as Steiner's pen name recalls Spencer Brown's, her scholarly work is clearly an image of *Laws of Form*—with certain fundamental revaluations. First, Steiner posits that mathematical language, rather than being more primary than everyday language, is in fact preceded and pervaded by it: " ' "counting," as it were, presupposes "language," and not the other way around' " (TN 255). This exactly reverses Spencer Brown's position that Boolean algebra transcends the representational forms from which it arose. Second, Steiner's model of language itself—as a complex collection of "noncommutative substitution loops"—clearly recalls Norema's experience of the endless substitutability of semiotic associations: which endlessness, we recall, critiques Spencer Brown's notion of a primary "content" (TN 254–55). Thus Steiner's text both logically frames *Laws of Form* (by revealing the hidden discursive ground of its mathematical argument) while remaining marginal to it (as its fictive image), its ambiguous relation to that other text as both image and critique rendering both texts equally problematic. Furthermore, because Steiner's linguistic model does not generate a simple nomenclature, but rather a complex set of intersecting metonymic loops, any translation utilizing this model must involve selecting from among many terms present in a given "loop." This suggests a provisional fictive explanation for the apparent gendering of "The Tale of Old Venn," since we know from the Appendix (not written by Steiner, but by *another* fictive academic) that Steiner may incline towards a feminist translation: "since the sex of the narrator of a sexually unspecified text is always a fifty-fifty possibility, I simply take my choice, which is consistent with the rest of my work" (TN 258). On the other hand, since Delany would have us understand that the tales are his *interpretation* of Steiner's translation, this perceived gendering may *reverse* Steiner's "real" translation (all of which recalls the editorial "tampering" in the final chapter of *Dhalgren*). Thus, the "explanation" the Appendix provides does not close the issue, but opens it further—finally eliminating the possibility of locating an original, privileged interpretation.

Near the center of the series—towards the end of the second book, *Neveryóna*—we find an image of Steiner's (and, by extension, Venn's) problematic project, as well as an unexpectedly direct statement of the relation of the series as a whole to its mathematical antecedent. At the conclusion to Chapter Eleven, the southern earl Jue-Grutn presents the heroine Pryn with a short discourse on the origins of writing. Reviewing in turn a collection of tokens, an image of those tokens inked on reed fiber, and a reflection of those images branded on a dried strip of flesh, Jue-Grutn speculates that each writing sample can be interpreted as an aesthetic artifact, an objective description, or an ideological construction. But to discern their relation to one another within a hierarchical order of authority—and thus to discern what pattern of appropriation might have obtained between them—one must decide which sample is the original: "Which one of the three inspired, which one of the three contaminated, which one of the three first valorized the subsequent two in our cultural market of common conceptions?" (N 302). Jue-Grutn will ultimately conclude that one cannot know. But prior to this conclusion, while speculating about what it might mean if the original writing had been a disinterested description of an objective state of affairs, Jue-Grutn—right in the center of his monologue—asks:

> "Suppose . . . another scribe was dazzled by the coolness of the disinterest enough to realize how beauty burns over and around that rigid, frigid abstraction and so created a scorching rendition to tease and terrify us with its ever-proliferating suggestions for further readings?" (N 303)

Standing outside the space of the novel, we know that this rhetorical question directly indicates that "other text" against which this text stands in a complex mirror-relation—though Jue-Grutn, "inside" the text, cannot know this. By the same token, we observe that Jue-Grutn's monologue, in reviewing three samples of writing and itself being embedded in a problematic fourth, is yet another image of Venn's discussion of tale-telling—but with a difference: while Venn might be able to recognize the pattern her fourth retelling generates, Jue-Grutn, completely constituted *by* that fourth text, cannot recognize it as we do. But even his incomplete description of an originary and pervasive archi-writing inspires in Pryn a vision of a potential infinity of meanings, which recalls both the image of Norema's childhood vision of the simultaneous opacity of the world and the unboundedness of the "space of examples," as well as an image from a tale which the adult Norema had told Pryn at the opening of *Neveryóna*—and presents an unnervingly accurate image of the staggering density and complexity of the reflections and counter-reflections we have been observing at this particular point in the text (N 305–8).

But if *Neveryóna* leaves us dazzled by a vision of unlimited semiosis, both *Flight from Nevèrÿon* and *Return to Nevèrÿon* present a considerably darker vision, in which images become counterfeits and reflections become distortions. These tales are veritable fugues of misrecognitions, misunderstandings, and misremembrances. To pick only the most obvious examples (one could go on indefinitely): the young smuggler's obsessive gathering of information about Gorgik the Liberator in "The Tale of Fog and Granite" mirrors the Master's quixotic quest for information about Belham the inventor in "The Tale of Plagues and Carnivals"; the Master's misremembering of events on his quest mirrors Gorgik's misremembering, in "The Game of Time and Pain," of the mines from which he himself had originally been liberated; and the smuggler's misrecognition of Gorgik in "Fog and Granite" mirrors the barbarian Udrog's misrecognition of him in "Time and Pain."

This last example is worth pursuing a little further. We know that the smuggler's and Udrog's misrecognitions both arise from the same source, namely, a highway thief who has been impersonating Gorgik in order to dupe unwary travellers. Furthermore, the thief knows that he can pass himself off as Gorgik in his later encounter with Udrog, because, even though he'd lost an eye to Raven's double-bladed sword in his earlier encounter with the smuggler, he still fits one of the many conflicting descriptions of Gorgik (RN 25). But what the thief does not know is that these conflicting descriptions have been deliberately engineered by Gorgik's one-eyed lover Noyeed (an image of his earlier lover, Sarg) gone out into the land to impersonate him and thus create an "all-pervasive fog" of confusion around him (FN 16). And what very few people in all of Nevèrÿon know, except perhaps the very powerful and the very marginal, is that Gorgik had originally appropriated this strategy of obfuscation from the absentee Lord Aldamir of the southern province, whom we have already (not) encountered in "The Tale of Potters and Dragons." Clearly, the double- (or is it quadruple-?) edged sword of reflection and appropriation has reappeared in these last tales with a vengeance. Even Gorgik, master appropriator though he is, admits that he is confounded by the proliferation of reflections that the world—and his own self—present to him:

> "All I could come to . . . was that, years before . . . I had looked into a mirror, recognized that mirror for what it was, and seized the image within it for my use. Now, at a sudden turn of chance, in need of an image to seize, I'd glimpsed that what I'd thought were mirrors and images and an 'I' looking into and at them were really displaced, synthetic, formed of intersecting images in still other mirrors I'd never noticed before—mirrors whose angle, tactility, and location, because there were so many of them, because they were visible only through what was reflected of them in other mirrors, I couldn't hope to determine (much less locate a coherent pattern in which to place them), much less determine which, if any, were real and which were merely intersections in others." (RN 93)

But where does this leave us, the readers? Are we, too, confounded by these reflections—blinded by their brilliance as Norema is blinded, briefly, by a reflection of sunlight from an Ulvayn belly-mirror (TN 104)? In the end, are we only able to apprehend each new image put before us as "some endlessly shimmering sign, whose clear and concise meaning in the weave and play of meanings is merely terrifying rather than illuminative" (FN 261)? Gazing into this hall of mirrors, what image within can we seize for our own use?

Here we would do well to recall Spencer Brown's reminder, near the end of his argument, that "we are, and have been all along, deliberating the form of a single construction . . . notably the first distinction" (LF 68). We must remind ourselves that we have, all along, been deliberating the relation between two constructions, Delany's and Spencer Brown's. To discern the value of our crossing through Delany's texts, let us return, briefly, to *Laws of Form*.

IV.

What is revealed will be concealed, but what is concealed will again be revealed.

G. Spencer Brown, *Laws of Form*

We recall that subsequent to its publication, *Laws of Form* became the subject of intense debate in the pages of the *International Journal of General Systems*, a periodical devoted to original research in the mathematical modelling of complex systems. Many of the contributors to the debate saw *Laws of Form* as an exciting and unprecedented contribution to the field of general systems, and used Spencer Brown's calculus to generate new models of networks and finite automata, and even to develop new axiomatic systems. Others saw *Laws of Form* as simply Boolean algebra written in a peculiar—and even misleading—notation. I submit that we can read this debate as an image of the debate that has grown up around Delany's work over the last few decades. I submit further that our reading can profit from precisely the exploration and critique of the content/image/reflection trope which Delany has undertaken, and which we have reviewed here.

Interestingly, both Spencer Brown's champions and his detractors often begin their arguments by translating his notation into more "familiar" algebraic forms; thus, the mark " ⌐ " becomes a "1," and the blank "   " becomes a "0," as in standard two-valued Boolean algebra. But if we accept this translation as valid, it becomes difficult to ignore the detractors, who offer convincing arguments that once it is reinscribed in classical notation, Spencer Brown's system is indeed isomorphic to Boolean algebra. But is this reinscription valid? Let us look to Paul Cull and William Frank's rather cantankerous critique of *Laws of Form*, which presents the most detailed discussion of the problem of translating Spencer Brown's typography. Although Cull and Frank actually change their minds in mid-argument about how to interpret Spencer Brown's calculus, both of their interpretations involve a general critique of Spencer Brown's use of the blank " " in his equations. They argue that equation (2), "⌐ = ", uses the blank space on the right side of the equation as if it is a symbol, not a true void—in which case it becomes possible to interpret any empty space in a given equation as potentially containing many "blank symbols."[7] But if Spencer Brown's equations are not to be "infinitely ambiguous," the blank must be interpreted as simply an unclear way of indicating a single constant, in which case one must interpret the mark and the blank as constants in a two-valued logic. Cull and Frank thus conclude, along with several other mathematicians in the debate, that Spencer Brown's calculus is merely a "confusing" or "obscure" way of writing ordinary Boolean algebra.

At this point I simply cannot resist quoting Delany's response to a particularly vituperative review of one of his own more "confusing" and "obscure" works: "I wonder if it doesn't mean something when the most violent detractor hits the point precisely."[8] For while Cull and Frank are correct in considering the blank problematic, they miss the mark, as it were, in interpreting the blank as a constant, and consequently miss what is truly radical about Spencer Brown's project. Louis H. Kauffman, in a brief and elegant refutation of Cull and Frank's argument in the *Mathematical Review*, provides the key to understanding both the real status of the blank and the reason why Cull and Frank must interpret it the way they do. Using a model Spencer Brown himself spends much time exploring (LF 69–76), Kauffman interprets the expressions in the calculus as representing collections of embedded circles on a plane—in which case it becomes immediately apparent that one cannot have a "blank space" without a circle somewhere demarcating it: the relation between the mark and the blank is not truly a binary relation, but a container/contained relation. Blanks become "ambiguous" only if one reinscribes the mark and the blank into a more classical notation which obliterates their fundamental relational property. The point is that "a notion of 'many blanks' has arisen the moment we use a symbol . . . for the blank. It arises in the descriptive context."[9] This explains why Cull and Frank, later in their argument, must resort to using parentheses to convey the concept of embedded marks and blanks:

one cannot literally embed a "0" inside a "1." Thus, Kauffman explains, the key to interpreting the calculus correctly lies in understanding that all expressions within it "stand for purely local situations that occur in larger collections" of expressions.

Do we find any equivalents to Kauffman's statement in *Laws of Form* itself? Yes, we do: immediately after his introduction of the concepts of content, image, and reflection, Spencer Brown mentions in passing that "an unwritten cross is common to every expression in the calculus of indications and so need not be written" (LF 43). Although Spencer Brown himself does not elaborate on this remark, we have just seen that it is absolutely crucial in preserving the coherence of his notation—and more specifically, that it does indeed refute Cull and Frank's argument, since the disquieting "blank space" on the right side of equation (2) turns out to be implicitly "framed" by an unwritten mark:

$$\overline{\overline{\,\rceil\,}} = \overline{\,\rceil\,}$$

But this new understanding will have an absolutely shattering effect on our interpretation of the calculus as a whole. For if every expression in the calculus is understood to be framed by an unwritten mark, then there is no limit to the number of outer frames in which a given expression can be said to be embedded:

$$\overline{\overline{\,\rceil\,}}\,...$$

Which in turn means that when we reduce an expression down to its "unique value," we are really only reducing it down to the value indicated within the unwritten mark. If we decided to write that mark in, the value would reverse itself; if we added the next one, the value would reverse itself again, and so on.

Thus, to reduce any expression in Spencer Brown's calculus down to a single value is equivalent to suppressing knowledge of a frame.

Clearly this is an image of the interpretive dilemma Delany's work presents to us. For, as we have seen, to try to trace out any single privileged interpretation through the texts one must in effect ignore the elaborate destabilizing frames which Delany has set up around/within them. And it is precisely this sort of interpretive activity that has led some of Delany's critics to insist—rather as Spencer Brown's critics have insisted that his calculus is just a typographically obscure Boolean algebra—that Delany's texts are merely stylistically obscure fantasies.[10] But this sort of interpretive activity is just an image of thematic criticism in general, which tries to isolate as an object of analysis—by interpretive methods which are restricted to what is allowable within one's given discourse—what is really a dialectical process of image and reflection. Thus it becomes clear why Spencer Brown's scholarly readers, operating within an institutionally sanctioned (and therefore conservative) discourse, *must* ignore the fundamental properties of his calculus and interpret it as a form of Boolean algebra, just as Delany's critics within the sf field must ignore the real readerly effects of his texts in order to interpret them according to a pre-existing template for the "well-formed" sf or fantasy story. Both Delany's and Spencer Brown's texts generate a situation which *reveals* a certain kind of interpretation to be equivalent to an act of *concealment*.

Along similar lines, we can expand on our earlier statement that finding a single value for expressions in Spencer Brown's calculus is equivalent to concealing the presence of a frame, and say that to interpret Spencer Brown's calculus as a two-valued logic is equivalent to concealing a relation that is not binary, but hierarchical. But this, of course, is an image of the concealment of hierarchy behind binarism that deconstructive criticism works to reveal. Spencer Brown's calculus can thus be read as a mathematical image of Derrida's logic of the trace, dropped into the binary stronghold of algebraic discourse—the effect of which has been the commencement of an ongoing dialogue between the conservative and progressive voices within, and the revelation of the discursive limits within which the dialogue operates. But Spencer Brown's text does not reside wholly outside the discourse, just as it does not reside wholly within it: as Delany's critique indicates, Spencer Brown's text is itself grounded in a conception of the metaphysics of mathematics which is not necessarily incompatible with the root-assumptions of the discourse it critiques—so any limit it reveals, it reveals at least partially from within. But this is just another image of deconstruction. In the Appendix to *Tales of Nevèrÿon*, Delany, ostensibly discussing Steiner's work (in the persona of the evocatively named conservative academic S. L. Kermit), addresses the problem of the status of Spencer Brown's:

> The question must finally be: Are Steiner's equations the expressions of a conservative collective speech, which would certainly seem to be the case with any probability work concerning myth and language; or, are they the expression of a radical individualistic authority—which seems, at any rate, to be the collective view of mathematical creativity, if not authorship/authority itself. (TN 260)

This self-deconstructing passage expresses the dialectic which Delany's analytical engine has set in motion, and, needless to say, of which it itself—neither wholly inside nor wholly outside its own discursive field—is constituted. And the readerly experience of this dialectical oscillation is not one of reassurance, of inevitability, of learning yet again what one already knows—but rather of ongoing recognition and revelation: that is, the experience of insight itself.

In *Laws of Form* we find a striking image of the kind of deconstruction/revelation that Delany's texts generate, as well as a model of the ungrounded ontology from which they generate it. Very early in his argument, Spencer Brown reminds us that just as expressions can be simplified, they also can be made more complex (LF 9–10)—which means that equations can be read from right to left as well as from left to right. Thus, by equation (1), any mark can generate an infinite number of "twins." And by equation (2), any blank (which we now know to be enclosed/defined by a mark) can be thought of as infinitely "productive," as concealing within itself an infinitely deep echelon of marks:

But if we connect this image with our earlier notion of the infinite number of unwritten frames which can be revealed to reside *outside* of any expression, then we see that any mark, and by extension any expression, can be understood to rest in a potentially infinite "corridor" of unwritten distinctions:

And this is quite literally an image of Delany's hall of mirrors. It is an image of what we are really doing when we call any distinction the first distinction, any content the primary content, any ontological ground *the* ontological ground: we are positioning ourselves within an unbounded field of possible revelations by performing a complex act of concealment. The act may be willed by us, or the act may be heavily determined by the discourse in which we are embedded (a dialectic with which we are now familiar); but in either case, we are suppressing revelation in the interests of intelligibility. But this process of reduction is just an image of language itself, which, as Delany says in his essay "Shadows," does not so much differentiate entities as indicate "any number of *different* things in the *same* way" (JHJ 117); thus it is also an image of any critical interpretation, any algebra, or any coin. The problem then becomes one of how to discern when this reduction shades over into oppression—for which a calculus grounded in the notion of ideal distinctions may not provide the optimum interpretive method. As Reverend Amy says in *Dhalgren*: "What we need is not a calculus of form but an analytics of attention, which renders form on the indifferent and undifferentiated plurima" (D 527).

Toward the end of his argument, Spencer Brown devises a complex method for generating infinitely extended expressions.[11] In these expressions he discerns a property which we have already seen to be potentially present in every expression in the calculus: namely, the property of indeterminate value. Such expressions, Spencer Brown argues, can be read as oscillating in time between two values, as alternately "transparent" and "opaque" to the space outside the expressions—an image of the dialectical process. Spencer Brown calls this property of oscillation a *subversion* (LF 62). But if every expression has this property, then every expression is a subverted expression—which Spencer Brown himself seems to realize, though he appears unwilling to pursue the idea. In his discussion of the phenomenology of distinction, following his discussion of subversion, Spencer Brown notes in passing that "in these experiments the sign ' = ' may stand for the words 'is confused with' " (LF 69). But this is just a restatement of the process of reduction-shading-into-oppression that we discerned above. And like his previous passing comment about the unwritten mark (are we now beginning to see why Spencer Brown can *only* make these comments in passing, why he *must* deprivilege them within the mathematical context which legitimates his argument?), this comment indicates a property which completely alters our view of the calculus as a whole: the property that not a single equating of one so-called distinction with another, be it the ideal first distinction, the mark, or the observer, is a perfect equating—that every equation in the calculus of indications is a subverted equation.

In her essay "A Cyborg Manifesto," Donna Haraway mentions her indebtedness to Delany's writing, and to *Tales of Nevèrÿon* in particular, for being part of a group of texts which had provided much of the inspiration for her own conception of a radical political project founded in the celebration of the "confusion of boundaries" and the "leaky distinction"—in the transgressive crossing of borders between realms of knowledge and practice which discursive and coercive systems would endeavor to keep separate.[12] Clearly, Delany's deconstruction of *Laws of Form* makes such a crossing. The value of that crossing to us, standing in the space of the humanities, is the illumination of a whole realm of mathematical discourse (and more importantly, its limits) that might otherwise have remained concealed and opaque. The brilliance of this illumination—and all of its reflections in other discourses, other texts—is a tribute to Delany's ingenious appropriation/contribution. But a critical essay such as mine can only present a much-reduced account of this illumination—and what it suppresses in that account may ultimately be more important than what it privileges. For an incomparably richer experience of this illumination, then, the reader must turn away from my reflections and—here I echo the words of K. Leslie Steiner in her (authorial? or authoritarian?) "Preface" to the whole series—return to Nevèrÿon.

Notes

1. All page references to the Return to Nevèrÿon series are to the Wesleyan University Press/University Press of New England editions:

> *Tales of Nevèrÿon* (Hanover: University Press of New England, 1993), abbreviated TN;
>
> *Neveryóna* (Hanover: University Press of New England, 1993), abbreviated N;
>
> *Flight from Nevèrÿon* (Hanover: University Press of New England, 1994), abbreviated FN;
>
> *Return to Nevèrÿon* (Hanover: University Press of New England, 1994), abbreviated RN.

All references to *Dhalgren* (abbreviated D) are to the Grafton Books edition, published in London in 1992.

Here I must give my heartfelt thanks to Samuel R. Delany himself, who very generously provided me with copies of his more difficult-to-find criticism and fiction throughout the writing of this essay.

2. James Joyce, *Ulysses* (New York: Random House, Vintage Books, 1986), 30.

3. The same can be said of epigraphs at the beginning of critical essays.

4. Reprinted in *The Jewel-Hinged Jaw* (New York: Berkley Publishing Corporation, 1978), 197–8 (abbreviated JHJ).

5. G. Spencer Brown, *Laws of Form* (New York: Bantam Books, 1973), xiv (abbreviated LF).

6. *The American Shore* (Elizabethtown, New York: Dragon Press, 1978), 229 (abbreviated AS).

7. Paul Cull and William Frank, "Flaws of Form." *International Journal of General Systems* 5 (1979): 202.

8. Delany is here responding, in *The Straits of Messina* ([Seattle: Serconia Press, 1989], 38), to Harlan Ellison's review of *Dhalgren*.

9. Louis H. Kauffman, review of "Flaws of Form," *Mathematical Reviews* 81e:00007 (May 1981): 1620.

10. See, for example, Darrell Schweitzer's review of *Neveryóna* in *Science Fiction Review*, Vol. 12, No. 3, August 1983: 46.

11. I would argue that Spencer Brown actually devises a much simpler method early in Chapter 6, with Consequence 4, interestingly named the "Occultation" or

"Conceal/Reveal" function. All one has to do is write in the unwritten mark around the expression, and one gets a construction identical to, and expandable in the same way as, the step-generating sequence in Chapter 11.

12. Donna Haraway, "A Cyborg Manifesto," in *Simians, Cyborgs, and Women* (New York: Routledge, Chapman, and Hall, Inc., 1991), pp. 173–78, 150, 152.

SELECTED BIBLIOGRAPHY

For a more complete bibliography see *Samuel R. Delany: A Primary and Secondary Bibliography, 1962–1979* by Michael Peplow and Robert S. Bravard, Boston: G.K. Hall & Co., 1980. A supplement to this, also by Peplow and Bravard, appeared in *Black American Literature Forum*, Summer 1984, Vol. 18, No. 2, ed. Joe Weixlmann.

Fiction

Atlantis: Three Tales. Hanover and London: Wesleyan University Press, 1995. (Also as a first, limited edition from Seattle: Incunabula, 1995.) Contains the novel *Atlantis: Model 1924* and two stories, "*Citre et Trans*" and "Erik, Gwen, and D.H. Lawrence's Esthetic of Unrectified Feeling."

Hogg. Boulder and Normal: Fiction Collective Two/Black Ice Books, 1995.

The Mad Man. New York: Richard Kasak Books, 1994.

They Fly at Çiron. Seattle: Incunabula, 1993.

Return to Nevèrÿon. Hanover and London: Wesleyan University Press, 1994. Corrected edition of the 1986 volume *The Bridge of Lost Desire*. Contains the novel *The Game of Time and Pain* and two stories, "The Tale of Rumor and Desire" and "The Tale of Gorgik."

Flight from Nevèrÿon. Hanover and London: Wesleyan University Press, 1994. Corrected edition of the 1985 volume of the same title. Contains the novels *The Tale of Fog and Granite* and *The Tale of Plagues and Carnivals* plus "The Mummer's Tale."

Neveryóna. Hanover and London: Wesleyan University Press, 1993. Corrected edition of the 1983 volume of the same title.

Tales of Nevèrÿon. Hanover and London: Wesleyan University Press, 1993. Corrected edition of the 1979 volume of the same title. Contains "The Tale of Gorgik," "The Tale of Old Venn," "The Tale of Small Sarg," "The Tale of Potters and Dragons," and "The Tale of Dragons and Dreamers."

Driftglass/Starshards. London: HarperCollins/Grafton Books, 1993. Collected short fiction. Contains "Of Doubts and Dreams, An Introduction," "The Star Pit," "Corona," "Aye, and Gomorrah . . . ," "Driftglass," "We, in Some

Strange Power's Employ, Move on a Rigorous Line," "Cage of Brass," "High Weir," "Time Considered as a Helix of Semi-Precious Stones," "Omega-helm," "Prismatica," "Ruins," "Dog in a Fisherman's Net," "Night and the Loves of Joe Diconstanzo," "Among the Blobs," *"Citre et Trans,"* "Erik, Gwen, and D.H. Lawrence's Esthetic of Unrectified Feeling."

Stars in My Pocket Like Grains of Sand. New York: Bantam Books, 1984.

Distant Stars. New York: Bantam Books, 1981. Stories.

Triton. New York: Bantam Books, 1976. Both *Triton* and *Dhalgren* are scheduled for reissue by Wesleyan University Press.

Dhalgren. New York: Bantam Books, 1975.

Equinox. New York: Richard Kasak/Rhinoc*eros Books, 1994. Originally published under the title *Tides of Lust.* New York: Lancer Books, 1973.

Driftglass. New York: NAL/Signet, 1971. Stories.

Nova. New York: Bantam Books, 1987. Originally published in 1968.

The Einstein Intersection. New York: Bantam Books, 1981. Originally published in 1967.

Empire Star. New York: Bantam Books, 1983. Originally published in 1966.

Babel–17. New York: Bantam, 1984. Originally published in 1966.

The Complete Nebula Award Winning Fiction of Samuel R. Delany. New York: Bantam Books, 1986. Omnibus volume containing *Babel–17, A Fabulous, Formless Darkness* (originally published as *The Einstein Intersection*) plus the short stories "Aye, and Gomorrah . . ." and "Time Considered as a Helix of Semi-Precious Stones."

The Ballad of Beta–2. New York: Bantam Books, 1982. Originally published in 1965.

The Fall of the Towers. New York: Bantam Books, 1986. One-volume edition of the trilogy of novels *Out of the Dead City* (originally published in 1963), *The Towers of Toron* (1964) and *City of a Thousand Suns* (1965).

The Jewels of Aptor. New York: Bantam Books, 1978. Originally published in 1962.

Nonfiction

Longer Views. Hanover and London: Wesleyan University Press, 1995. Contains six essays: "Wagner/Artaud," "Aversion/Perversion/Diversion," "Reading at Work, and Other Activities Frowned on by Authority: A Reading of Donna Haraway's 'Manifesto for Cyborgs'," "Shadow and Ash," "Atlantis Revisited," and "Shadows."

Silent Interviews: On Language, Race, Sex, Science Fiction, and Some Comics. Hanover and London: Wesleyan University Press, 1994. Selected written interviews.

The Straits of Messina. Seattle: Serconia Press, 1989. Essays.

Wagner/Artaud: A Play of 19th and 20th Century Critical Fictions. New York: Anzatz Press, 1988. 80-page monograph.

The Motion of Light in Water: Sex and Science Fiction in the East Village, 1957–1965. New York: Arbor House/Morrow, 1988. Autobiography.

The Motion of Light in Water: East Village Sex and Science Fiction Writing, 1960–1965. London: Grafton Books, 1990. This British edition is thoroughly revised and expanded by more than a hundred pages.

The Motion of Light in Water: Sex and Science Fiction in the East Village. New York: Richard Kasak/Masquerade Books, 1993. A further revision of the British edition above.

Starboard Wine: More Notes on the Language of Science Fiction. Pleasantville, NY: Dragon Press, 1984. Essays.

The American Shore: Meditations on a Tale of Science Fiction by Thomas M. Disch—"Angouleme." Elizabethtown, NY: Dragon Press, 1978. Book-length semiotic analysis of Disch's story.

The Jewel-Hinged Jaw: Notes on the Language of Science Fiction. Elizabethtown, NY: Dragon Press, 1977. Essays. A corrected edition was published by Berkeley-Putnam/Windhover Books, 1978.

Heavenly Breakfast: An Essay on the Winter of Love. Flint, MI: Bamberger Books, 1995. Memoir of various urban communes and co-ops during 1967. Originally published in 1978.

Secondary Works

Barbour, Douglas. *Worlds out of Words: The Science Fiction Novels of Samuel R. Delany.* Frome, England: Bran's Head Books, 1979.

Fox, Robert Elliot. *The Conscientious Sorcerers: The Black Postmodernist Fiction of LeRoi Jones/Amiri Baraka, Ishmael Reed and Samuel R. Delany.* New York: Greenwood Press, 1987.

McEvoy, Seth. *Samuel R. Delany.* New York: Frederick Ungar Publishing Co., Inc., 1984.

Moylan, Thomas M. *Demand the Impossible: Science Fiction and the Utopian Imagination.* London: Methuen, Inc., 1986.

Peplow, Michael W. and Bravard, Robert S. *Samuel R. Delany: A Primary and Secondary Bibliography, 1962–1979.* Boston: G.K. Hall & Co., 1980.

Slusser, George E. *The Delany Intersection: Samuel Delany Considered as a Writer of Semi-Precious Words.* San Bernardino, CA: Borgo Books, 1977.

Weedman, Jane Branham. *Samuel R. Delany.* Starmont Reader's Guide Series, No. 10. Mercer Island, WA: Starmont House, 1982.

CONTRIBUTORS

Russell Blackford holds a Ph.D. in English literature from the University of Newcastle, N.S.W., has studied law at the University of Melbourne, and is currently Executive Director of the Australian Higher Education Industrial Association. A well-known critic of science fiction, he has contributed to standard reference works such as the *Encyclopedia of Science Fiction* and to critical journals such as *Science Fiction, The Journal of Popular Culture, Foundation* and *The New York Review of Science Fiction*.

Mary Kay Bray has carried a childhood interest in science fiction throughout her academic life, from the University of Colorado to Texas Tech University and Wilmington College of Ohio where she is currently on extended leave. She has published articles on Dick, Elgin and Delany, and has presented papers on Delany and others at various academic conferences. She first began reading Delany in the early 1970s, becoming a devotee with her purchase and first reading of *Dhalgren* in 1975.

Ray Davis has published fiction in Paul McAuley's and Kim Newman's *In Dreams* and criticism in *The New York Review of Science Fiction*, where an earlier version of this essay appeared. He lives in San Francisco, works in the multimedia software industry, conducts Web publishing workshops and "distrusts taxonomic arguments."

Robert Elliot Fox is Associate Professor of English at Southern Illinois University at Carbondale. He is the author of two black-writing studies from Greenwood: *Conscientious Sorcerers: The Black Postmodernist Fiction of LeRoi Jones/Amiri Baraka, Ishmael Reed and Samuel R. Delany* (1987) and *Masters of the Drum: Black Lit/oratures Across the Continuum* (1995).

Jean Mark Gawron lives in Half Moon Bay, California. As a linguist specializing in semantics, he has written widely on anaphora, quantification, focus, lexical semantics and dynamic semantics. He has also written three remarkable science fiction novels, the most recent of which is *Dream of Glass* from Harcourt-Brace; he is currently at work on a fourth, *Shadow of Heaven*.

218

Ken James is a writer and filmmaker currently living in Maine. He graduated *summa cum laude* from Cornell University in 1990, in 1992 received his M.A. in American Studies from the University of Michigan, and is now completing his M.F.A. in Film and Media Arts at Temple University. James conducted one of the finest interviews with Delany, reprinted in *Silent Interviews*; more recently he wrote the introduction to Delany's collection of essays, *Longer Views*.

Carl Malmgren teaches twentieth-century literature and literary criticism and theory at the University of New Orleans. His books include *Fictional Space in the Modernist and Postmodernist American Novel* (Bucknell UP, 1985) and *Worlds Apart: Narratology of Science Fiction* (Indiana UP, 1991). He is currently working on a study of mystery and detective fiction.

James Sallis, one-time editor of the landmark science fiction magazine *New Worlds*, is author of five novels (including three in a series of acclaimed mysteries), of two collections of short stories, and of studies of music and literary history as well as a highly praised translation of Raymond Queneau's novel *Saint Glinglin*. His poetry, stories, translations and essays regularly appear in such publications as *Poetry East*, *The Georgia Review*, *Book World*, *North Dakota Quarterly* and *High Plains Literary Review*.

David N. Samuelson has published over 200 articles and reviews on SF, fantasy and utopian literature. Professor of English at California State University, Long Beach, since 1966, he has taught established courses in folklore and mythology and in British, world and contemporary literature while developing new courses in Joyce and Yeats, future studies, and SF, fantasy and utopian literature. He is currently writing a book on Delany as well as one on "hard" SF.

Kathleen L. Spencer teaches literature and composition at Cincinnati State Technical and Community College. A scholar of science fiction and Victorian and twentieth-century fantastic literature, she has published, in addition to her work on Samuel R. Delany, articles on Ursula Le Guin and Joanna Russ, *Dracula*, Charles Williams, and science fiction narrative theory. Since 1988 she has served as editorial consultant for *Science-Fiction Studies*. Other scholarly interests include women's studies and Afro-American literature.

INDEX

Aldiss, Brian, 117
Alternate-society science fiction, 3–4, 13–14, 19–24
Amis, Kingsley, 3
Anger, Kenneth, 100
Antonioni, Michaelangelo, 172
Armstrong, Neil, 103
Arnold, Matthew, 115
Ashbery, John, "The Instruction Manual," 78
Asimov, Isaac, 3, 120; *Foundation* trilogy, 114
Asturias, Miguel Angel, *Mulata*, 103
Auden, W. H., 104, 163
Austen, Jane, 115

Baker, Russell, 178
Ballard, J. G., 115; *The Burning World*, 103
Baraka, Amiri, 106
Barbour, Douglas, 121–22
Barth, John, *Giles Goatboy*, 102, 103
Barthes, Roland, 52, 57, 93, 131
Bataille, Georges, 173
Bellona (sister of Mars), 99
Berkeley, George, 67
Blake, William, 169, 179
Blaser, Robin, *The Practice of the Outside*, 54
Blish, James, 119
Boolean algebra, 192–93, 194, 204, 207–08, 209–10
Borges, Jorge Luis, 118

Brown, G. Spencer, 132; *Laws of Form*, 191–97, 198–99, 202, 204, 207–13
Budrys, A. J., 119
Bunyan, John, *Pilgrim's Progress*, 130
Burgess, Anthony, *A Clockwork Orange*, 4
Burroughs, Edgar Rice, 117

Califia, Pat, 163
Calvino, Italo, 118
Canetti, Elias, *Auto-de-fe*, 103
Censorship, 51
Cervantes, Miguel de, *Don Quixote*, 104
Chernoff, John Miller, 46
Chomsky, Noam, 72
Clarke, Arthur C., 118
Coleridge, Samuel Taylor, 14
Conrad, Joseph, 122
Cooper, Dennis, 175
Cull, Paul, 208–09

David, Charles, 53
Deconstruction, 152–58, 210–11
Delany, Samuel, autobiographical elements, 120–22; on science fiction, 112–23, 191; on sword-and-sorcery, 191; on teaching, 119–20; on his writing, 51, 71, 103, 111, 158
Works: "About 5,175 Words," 112; "The *Algol* Interview," 114, 115; *The American Shore*, 93, 110, 113, 116; "Aye, and Gomorrah," 43, 165–66; *Babel–17*, 5–14, 43, 50, 109–10,

221

131, 165; *The Ballad of Beta–2*,
109; *The Bridge of Lost Desire*
(*Return to Nevèrÿon*), 157, 205–06;
Camp Concentration, 168; "Crazy
Diamonds," 120; *Dahlgren*, 41, 43–44,
48, 49, 51, 62–63, 64–95, 97–106,
110, 127, 166, 189–90, 191, 196–97,
211–12; "Discourse on Desire," 111;
The Einstein Intersection, 43, 68, 100,
109–10, 131, 165, 167; *Equinox* (*Tides
of Lust*), 44, 48, 49–57, 100, 104, 110,
164, 165, 166–72, 182; *The Fall of the
Towers* trilogy, 102, 109, 165; *Flight
from Nevèrÿon*, 157, 190, 191, 205–07;
Heavenly Breakfast, 100, 111; "Helix,"
119; *Hogg*, 100, 110, 164, 172–77,
179, 184; *The Jewel-Hinged Jaw*, 110;
The Jewels of Aptor, 102, 109; *The
Mad Man*, 162, 164, 165, 177–85, 186;
The Motion of Light in Water, 100, 111;
Neveryóna, 51–52, 157, 200, 204–05;
"A Note on the Anti-Pornography of
Samuel R. Delany," 51; *Nova*, 102,
110, 167; "On the Unspeakable,"
172; Return to Nevèrÿon series, 42,
110, 114, 157–58, 166, 190, 191,
196, 197–207, 213; "The Rhetoric
of Sex, The Discourse of Desire,"
185; "Shadows," 110, 111, 211; *Silent
Interviews*, 110; *The Splendor and
Misery of Bodies, of Cities*, 26, 27;
Starboard Wine, 110; *Stars in My
Pocket Like Grains of Sand*, 17–15,
26–42, 110; *The Straits of Messina*,
110; *Tales of Nevèrÿon*, 26, 51, 127–28,
133, 135–44, 145–52, 153–58, 189,
210, 212; "Time Considered as a Helix
of Semi-Precious Stones," 102, 110,
166; "To Read *The Dispossessed*,"
120; *Triton*, 17–18, 43, 44–49, 50,
51, 54, 56, 57, 99, 110, 128, 132–33,
141, 152, 166, 167, 178, 179, 203;
Wagner/Artaud, 110; "We, In Some
Strange Power's Employ, Move On a
Rigorous Line," 100
De Man, Paul, 112; "Pascal's Allegory of
Persuasion," 128–31

Derrida, Jacques, 112, 121, 128;
"Borderlines," 128, 129, 131, 144, 151,
152–53, 154, 155, 156–57, 210; *Of
Grammatology*, 152, 155
Dick, Philip K., 120
Dionysus, 102
Disch, Thomas, 110, 113, 116, 119, 121;
334, 114; *Camp Concentration*, 55
Douglas, Mary, 132; *Natural Symbols*,
48–49
Du Bois, W. E. B., 50

Eagleton, Terry, 54–55, 116
Elgin, Suzette Haden, *Native Tongue*, 14
Escher, M. C., 94

Fantasy fiction, 103, 112, 114–15, 117
Faust myth, 49, 50, 51, 53, 56, 57,
168–69, 170
Felman, Shoshona, 112
Fish, Stanley, 112
Fitting, Peter, 118
Forster, E. M., 178
Fort, Charles, 103
Foucault, Michel, 50, 112, 132
Fox, Robert Elliot, 167
Foyster, John, 114
Frank, William, 208–09
Frazer, Sir James, 102
Freud, Sigmund, 116

Garcia-Marquez, Gabriel, *One Hundred
Years of Solitude*, 104
Gates, Henry Louis, Jr., 53, 106
Gender, in Delany's fiction, 33–34, 43,
47–48, 54, 137–38, 146–51, 174–75,
201, 202
Genet, Jean, 173
Gernsback magazines, 117, 118
Gide, André, 71; *The Counterfeiters*,
67–68
Gillespie, Bruce, 27
Goodman, Paul, 43
Gothicism, 105, 117
Gramsci, Antonio, *Prison Notebooks*, 49

Hamilton, Edmond, 118